AF557753

WOMEN POWER IN TWENTY FIRST CENTURY

WOMEN POWER
IN
TWENTY FIRST CENTURY

KANTA SHARMA

ANMOL PUBLICATIONS PVT. LTD.
NEW DELHI - 110 002 (INDIA)

ANMOL PUBLICATIONS PVT. LTD.
4374/4B, Ansari Road, Daryaganj
New Delhi - 110 002
Ph.: 23261597, 23278000
Visit us at: www.anmolpublications.com

Women Power in Twenty First Century

First Published, 2004

ISBN 81-261-2004-5

PRINTED IN INDIA

Published by J.L. Kumar for Anmol Publications Pvt. Ltd., New Delhi - 110 002 and Printed at Mehra Offset Press, Delhi.

Contents

Preface

Women Power is a great reality. It's a force behind all movements and activities in society. The sociologists and social activists are bound to recognise the vitality and significance of the Women Power.

Mahatma Gandhi was the first in India to acknowledge the women's force and power. He mobilised the female masses in villages and towns and motivated them to take part in freedom movement through various agitations.

Today, in our country, the women-folk have emerged as a powerful class in their own right. They make their presence felt, everywhere—in agricultural sector, industry, business and service, including administration and of course in politics.

Earlier, women were a neglected lot in our social system, but now, they have a defined and definite role in all walks of life. There is a strong presence of women in all areas and fields. They suffered for centuries, but now they have awakened and are well aware of their rights and strength.

Over the decades the scholars and researchers have been engaged in measuring and assessing women's value and weightage. They have also recorded their conclusions—and as a result—there are numerous books on different issues concerning women. Still, there is a dearth of good, and authentic books on the subject. Hence, this writer chose to present a comprehensive book on Women Power, which is relatively a new concept.

This work may be accepted as a modest effort, in the direction, where the ultimate goal can be fixed as making people realise the vitality of Women Power and salute them as the achievers.

The undersigned is confident that this endeavour would be accorded due acknowledgement by all concerned including scholars, academics and the common people.

—Editor

1

Introduction

In contemporary feminist literature, the word 'women' has been replaced with the term 'gender' as a new category of analysis to assert that much of sexual differentiation is a social and political construct, related to but not determined by biological sex difference. It (Gender) "is seen as the process by which individuals who are born into biological categories of male or female become the social categories of men and women through the acquisition of locally defined attributes of masculinity and femininity". Therefore, the feminists argue that this replacement (from women to gender) provides deeper analysis of present inequalities, and thus challenges the structure of current social, economic and cultural processes.

In fact the invention of this new word 'gender' is the result of two decades of intensive thought and research. In its most recent usage, gender seems to have first appeared among American feminists who wanted to reject biological determinism implicit in the use of such terms as 'sex' or 'sexual difference'. Two major theories of gender are prevalent today- the psychologically focused theory of gender, and the historically and anthropologically focused explanation of gender.

The former is represented in the writings of Simone de Behaviour, who says: "One is not born but rather becomes a woman." She claims that it is a whole process by which femininity is manufactured in society. To quote her, she is defied and differentiated with reference to men and not he with reference to her; she is the incidental, the inessential as opposed to the essential. He is the subject, he is the absolute - She is the Other.

Simon Behaviour argues that it is the child-bearing role, of women which excluded them from the productive process, and prevented her from seeing themselves as subjects in their own right. Thus, an artificial idea of womanhood was created by the society. She exhorts: "No biological, psychological or economic fate determines the figure that the human female presents in society, it is civilization as a whole that produces this creation, intermediate between male and eunuch who is described female."

Nancy Chodorow also subscribes to the above viewpoint and substantiates her argument from a psycho-analytical point of view. She argues that since women have always been assigned the responsibility of primary parenting and nurturing, she develops a psychology of being more suited to the task of nurturing and caring and thus herself chooses the role of a care-given and confinement to the private. On the other hand, man from the very beginning is encouraged for more and more individualisation and attaining status resulting into such personality traits impelling him to associate himself with the public.

The second theory of gender, based on historical and anthropological explanation, proclaims that in most of the societies so far, gender has been a socially constructed category rather than biologically determined. However, the proponents of this theory have also stressed that the nature of this social construction differs from one society to the other. So, there cannot be any uncausal, unavailable and a historical explanations of it. Anthropologist Michelle A Rosaldo supports this theory on the basis of her cross-cultural research which reveals that women are subjected to the authority due to the existing dichotomy between the public and the private.

Historian Linda J Nicholson also rejects the unicausal explorations of inequality of sexes. She also emphasises, that it has been affected by various causal factors in different social contexts. She stresses the need to fight against the powerful tendency present in political theory to reify the public-private distinction and to perceive it as rigid. She believes that one can comprehend this distinction only through the study of history for the gender structure irregular time and place is less affected by other contemporary stressors, such as political, economic, than by the previous history of gender. Joan W Scott also stresses the centrality of history in analysing different aspects of the construction of gender. She explains (a) how cultural myths and symbols justify the suppression of woman: (b) how these symbols create the 'binary opposition of masculine and feminine, male and female; (c) how social institutions family, labour markets, educational instructions, and polity reinforce this dichotomy-, and (d) how the subjective identity formation of individuals is psychologically determined.' She, therefore, emphasizes the need to expose the social construction of gender by deconstructing it. 'Ibis calls for:

> "....a refusal of the fixed and permanent quality of binary opposition, a genuine historicization and deconstruction terminism cannot be monolithic in its issues, goals and strategies, since it constitutes the political expression of the concerns of women from different regions, classes, nationalities and ethnic backgrounds. There is and must be a diversity of feminisms, responsive to the different needs and concerns of different women and defined by them for themselves.

The most positive part of the whole discourse is that these concerns are reflected in practice also. Women involved in different social movements are fighting against injustices on their own cultural terms. Environmental activists, such as Vandana Shiva are speaking of the need to decolonize northern assumptions such as the concept of sustainable development and appeal to save environment through knowledge based on poor women's experience.

Thus, feminist scholarship has brought sweeping changes to social and political theory. It has cautioned us against constituting gender as a super-ordinate category of analysis. It should neither be an automatic starting point of analysis of adjustment, nor should it be ignored as a potential starting point. We must avoid approaches that are gender-blinded or gender-blind. Then only we can have true meaning of democracy and participation.

This has eventually led to the dichotomy between morality and power. Women in the name of being more moral have been excluded from the public realm. Even the suffragists argued in favour of women's franchise by claiming women's superior morality as it would usher the state in a reign of peace. This is why Elshtain alleges that suffragist instead of challenging the separation of the public and private, merely "perpetuated the very mystifications and unexamines presumptions which served to rig the system against them."

Against this background, one can understand the significance of the feminist slogan; The personal is the political.

The feminists argue that public realm of politics can be rational, noble and universal as the messy content of the body, meeting its needs providing for production, caretaking and attending to birth and death, are taken care of elsewhere.

So a modern reflective political theory should recognize that the glory of the public is dialectically, entwined with the exploitation and repression of the private and the people restricted to that sphere so that they can take care of people's needs. In view of this, feminists conclude that 21st century politics requires a basic rethinking of this distinction and its meaning for politics.

Feminists are tying to develop a theory, of social practice on the following premises: First, there should be no sexual division of labour in workplace and in political organizations of all ideological persuasions: second, it believes in a differentiated social order within which various dimensions are distinct but not separate or opposed, and which rests on social conception of individuality, which includes both women and men as biologically differentiated but not unequal creatures.

We must expand conception of politics, based on the understanding that power relations between men and women are not confined to the 'public' world of law, the state and economics, but that they pervade all areas of life. This means that, contrary to the assumptions of traditional political theory, the family, reproduction and sexuality must be included in political analysis.

The question arises how far this public/private dichotomy and its deconstruction is relevant to the women of the Third World? Can this empowerment epistemology be rooted In White women's experiences, subjectivity and identity fulfil the interest of Third World women?

However, in the post colonial discourse, women of North have themselves understood the significance of Third World women's realities and they have themselves rejected the monolithic nature of earlier feminist discourse on the grounds that it ignores difference, indigenous knowledge, and local expertise. For example, modernity is equated with Westernization, industrialization, and superiority, whereas non-modernity is equated with non-Western countries, tradition and inferiority. In the 1970s, Ester Boserup's pioneering work Women's Role in Economic Development asserted that modernization had marginalized women and their contributions in the Third World. Chandra Mohanty also questions the Western approach. How, she asks:

> "...is it possible to refer to 'the' sexual division of labour when the content of this division changes radically from one environment to the next, and from one historical juncture to another? At Its most abstract level... concepts such as the sexual division of labour can be useful only if they are generated through local, contextual analysis. If such concepts are assumed to be universally applicable, the resultant homogenisation of class, race, religious, 'and daily material practices of women in the Third World can create a false sense of the commonality of oppressions, interests, and struggles between and among women globally."

Sen and Crown too cautions against adopting a concept of gender that ignores difference and diversities. They believe this diversity is built on gender oppression and hierarchy. He exclaims:

> "The most fundamental and general of these opposition associates women with nature and men with culture. Nature is always seen as of a lower order than culture. The feminists like Ortner argue that the opposition between women/nature and men/culture is itself a cultural construct and not given in nature. Firestone in her work Dialectic of Sex argues against this separation of private and public. Women necessarily suffer from a fundamentally oppressive biological conditions. It is their role as reproducers that has handicapped women over the centuries and made possible men's patriarchal power."

The consequences of the public-private dichotomy are disastrous. Due to this, only women have been deprived of political power and effective participation. Citizenship for women is always seen as "an elaboration of their private domestic task." Thinkers like-Ruskin could argue that "man's duty as a member of the commonwealth, is to assist the maintenance, in the advance, in the defence of the state. The women's duty as a member of the commonwealth is to assist in the ordering, in the comforting, and in the beautiful adornment of the state."

2

State of Affairs

The political scenario in India today is characterised by a rather curious feature with most of the political parties and combination of parties accusing one another of striving to subvert democratic institutions. The Narora document has done the right thing to focus on the central fact that politics in India today faces grave threats. It is also correct in underlining the fact that most of the political issues the country is agitating on, are directly or indirectly related to this central fact.

For a proper understanding, however, of the current turmoils and conflicts in this vast country of nearly 900 million population, into which gigantic social forces are being inexorably drawn, it is necessary to start with an analysis of the real nature of politics in India, and its active role in the course of sociopolitical development. Only an examination of the nature and role of the existing political institutions can lead to an understanding of the nature of subversive attacks on them and, consequently, of the imperatives for overcoming them. The debate on women's entry into politics in India is closely related to this analysis, In order to start this debate, one has to look at the nature and working of politics in India.

Female Dominance

The basic nature of a political system is judged not by the speed of its ways, nor even by the proclamations it may have chosen to make, it has to be judged by its actual working-by the resultant of the social processes it seeks to encourage, control and repress. Earlier, even before the transfer of power, on January 22, 1947, a resolution moved by Jawaharlal Nehru in the Constituent Assembly of India, which set the objective of framing a Constitution – "wherein shall be guaranteed and secured to all the people of Indian justice, social, economic and political; equality of status, of opportunity, and before the law; freedom of thought, expression, belief, faith, worship, vocation, association and action, subject to law and morality". The Preamble of the Constitution proclaims the resolution on the same lines. Devices like confided Fundamental rights, Directive Principles of State Policy, special safeguards for minorities, Scheduled Castes and Tribes and so on, have added to the attractive look of the Constitution. The democratic and egalitarian appearance of the political power in India has been further reinforced by the adoption of the socialistic pattern of society as the goal, still later by the full-threaded declaration of war against mass poverty----'garibi hatao' and, finally, by the 42nd amendment of the Constitution to declare the Indian Republic as a socialist and secular state. However, observers within the country and from abroad have refused to take these proclamations at their face value. They have clearly and categorically characterised the existing political power structure in India as exclusive and elitist.

For instance, Professor V K Rao, a former Union minister, identifies the locus of political power in India in "a political alliance of the intermediate classes with the upper classes, resorting to socialist ideology only to win mass support but using all levers of power to facilitate a type of capitalist development in the interest of a narrow section of Indian society". Another Indian analyst says, "whether in agriculture or industry or infrastructure or even scientific research, the advantage has invariably gone to that segment of power elite, which holds the political levers of parliamentary democracy. The present power structure constitutes the greatest stumbling block to any successful effort to relieve the poverty of the poor. According to Gunnar Myrdal, "India is ruled by a select group of upper class citizens who use their power to secure their privileged positions". He defines the elite groups as the product of a linking up of the vested interests of business, permanent officials and political leaders.

Caste Factor

The process of politics is one of identifying and manipulating existing structures in order to mobilise support and consolidate positions. When the caste structure provides one of the most important organisational clusters in which the population is found to live, politics must strive to organise through such a structure. The alleged casteism in politics is thus no more and no less than the politicisation of caste. Caste in contemporary Indian politics plays a very important role behind the facade of parliamentary democracy. The political behaviour of people is influenced by caste considerations as is quite evident at the time of distribution of tickets by political parties for elections and composition of ministries. As far as possible and practicable, the people prefer a candidate of their own caste, irrespective of his merits and demerits. Similar regard is paid when the list of party's office-bearers is prepared. When a single party is not in a position to have its own candidates, alliances are formed on the basis of caste to recommend the name of a person after arrangements of 'give and take' are made to the satisfaction of the constituents. The central discovery is that politics is more important to caste and castes are more important to politics than before. There is a widespread impression among educated Indians that caste is on its last legs and that, educated, urbanised and westernised members of the upper classes have already escaped its bond. Both these impressions are wrong. These people may observe very few dietetic restrictions, marry outside caste and even religion, but this does not mean that they have escaped the bonds of castes entirely. They show caste attitude in surprising context. That is the reason no political analysis of Indian politics that neglects caste is worthwhile. In fact, caste has become a factor to be reckoned with and none of the political parties, including Congress, Bharatiya Janata Party (EUP) and Communist, can ignore it. Some of the political parties are organised purely on caste basis. For example Dravida Munnetra Kazhagarn (DMK) and All-India Anna Dravida Munnetra Kazhagarn (ALADMK) are anti-Brahmin parties, National Democratic Party of Nair community, Socialist Republican Party of Ezhava community, Kerala Congress of Catholic community and Bahujan Samaj Party (BSP) of lower caste communities are purely casteist parties. In Madhya Pradesh, it is a general observation that whenever there was Thakur Chief Minister, the Yadava, Kurmi and Brahmin legislators felt themselves neglected. Thakur officers were being promoted out of turn, despite the fact that some of them had adverse service records and inquiries were pending against them. Furthermore, few of the senior IAS Brahmin officers have been suspended. More or less, this has been observed all over the country.

To a limited extent, caste system was recognised by the framers of the constitution when they reserved seats for Scheduled Castes and Scheduled Tribes in the House of People and Legislative Assemblies of the states, made a provision for the appointment of a special officer for Scheduled Castes and Scheduled Tribes to investigate matters relating to the various safeguards provided for them in the Constitution and also by providing for a minister in charge to look after the welfare of Scheduled Castes, Scheduled Tribes and other backward classes in the states of Bihar, Madhya Pradesh and Orissa. There is also a provision which empowers the President/Parliament to indulge/exclude certain castes or groups therein in the category of Scheduled Castes. Subsequently, the Constitution was amended in 1951, and a provision was also made for protective discrimination in favour of Scheduled Castes, scheduled tribes and other socially and educationally backward classes of citizens in services. Keeping in view the social hierarchical caste based structure, which exploited the weaker sections of society, there was and is a justification for such a provision in the Constitution, but only to limited extent for a limited period. However, while doing so efficiency of administration should also not be blindly ignored, otherwise, their condition would become more miserable. It is important to note that the expression 'Scheduled Castes and Scheduled Tribes' as used in Article 338, include "such other backward classes as the President may, on receipt of the report of a commission appointed under clause (1) of Article 340, by order specify and also the Anglo-Indian community". About reservation, it should be remembered that reservation can neither be made on communal considerations nor more than 50 per cent seats be reserved. While caste has been politicised, in the process it has provided the Indian politics with processes and symbols of political articulation. Thus, within the new context of political democracy, caste remains a central element of Indian society even while adapting itself to the values and methods of democratic politics.

Class Factor

In a literal sense, castes and classes have different implications. But in the politics of our country, they have come to be identified with each other. Even courts have accepted the view that in certain situations, the class as a whole may be taken as a caste and thus, caste may be entitled for the benefits of reservation that are available to a backward class.

We find that most of the tensions and conflicts have their source in social stratification and, for this reason, a possible solution to such political problems should be discovered in the rectification of the balance between different classes. The dialectics of Indian politics demand grappling with complex and contradictory trends in the country which has shown many positive and negative features during the past few years. Simply stated, the term 'class' signifies an aggregate of persons within a society possessing approximately the same status. It is a set of relationship constituted by the granting of deference of individual roles and institutions in the light of their place in the system of power and occupation. What really makes a class is the factor of economic interest. The factor of economic interest is so deep that, as suggested by Karl Marx, it differentiates between the rules and the ruled, the exploiters and the exploited. Marx, however, makes the meaning of the term 'class' very rigid by applying the criteria of ownership and control over the means of production and distribution of goods. It may also be added that in common parlance, this term is used in greatly varying senses as upper or middle classes, propertied and non-propertied classes, educated and uneducated classes, even productive and unproductive classes. Liberal writers dwell upon the doctrine of three broad stratas of society-upper, lower and middle-living in harmony and peace. Max Weber takes a middle view in this regard and while dealing with the objective and subjective dimension of this important issue, builds the concept of class on three factors-possession of economic means, external standard of living, and cultural and recreational possibilities.

The struggle of the members of different classes, for the sake of protecting and promoting their specific interest, leads to the creation of conflicts and crises that demand their solution, sooner the better, and thereby the relationship between social set up and political system is established. In the context of Indian politics, class cuts into caste and is also cut into sub-caste by it. Low standing in the social hierarchy has been commonly taken as a sufficient indicator of backwardness. The cause of most of the social conflicts and tensions lies in the want of economic justice.

For Want of Education

The socioeconomic analysis of educational advance in the post-independence period is available from a number of village surveys. From these, it is clear that the spread of literacy and education is much in evidence among the more affluent and socially advance sections of society than among the poorer and more backward sections. The traditionally upper castes are almost all literate and have progressed much further in higher education, the middle castes have registered significant educational progress; but the lower and other backward sections of the population are lagging considerably behind. Literacy is crawling at snail's pace, and female education has not even touched these sections of society particularly in rural areas. Thus, backwardness in education is closely related to the economic and social backwardness and bears the same hallmarks of a society divided against itself. The benefits of high agricultural productivity have not trickled down to the lower castes, the majority of whom work as agricultural labourers. The rigidity of social customs and the relatively poor bargaining power have kept the lower castes in their caste-ordained position.

The economic and political power essentially belongs to the propertied classes, mostly from the upper castes, who have continued to monopolise education and culture too. The vast masses at the base of the social pyramid are not only deprived of the real power, but the power mechanism so works as to perpetuate and intensify this deprivation of the masses lower down. Lower caste segments of population who have historically constituted the most oppressed and exploited mass of the Indian people, practically deprived of any share in the economic, political and educational cultural developments in the country, continue to live in almost the same socioeconomic conditions, some symbolic improvements in certain sectors notwithstanding. Can a nation of 960 million catch up with the rest of the world with nearly 48 per cent of its population totally illiterate? It cannot, if it does not take up bold measures to tackle the chronic problem within a timeframe. Though we have impressive statistics on education: 590,421 primary schools, 171,216 upper primary and 98,134 high schools, 6,596 colleges for general education, 1.354 professional colleges and 226 universities, for the 150.7 million children enrolled in the age group of 6-14 years, there are 2.90 million teachers. But India of 1999 is caught between the paradox of high technocrats. IIT professionals, MBA, graduates and other literate and another India overflowing with an illiterate population of more than 400 million.

Financial Factors

Economic power has paved the way for capturing political power and thereby using state apparatus for suppressing the opponents belonging to the poor and backward class. For instance, it is the power of money that purchases the vote bank and thereby manages to have the induction of legislators and administrators, who protect and promote the interests of the rich and upper class. Likewise, in rural areas, the rich peasants have established linkages with the administrative apparatus that work against the rural poor who are immensely vulnerable because they are non-owners and the power-wielders are supported by their ownership of land. Corruption breeds corruption. When it sets in, it grows like weeds in a garden. There is no known antidote for it except exposure and punishment.

Due to expensive elections, degeneration of moral values, and the desire to be rich overnight, political corruption has now become a great threat to our political system. It has diluted moral and ethical standards over the years, has seeped into all walks of life, and hampered the economic development of the country. Since Independence, all the Prime Ministers not only ignored, but actively helped some of the politicians who were very close to them in the matters of financial improprieties. This approach of Prime Ministers of not only shielding but also promoting the corrupt politicians, had its adverse impact on the Indian political system because it encouraged political corruption and hence, corruption started spreading from top to bottom. It is interesting to note that on the one hand Prime Ministers refused to appoint a commission of inquiry against their ministers or chief ministers, belonging to their party, but were quick in appointing such commission whenever a minister or chief minister belonging to some opposition party was involved. This shows that all the Prime Ministers have dragged their feet in appointing commissions of inquiry when their own kith and kin or lieutenants were involved. With the passage of time, links with the underworld of gamblers, smugglers and FERA violators on the one hand, and further deterioration in moral and political standards on the other, has further increased corruption in political life. When politicians indulge in corruption on a large scale, bureaucracy cannot remain far behind. The selling, of national secrets by officials occupying sensitive places is a sad commentary on the political and bureaucratic leadership of the country. Public Service Commissions and other recruiting agencies in some of the states have also become dens of corruption. One of the most disturbing developments which has encouraged corruption is that politicians have undermined the process of rule of law by withdrawing cases of corruption lying in the courts of law. It follows that when politicians who amass wealth by misusing their powers and position and are still not punished, then how can bureaucrats who are stunningly corrupt and serve their political masters, be punished? In fact, Indira Gandhi had once said that corruption is a worldwide phenomena. She had also admitted that it is not true that the Congress alone gets the money or gives the favours.... We do collect money, but everybody does". According to Viren Shah, the ex-president of the Indian Merchants' Chamber of Commerce, "Can we say that we have not contributed to corruption by bribing those in authority or making clandestine contributions to party funds?"

It is important to note that the history of many Third World countries tells us that when corruption and crime jointly act upon economic and political institutions and state power is employed for partisan political objectives, the result inevitably is both massive violence and authoritariatism and this is exactly the direction in which Indian polity is now heading which is very dangerous and unfortunate.

Criminal Angles

Nani A Palkhivala, the eminent constitutional expert observes, "I do not think India, in its entire history of five thousand years has ever reached a lower level of degradation than it has reached now.... The picture that emerges is that of a great nation in a state of moral decay, of which crime, chaos and corruption are three of the several facets." In order to protect themselves, citizens in some parts of the country have begun to organise private armies. Sooner or later, all developing countries become difficult to govern, and over the past two decades, India has been moving in that direction.

The much talked report of the Vohra panel categorically points out that crime syndicates mafia. Organisations have developed muscle and money power and established linkages with government functionaries, political leaders and others. The CBI has reported that the nexus between the criminal gangs, police, bureaucracy and politicians has come out clearly in various parts of the country. There has been a rapid spread and growth of criminal gangs, armed sertas, drug mafia, smuggling gangs, drug peddlers and economic lobbies in the country, which have, over the years, developed an extensive network of contacts with the bureaucrats/government functionaries at the local levels, politicians, media persons and strategically located individuals in the non-state sector. In certain states like Bihar, Haryana and Uttar Pradesh, these gangs enjoy the patronage of local level politicians, cutting across party lines and protection of government functionaries.

The big smuggling syndicates with international linkages, have spread into and infected the various economic and financial activities including hawala. Transactions economy causing serious damage to the economic fibre of the country. The network of mafia is virtually running a parallel government, pushing the state apparatus into irrelevance. The cost of contesting elections has thrown the politicians into the lap of these elements. Another feature in the political culture of the ruling class is the politicisation of crime and of politics. Politicisation of crime involves competitive use of anti-social forces for the mobilisation of party funds, for managements of elections, for organising meetings and conferences and even for recruiting workers at lower levels from among anti-social elements. It also means the misuse of criminal intelligence as a political tool for black mailing political opponents.

Criminalisation of politics means direct entry of criminals into political parties and legislatures, including Parliament. Today politics is no longer decent: hooligans and hoodlums are gaining control of public life. The notorious criminals, history-shelters, smugglers and murderers are swarming into politics. Formerly, they were on the periphery of Indian political life, now they have moved considerably towards the centre to manipulate the gears and levers of political machine.

Kuldeep Nayyer wrote that according to the Chief Election Commissioner, 180 out of the 425 members of Uttar Pradesh Legislative Assembly had criminal records and the last general elections in Bihar were contested by as many as 243 candidates against whom charges were pending. According to India Today, "of the 424 members of the Vidhan Sabha, 132 are suspected criminals, 16 of them now actually sit in cabinet meetings. Election Commissioner G V G Krishnamurty, while addressing press persons on August 20, 1997, said as per records, 40 members of Parliament have criminal cases pending against them while nearly 700 members of state assemblies out of 4,072 are named in criminal cases, though It was an international accepted norm that 'law breakers cannot be allowed to be lawmakers", which India must also follow.

In a historic judgement on March 20, 1997, the then Chief Justice of India, A M Ahmadi, warned the nation of the emergence of new crime syndicates with a very strong nexus with politicians, bureaucrats, media, personalities and even members of the Judiciary. It is unfortunate that no counter moving force to check criminalisation of politics is emerging. The historic resolution passed by the Lok Sabha at the special session of Parliament on the occasion of the golden jubilee of Independence, August 26 to September 1 1997 observes: "The meaningful electoral reforms be carried out so that our Parliament and other legislative bodies be balanced and effective instruments of democracy and further that political life and processes be free of the adverse impact, on governance of undesirable extraneous factors including criminalisation."

Women of India are paying a heavy price in terms of a rising tide of violence and assent on their honour just because of distorted social values, a band of politicians, hand in glove with criminals and anti-social elements, caste conflicts, etc. Crimes against women are on rise despite all sacrosanct provisions in the Constitution, criminal law, Parliament, judiciary, police, media coverage, the National Human Rights Commission and the National Commission for Women. Perhaps every segment of India has to own the blame and should dip its head in shame for the continuing assault on womanhood in India.

Women's Condition

The women of India have been exposed to greater insecurity, to poverty, illiteracy, casteism, orthodoxy unhealthy living conditions, traditionalism, backwardness, corruption, criminalisation and male dominance in most of the fields. They have been affected by lack of opportunities and facilities owing to the innate discrimination prevalent in the society. In the last 20 years, there has been a global effort with a strong support from the United Nations to understand the discrimination and restore a status to women of the world. The slogan has been equality, development and peace.

The United Nations General Assembly declared the International Year of Women in 1975 followed by the International Women's Decade and organised three world conferences-Mexico in 1975, Copenhagen In 1980 and Nairobi in 1985. The Nairobi conference decided strategies for the advancement of women upto 2000 AD. The world has consciously marched forward with various instruments for eliminating discrimination against women during the 20 years. The fourth world conference on women held in Beijing in 1995, focused on the structural changes that are necessary in the society. It emphasised that no enduring solution to society's most threatening social, economic and political problems can be found without the full participation and full empowerment of the women. India's strategies and action plans are to eliminate all discrimination against women; remove the chasm between legal status and defect status; create an environment of harmony and partnership of men and women.

There are countries like Sweden, Finland and Norway, where women make up almost half of the national legislatures. Stories of smooth succession of power from husband to wife are in plenty. Commenting on how widows and daughters have been thrust into power by dynastic imperatives in Asian countries like Philippines, India and Indonesia. Rounaq Jahan, a Bangladeshi political scientist had observed, "They think that they can manipulate these women. But every time they were surprised that once in power, Women handled the men and mastered old style politics."

But behind most successful women leaders in India, there has been the hidden hand of a man. Just as Jawaharlal Nehru groomed Indira Gandhi, MG Ramchandran did for his screen partner Jayalalitha and Kanshi Ram is doing for his acolyte Mayavati. Even Laloo Prasad Yadav is not far behind these veterans in propping up his wife Rabri Devi, who confidently faces the camera today instead of taking shelter in her kitchen. There may be a sharp variance in their life style, levels of political sophistication, in their dress sense, but they have one thing in common, that is, their valuable grooming in a political career by their mentors. Grooming Includes training in developing their ethos, political issues and marketing them to their selected audience (voters). Many of them would be raw, without a political or famed godfather to lend support. Like one-third reservation for women at rural and urban local bodies, 33 per cent quota may help women in increasing their numerical strength to 181 in the Lok Sabha, it certainly may not be enough in attaining empowerment in the real sense, which would still remain a far cry. After all the road to empowerment is circuitous. Attaining political power may not mean enjoying or utilising it for the betterment of the country or her constituents, till they are trained to cross the rough and tumble of Indian politics.

Therefore, the present political scenario and demand for women's quota have generated a need for starting grooming courses for women politicians in India. Just as the path of empowerment became easy for the American women by mastering political skills. The Indian women can also attain empowerment if only they are groomed well. For women in the West, there are no reservations on the road to political empowerment. But they have the 'primaries' and other sundry opportunities to make themselves hard enough for the long grind in the political arena. Strangely, the idea has not struck us, where women advancement in the political domain is just a matter of time. A politically ambitious woman in our country is just thrown in the thick of things, to fend for herself. As more and more women get into the thick of things there is an urgent need to evolve a system that will prepare them for this opportunity. Though there are many examples of women who have come through the system, they are seasoned, and experienced. But they have never been to any finishing school. What they have learnt is through sheer experience. There are no caucuses and no primaries where they can cut their political teeth. In effect, they have to behave, react and act as a politician from the word go. It is not an easy task. There are few women in public offices because few of them run for elections. The reservation in panchayats and municipalities will gradually bring more and more women into the political field. They will gather experience at a level, which will teach them the indispensability of a plural society. Among the women at the local institution level, those who want to adopt politics as a full-time career, will move up to the higher bodies in course of time, and their male colleagues will regard their ascent as a natural and legitimate progression. The training institutions or organisations will teach these political women not only the finer things of decision-making and use their power properly, but also the awareness, understanding of outer world, public dealings and if required, literacy, can also be taught to them. Such a process will not cause any political or social upheaval. The benefits of empowerment would also come in due course without the element of confrontation with other groups.

At present, like other Asian countries, there is very slow rise in the percentage of Indian women in Parliament, central ministry, administration, higher education and technical Institutions.

The Union government obviously thinks this call for affirmative action as is evident from its decision to introduce the Constitution (81st Amendment) Bill in the Lower House. If passed by Parliament, the amendment will have a third of the seats reserved for women in the Lok Sabha and the state assemblies. In this situation, the need for grooming institutions becomes very relevant.

Mohini Girl wrote, "the country is facing, as never before, a torrent of crime due to various socioeconomic reasons not to speak of infiltration of illegal migrants, besides other state sponsored terrorism, much of these kinds of heinous crimes and atrocities have their roots in the drug mafia, foreign patronage and other country strategies to destabilise civilian population." Criminalisation is a big problem as most Asian cities are unsafe to live in despite the economic growth in the region. Compared to them, the law and order situation in Indian metros is better. The crime rate in Bangalore and Delhi is much lower than that in Seoul or Tokyo.

Apart from this situation, women's status in Asia is clearly in flux. Democracy seems to have helped by creating an environment in which autonomous women's groups could form, network and develop some political influence. Progress in terms of formal political representation of women has been much more gradual in most Asian nations. The practice of reserving parliamentary quotas for women seems to be spreading, although this obviously is a lengthy process. Women in Asia, therefore, face substantial political challenges with significant, but limited resources at their disposal.

Fortunately, in recent times, women have awakened to the fact that in order to break gender-barriers and overcome social bias, women's participation in the political process is essential. Though women constitute nearly half of the total population, politics has all along been men's domain. A February 1997 report on inter-Parliamentary unions says that Indian women hold only 7.2 per cent seats in the Lower House and 7.8 per cent seats in the Upper House. This can be called as token representation.

The percentage of women MLAs in state assemblies is also not very encouraging. Though in comparison to 1952, the percent age in the years from 1993 to 1998, has been certainly increased but still it is insignificant.

The truth is that except for mouthing political platitudes during elections, men are not prepared to give political space to women. One must realise that advancing the status of women is not only a moral imperative, but women's presence at the decision-making level is sine quanon for strengthening democratic traditions and fighting against injustice and oppression.

However, laws alone do not lead to social transformation unless followed by resolute action and socialite awareness of the wrong that have been perpetuated on women from time immemorial. But first of all there should be a revolution of consciousness in the minds of women-in the way they thought about themselves. Women must realise that gender deprivation is inconsistent with the basic human rights of women. They must realise that they have constitutional rights to equality, health care, economic security, access to education, employment opportunities, pay equity and political *power*. As India has celebrated more than 50 years of its Independence, this is a historic opportunity to invest in India's future for when a woman thrives, her family thrives, when families thrives, communities flourish and the nation reaps the benefits.

3

Societal Control

It is a global experience that in any political system, right from the developed to the developing countries, women's presence in the political process is marginal and low except a few countries (the Nordic countries). Women's movements for their rights started in the later half of the 19th century and continued till the first half of the 20th century, ultimately crystallising to a demand for the 'right to vote'. Women in many countries had to wage long and grim battle to get this right. In most countries, they got this from the second decade of the present century. Despite their struggle for a long period, women have, not yet been able to attain a rightful position in the arena of politics.

Radical feminists have gone beyond just the right to vote, maintaining that the demand for right to vote came from women of the elite class to find some room for themselves in the established power structure. There is now an emphasis on the right to participate in the political decision-making. And it is here that the crunch lies. The percentage of women as voters has increased considerably in most of the countries, but they have not been able to create a niche for themselves in the policy-formulating and decision-making bodies. Their political status remains secondary.

Barbare Nelson and Najma Choudhury, the editors of the book: Women and Politics Worldwide, maintain that a study has been carried out in 43 countries on women's political engagement, which reveals the fact that women everywhere have a secondary political status. They maintain that there have been women of substance in politics, holding on their own, but such women are exceptions and it's not the rule. They also imply that it does not mean that all women experience their subordinate political status in a similar way, or all groups of women are subordinate to all groups of men in a similar way. In most cultures there is a complex matrix of political power, composed of many social hierarchies, of which gender is only one component. Nevertheless, men of any group are more able to be active in politics than women of their group. They emphasise that the ubiquity of women's secondary political status demonstrates how politics is intertuned with other aspects of life. They see politics, economics, culture, religion and law as mutually constitutive, each creating itself and the other at the same time. The secondary position of women in each realm is reinforced by the total pattern of male privileges. But each sphere of society also creates unique elements of gender inequality and its own opportunities for resistance, innovations and transformation.

Women's political participation has to be discussed in the context of gender and patriarchy. Gender is defined as the social construction of relations between women and men and among various groups of women and men. Feminist scholarship places gender as the "sociocultural manifestation of being a man or women- at the focus of inquiry in research and study and arrived at a 'gendered' understanding of society. It has been a long battle to show that a woman is not a mere composite of female anatomy and physiology, sex and gender are not identical. Sex connotes a biological difference between the male and female. The difference between sex and gender is at once a liberator as well as an explorator, for if we are convicted that discrimination, oppression and exploitation that are ascribed to natural difference are false deduction, and that body differences do not warrant these differentiation, and they are socially produced, then we have a basis for action. Gender is the most potent, significant and enormously useful analytical concept that feminists have thrown up. It is a matter of social ascription, a socio-cultural construction and provided a deeper analysis of inequalities existing between male and female. The feminist scholars through the application of the concept of gender have challenged the structures-socio-economic political and cultural processes. Simon de Bearnvoir maintains, "one is not born but rather made a women". To quote her, "she is defined and differentiated with reference to men and not with reference to her; she is incidental and unessential as opposed to the essential. He is the subject, he is the absolute she is the other". Nancy Chodorow maintains that since women have always been assigned the responsibility of primary parenting and nurturing, they develop a psychology of being most suited to the task of nurturing and caring, and thus, themselves choose the role of the care-giver and 'confinement to the private'. Rosaldo supports the theory that in most societies, so far gender has been a socially constructed category rather than biologically determined. Unda Nicholsan maintains that the gender structure in a particular time and space is less affected by other contemporary structures such as political, economic etc. more by the previous history of gender.

The concept of gender, thus, explains the division of spheres of action into private and public. The private sphere belongs to women while the male is assigned the public spheres. Firestone argues against this separation of spheres of activity.

This public/private dichotomy has resulted in women being marginalised in all spheres of activity - social, economic and more specifically, political. Rationality, self-discipline, competition, universality to mention a few are the priced qualities of political parlance. These are inherent in male. On the contrary, irrationality, indiscipline particularly, submissiveness, impulsiveness are some of the qualities associated with female nature.

Patriarchy looms large in feminist debate. Patriarchy implies that power is imperative in gender relations. As a substantive, it usually refers to some form of systemic male dominance. Kata Millet in Sexual Political and Shulasmith in The Dialectic of Sex sees patriarchy as a broad system of power of men over women. This patriarchal character of society pervades ideology and culture.

Millet, Firestone, Mackennon and the whole movement behind them have drawn our attention to the pervasiveness of sexual domination and the role of force and male violence as a major social-historical reality.

The origins of the concept can be traced to the 19th century women's movement and in Marxism. Mark and Engels in their German Ideology had incorporated crucial insight about women. Engel's major contribution was to bequeath to the working class movement, a conceptualisation that women were not naturally the, second sex. They were in fact being exploited within an oppressive family structure. Though, he used the term 'father right, this was essentially a conceptualisation of patriarchy.

Contemporary feminist theories of patriarchy emerged primarily in reaction to and in confrontation with the mechanical materialistic form of Marxism that had developed. This was because in the Marxist tradition concepts 'patriarchy' was retained in, however, inadequate a form. It has avoided biologism and retrained the nation of a separate male-dominated family/reproduction system. Radical feminism has sought to replace economic class struggle with a nation of sexual class struggle.

Without going into the detailed analysis of the various theories of patriarchy and later its downfall, we can for our purpose of study infer that power is imperative in gender relations, in producing gender relations and in maintaining these in some way or other.

In actual practice, the rule of the patriarch over the household and family has been extended into the rule of the male over the female in wider society, economy and politics. Experiences in various political systems with very different hierarchy and cultural patterns proves the patriarchal mindset of the male over female in all spheres of life and its activities. The resistance of female participation in politics is also a direct result of this mindset. The resistance to female participation in politics is a direct result of this mindset, although other environmental factors cannot be ignored. Even the definition of politics for centuries has been the result of gender-patriarchy considerations. The feminist academics have questioned the traditional definition and constituents of politics, and charged it with gender bias. Before going into the details of efforts at a redefinition of politics from feminist perspective, we turn to the conventional definition and constituents of politics.

Politics has been defined in various ways, but there is a common thread running through all of them, that it is inevitable in any society. It is about representation, policy, position and power with government as its area. Miller maintains that it is the activity which aims at bringing government to bear in a particular direction, to secure particular results. Laswell maintained that political process is the shaping, sharing and exercise of power. Involvement in politics is directed towards influencing power channels and elites for protecting one's rights and self-interests and giving legitimacy to political elites and their decisions. Conventionally, politics deals with the formal political structures but it has now been wined by political theorists to include movements, protests and struggle as legitimate expressions of political behaviour. Political sphere, thus, includes the "spheres in social relations, where power relations are generated, institutionalised and used to encourage, control or move people's attitudes, beliefs in a specified direction to control and regulate the distribution of resources."

Feminist scholars have been very concerned about what constitutes politics, that it is basically male activity. They have challenged the dominant hypothesis that politics is confined to public sphere. They maintain that traditional Politics legitimises women's exclusion or absence from the power spheres and also devalues women's concerns.

Feminists also argue for a redefinition of politics. An important feature of their efforts have been to proclaim the Political nature of private life and the relation between sexes, which has brought traditional political science into question and has forced the authorities to take account of Problems hitherto regarded as belonging to private life. Political participation has to be discussed and understood in this light.

Operating in All Fields

Political participation has been defined in various ways, but in nutshell it refers to the participation of individuals in the political process, and that it ensures that individuals are able to take part in deciding the common goals of the society and the best ways of achieving it.

Kazenstein Mary Fainshod conceptualises political participations as public membership of citizen 'sharing' justice and orienting their action towards a public or a common good. Political participation also connotes activities for protecting one's rights and duties and advancing interest through competition.

The concept of participation as an instrumental action for having a close link with power is postulated by Laswell and Parsons Verba. Nie states political participation as "the activities by private citizens that are more or less directly aimed at influencing the selection of governmental personnel and/or the action they take. Political participation as instrumental action is close to 'exchange theory'. Politics is depicted in the language of bargaining, exchange and efficiency. A rational citizen is considered to be a consumer of private benefits. Participation is thought of as cost incurred in the political market only when one's vital interests are at stake. The result is a cost-benefit account according to which rational citizens minimise costs and maximise benefits. Rayon terms such action as rational. It may be assumed that participation is rational in the sense that it consists of the examination of alternative actions and the selection of that alternative, which yield the greatest expected utility. Self-interest, thus, is the main base for choice of ones action.

These two concepts are two different ways of representing rationality of political participation.

Milbrath maintains, "every person participates atleast passively in the political system in which he lives.... There is no such thing as not behaving. Thus, apathy or passivity is a form of Political participation for some.

In liberal democratic political systems, it is regarded as essential that more and more people participate in the system. However various studies have revealed that only a very small percentage, even less than 10 per cent participate in the political process. Actually participation and its extent is related to various factors - the psychological make up of the person, his total personality and external environment the social, economic, cultural, individual response to such stimuli, but his political attitude is outcome of his social Personality and his Political options reflect the characteristic modes of his adjustments to life.

Milbrath holds that political participation differs in relation to four major factors: (i) the extent to which the individual receives political stimuli; (ii) the individual's personal characteristics; (iii) social characteristics: and (iv) the political environment in which the individual finds himself. Dahi is of the opinion that some people are indifferent to politics, others are more deeply involved. Even among those who are deeply involved, Only some actually seek power and among the power seekers, some gain power more than others.

Milbrath basing on the intensity of participation divides input Political activity mainly into three categories (i) active: (ii) passive or supportive; and (iii) apathetic. Active political activity is again categorised into conventional and unconventional. Participation in protest process, is regarded by Milbrath as unconventional.

Why at Low Ebb ?

Participation of women in the political process has been very low. Their presence in the legislative and decision-making bodies is scarcely above 10 per cent except some Nordic countries. It has been often stated that the personality traits of women (lack of self-esteem to be precise) and the socio-economic cultural environment and, on the other hand, the political environment is to a great extent responsible for women's Marginal participation in politics.

Preceding observations reveal that self-esteem, standing in the society, the culture which puts maximum premium on the male and the political environment of instability, criminalisation and absence of political ideology are factors which influence the extent of political participation.

Women fall mainly into the group of those who are apathetic to politics because of the group of those who are apathetic to politics because of their low status in society (ii) lesser exposure to education (iii) very low economic status (iv) the restraining, cultural norms and, (v) the unhealthy political environment, the nature of political structure, such as party structure, process of political succession, which supports or opposes the recruitment of women to political offices.

In nutshell the socio-political environment determines the participation and involvement of women in politics. Culture is a very dominant factor. It deprives women of the self-esteem necessary for political leadership. Jean J Kirkpatrick observes "in a culture which values the male more highly than the female, women may never acquire the confidence and autonomy required to seek power and wield it effectively." Culture decides role choices, "The transition from the roles of housewife and mother to the role of political decision-maker is riot easy, and has not been frequently attempted. The roles of housewife, mother, law-maker etc, do not have what Eulau and Spranger have called professional convergence". Kirkpatrick refutes the established relationship between power, politics, and maleness. According to her, the female psychology is no more a disqualification for politics. She maintained that in the ultimate analysis, "to many radical feminists culture, ideology and social structure are conspiracy. The enemies are male and female are the most oppressed political caste in history."

Various Streams

The most prevalent political action is voting in elections. Although the 'right to vote' was won after a grim battle in most of the Western liberal democracies, at present women constitute a reasonable percentage of total voters in almost all political systems with the exception of some Middle East Muslim states.

Although there has been a global awareness and realisation that political participation does not only mean the right to vote (right from the Mexico conference in 1975 through Copenhagen, Nairobi and Beijing), yet women's presence in legislative bodies is scarce despite the absence of legal constraints.

So women have been accepted as voters but not as policy formulators and decision-makers. Women's movement has for the last two or three decades been demanding more space for women in the representative bodies, but things have scarcely changed. Demands for affirmative action/reservation as an instrument for ensuring more space to women has been repeatedly turned down in many countries. The ERA never got passed in USA. In India, although 33 per cent reservation was provided for women at grass-root level and local institutions through the constitutional amendment in 1993, the bill providing for 33 per cent reservation to women in the Lok Sabha and the state assemblies was not passed in 1996. It was not allowed even to be tabled in the Lok Sabha in 1998. This speaks a lot about the rigid patriarchal approach of the male political leaders. They will not let any effort for giving more space to women in politics go waste.

Even though democracy has made great gains in the 1990s, women average only 11.6 per cent of the world legislatures (inter-parliamentary union, 1997). Women essentially are appointed by men leaders in at least 37 undemocratic countries or are entirely missing from the national legislatures. In an additional 49 nations the new democracies or the partially developed ones – men parliamentarians dominate the legislature with 93 per cent membership. Only in the 27 long-established but unfinished democracies do women have the greatest opportunity for equality in representation. Yet, women members of these Parliaments average only 15 per cent.

Government of the people, by the people and for the people - Abraham Lincoln's concept of democracy - is an ideal which remains unachieved in the world specially in the context of half the population of any country, the women.

Democracy falls short when women of whatever colour or ethnic groups cannot vote or caste votes, and cannot expect success in electing representation of their choice, or being elected to the legislative bodies, and have little hope for enactment of laws they believe are critically needed.

The reasons - narrow gender roles, restrictive religious doctrines, unequal laws and education, discriminatory socio-economic conditions, male biased leaders or other political elites and women-unfriendly election system. The barriers, while varying among countries typically are interrelated and mutually reinforcing.

Anne Phillips in her The politics of presence maintains that the shift from direct to representation democracy has shifted the emphasis from who the politicians are to what they represent. She further maintains that men may consciously stand for women when what is at issue is the representation of agreed policies or programmes on ideals, but how can men legitimately stand in for women when what is at issue is the representation of women par se.

Phillips speaks about gender parity and accounts that a significant number of political parties have adopted the measures to raise the proportion of women elected. She recounts the experiences in South Africa and European countries like UK, Germany, the

Nordic countries where, when one party adopted a gender quota other parties also followed suit. The green party in Germany contributed to the quota - the Christian Democratic Party was adopted in 1986. There is consensus among major political parties in UK, atleast at the central level, in favour of selecting more women candidates.

She maintains that changing the gender composition of elected assemblies is a major and necessary challenge to the social arrangements, which have systematically placed women in a subordinate position and whether we conceive of politics as the representation of interests or need (or both) a closer approximation to gender parity is one minimal condition for transforming the political agenda. But she also mentions that this change cannot guarantee anything. The case for gender parity among our political representatives inevitably operates in a framework of pobabilities; rather than certanities. She maintains that politics of presence points towards rather different policy recommendation depending on the nature of the excluded group. In relation to women, a straight-forward quota seems entirely appropriate. In comparison to racial or ethnic quotas, the introduction of minimum quota for women and men is less inherently problematic because there are self evidently two sexes.

Phillips is, thus, in favour of politics of presence. It can ensure that there is a possibility of gender parity, as politics of presence can provide separate recommendation for the excluded group.

A Continued Journey

Women in India entered the political process in the early decades of the present century, through their massive participation in the national struggle for freedom under the leadership of Mahatma Gandhi. Gandhiji was able to reach out to women and draw them Into the vertex of the freedom movement. Though Gandhi could not fully abandon gender bias and in some way perpetuated the traditional image of the Indian women he did manage to appeal to women to join the movement. Women played a very important role in the Civil Disobedience Movement, the salt satyagraha and the Quit India Movement of 1942. Together with their Participation in movement against the colonial rule, the educated women were simultaneously struggling to get the right to vote and right to get elected. Generally, It is maintained that the women participating in the struggle especially, those who were in key positions were from the elite class. Not much has been written about thousands of Infamous women, who were poor and had rural background, but who In their own humble way had participated in the national freedom struggle.

Some women leaders were very articulate in their ideas and their awareness of the situation was prevalent. For example, in 1917, even before women in England got the right to vote. Sarojini Naidu had petitioned to the British Parliament the Indian women's demand for equal voting rights with men.

Gandhi had said as early as in 1929, "women must have the right to vote and equal legal status. But the problem does not end there. It only commences at the point where women begin to effect the political deliberations of the nation."

Gandhiji brought an absolutely new dimension into the debate on women's problem. He began from the basic issue that subjugation of and exploitation of women was the product of "men's teaching and women's acceptance of them, and thereby broke away from the reform tradition by preaching the philosophy not only of absolute equality of rights between the sexes, but the pragmatic necessity of enrolling women's support to transform the nationalist struggle for the transfer of power from the British to India through social revolution.

There is little doubt that it was the willing and spontaneous participation of women in the Civil Disobedience Movement rather than the radical ideas of sexual equality that finally tilted the balance in favour of political equality between the sexes within the Congress party and later in the Constituent Assembly.

The Constitution of free India saluted the massive participation of women in the freedom struggle by equal rights to enter into politics irrespective of gender and other factors.

It is now nearly 49 years since the Constitution was adopted in 1950. Despite the opportunity of equal access to the political process guaranteed by law, the presence of Indian women in politics is still scarce. Their representation has never gone beyond 9 per cent in Parliament, 10 per cent in state assemblies and 15 per cent in the Council of Ministers. Even though India had a Prime Minister like Indira Gandhi - the longest surviving women Prime Minister- women have not been able to find space in the representative and decision-making bodies.

Women's movements in India have been struggling for women's political rights for nearly five-six decades, yet women could only managed to get their demands for quota/reservation in Parliament and state legislatures included in election manifestoes of the political parties in 1991, 1996 and 1998 general elections.

The parties despite their promises have displayed their gender bias in giving tickets to women to fight elections. The Congress (1) has not been able even to put 15 per cent women candidates, although the party has the record of putting up comparatively the highest number of women candidates.

A major reason forwarded by all political parties is that the chances of women candidates winning are very thin compared to male candidates. However, the election reports display that the percentage of women winning in relation to their total candidates is much higher than male.

April 23, 1993 was a red letter day for Indian women, when the 73rd Constitutional Amendment gave statutory status to panchayats and provided 33 per cent reservation of seats to women at every tier of the grassroot political institutions. The elections have revealed that the number of women in gram panchayats is increasing steadily.

The granting of reservation to women at grass-root-level institution inspired women to make a similar demand with regard to Lok Sabha and state legislatures. Women activists and academics have been intensifying their demands in this regard, but it is being met with a constant protest by the males, as displayed in 1996 and 1998 by male members cutting across party lines.

Adequate representation in representative bodies is very important for women's empowerment in the political process, and reservation/affirmative action is being seen as the most potent strategy. The negative aspects are being heatedly debated not only by men, but also by some women activities. The debate still continues.

An important shift is being noted in the last couple of years from representation to governance. The Centre for Women's Development Studies, New Delhi, organised a meeting on gender democracy and governance In September 1997, in which Rajni Kothari opined in his paper that from focus on representation to focus on governance was an important transition. Why this emerging interest in governance? Because representation without participation in governance will only underscore the existing order. All feminists agree that gender represents a system of power relation. In Indian history, however, it can only be defined as an instrument to maintain a hierarchical social order designed to perpetuate inequality and diversity of a multiethnic, multi-lingual and multi-cultural population, said Vina Majumdar.

Caste is an important factor in Indian politics. Social scientists have been grappling with the phenomenon of caste for a long time, but only few have appreciated that the major instrument for maintaining the hierarchy even more than diversity is the subordination of women. Srinivasan's theory of Sanskritisation with increasing subordination/control on women believed to be applicable only to upwardly mobile. The studies by the Centre for Women's Development Studies, New Delhi find it equally manifest among all other groups, including the tribals, generally believed to be more generous in recognising women's right.

Women by and large have demonstrated their stake in democracy, especially when they threw out Indira Gandhi's government which was the first major attack on democracy since Independence. With the resurgence of women's movement since the 1970s. it advocates that "transformational politics" have increasingly recognised the potential of the movement to deepen democracy in India. Most analysis however, continue to harness the fear that women's large scale entry into power structures will only result in cooperation instead of changing the undemocratic and corruptive elements in these structures.

Vina Majumdar suspects that these fears are based on the continued undemocratic view of power and a narrow understanding of politics.

Majumdar writes about 'social engineering' as democracy in India was a radical departure from the inherited social system. At present, social engineering has become politically incorrect and nation states are being asked to reduce their interventionist roles. In the kind of democracy India has this weakening and extremely negative impact on the quality of governance or the management of power.

The role of women in the political process in India within the conceptual framework of gender and patriarchy. Women's role in the national freedom struggle has been analysed, and it has been found that gender equality was never the concern of our reformers in the late 19th century or our political leaders of the movement. They wanted a better place for women in the society, but for they never considered women's right as "individuals".

Similarly, the participation of women in formal political institutions and process has been severely restricted by gender considerations. The socio-cultural norms still restrict the movements and behaviour of women. Despite all the changes, women's behaviour is still restricted by the private female and public/male dichotomy. A very recent example is from Haryana where girls of 18 years are not allowed to cast their vote if they are unmarried. They can cast their votes only as married women if their husbands and family members permit and in the manner they want.

The opposition to women's reservation showed by the 81st Constitutional Amendment in 1996 by the male MPs and again in 1998 and onwards clearly mirrors the patriarchal attitude of our men in politics. It is very clear that they will not permit the loss of nearly 180 seats in Parliament to women, which will happen precisely if 33 per cent seats in Look Sabha are reserved for women.

The gender and patriarchal norms have perpetuated the subordination of women in the family and extended their subordination in the wider society, economy and polity. The environmental deterrents - social economic, cultural as well as political factors are in a close way related to these norms. India is characterised as a nation which is poor, has low level of education and awareness, is overridden by the feudal considerations. It is a multi-ethnic, multilingual and multi-religious society, and not all groups have equal access to the arena of politics. Yet, among all groups men have better enhances of access than women. The present Parliament in India consists of a majority of members from the backward castes and Dalits, but has the number of women of these groups or communities accordingly increased?

True, women need to be made conscious of their role in politics, the importance of their participation in parties and women's groups are continuously trying to train and mobilise them but centuries of subordination and passivity cannot be wished away in two decades. More than 50 years of Independence have not been able to ensure reasonable space for women in the representative bodies. It has not gone above 10 per cent. Therefore, there is a need for affirmative action in the form of quote/reservation for women. It is the prime need of the time.

4

Factors at Work

The Indian world is a male world with ambivalent attitude towards female. She is visualised as good and noble as well as bad and degenerative. Her reproductive functions are worshipped, but her sex is considered as a pull towards hell. She is respected as mother but hated as charmer. Still the Indian male wishes to enjoy her sex in every conceivable manner as is depicted in temple designs, architecture, erotic texts and in the pornographic material. Literature depicts his enjoyment; his keenness to impregnate her and to father many children even though they may be deprived of food and milk and live in abject poverty. The female submits herself to the male's demands because she believes she must serve him and raise the offspring she is destined to bear. She is absolutely dependent on male for her well-being. The willingness of the female for male domination, for letting him enjoy her body without her desire for it, for bearing children without having strength to endure pregnancy or money to feed them is explained by the fact that her life is woven into the myth of motherhood and service to man whom she has been conditioned to be economically dependent. Her weakness makes it obligatory for her to seek male protection and male in turn considers it as his birthright to hold the positions of power and authority over her.

The most vital questions which the modern psychologists and sociologists are concerned with are: Why are Indian women, even the educated ones, not prepared to emerge free from their mythical existence? Why are they submitting to the irrational male domination? Why are the Indian women still not prepared to lead a free and independent life? To seek answers to these questions we will have to peep into the psyche of the Indian women. To do so we will have to revert back to the women in ancient India.

There is no doubt in it that the ancient Aryan women were strong willed and dominating. The traces of domination can be found in the lives of the famous and respected women of ancient India. Hence it may be possible that the psyche of the Indian women is an offshoot of an urge to dominate. This may sound to be a view very much different from the prevailing opinion. But it has many elements of truth. We will present some arguments and facts in favour of this viewpoint.

The powerful and strong women of ancient India, when controlled by scheming males contrived a way to seek satisfaction. Pardweshi, the wife of blind Rishi Drighatamas, threw him in the river when he proposed legislation that a woman should have only one husband in her life. She was not prepared to subordinate her sexuality to the whims of one male. Drighatamas saved himself by clinging to a raft and lived long enough to put through his proposals. Later women were bound by this law and were unable to physically revolt, because of weakness due to frequent pregnancies and domestication. These women learned to achieve supremacy not by trying to break the myths, but by strengthening them. They did not make demands, but submitted to the demands of men. As the men continued to assert themselves, the strands of the web increased and women internalised their domination and externalised their subordination until their external life became miserable and their internal life gained expression through entirely different channels.

Indian woman serves her husband and rears her children and finds happiness in being half-clad and half-fed so that her husband and children get the best. Then her son marries and she demands a great price for rearing him up in the form of dowry. When the daughter-in-law enters the house, the mother-in-laws dominant attitude becomes explicit. Many stories depict the harshness with which the mother-in-law treats her son's wife. In some marriage customs, the mother of the son runs out of the house and sits on the edge of a well ready to jump in until the son and daughter-in-law offer their devotion and shower her with gifts. Thus the urge for domination which she has repressed when she entered the house as a young bride now finds as outlet, as she becomes the domineering mother-in-law.

The strict supervision and harsh moral codes under which women rear their daughters may also be outlets of the dominant urge. The Indian woman judges other women's behaviour patterns under strict social norms. Any failing on the part of another woman is a delight because it establishes her own moral superiority. By scandalising other she obtains a sense of power. No wonder that women gossip has become such powerful instrument for the maintenance of the status quo. Any change in existing norm releases dormant energy for domination.

We have made an earlier reference to the predominance of an element of masochism in the Indian female. This element is her weapon for dominance. She stoops to conquer and often become successful. Consequently, her husband becomes more sadistic and tries to crush her further. She submits to his cruelty and thus shows superiority in endurance, thus, a vicious cycle ensues.

Women's desire for dominance is a secret hidden desire. It is not evident at the external level of her existence but an analysis of her behaviour pattern throughout her life reveals it. Woman learns from early life that she is liked if she is helpless and dependent. She gets her needs met from her father and brothers when she subordinates herself completely and serves them devotedly. She learns that her path to any type of fulfillment lies through them. She also notices that her prestige and way of life depend on her docility. She, therefore, represses her will for independent thinking. She becomes completely domesticated and all her desire for dominance finds an outlet in leading a subordinated home life.

Carstairs while carrying on her study of "village women of Rajasthan" was warned by the men of the village that their submissive women were really quite strong-minded and often get their own way. The women even employed witchcraft. Carstairs says: "At first, I found it almost inconceivable that these meek, seemingly unassertive women could be seen as powerful agents of the supernatural; but on 7th March, 1950, 1 witnessed a scene which revealed them in a rather different light". ' That night when all the men of the village, except Carstairs and an invalid old man, left the village for joining a wedding party the women came out of their houses and with gay abandon indulged in dancing, singing, abusing and rehearsing many of the sexual acts. They were unbridled, strong in their expressions; and as fully emancipated as women in any part of the world can be. The next day Carstairs found their behaviour dull and demure. Carstairs writes: "Next day the wedding party returned from Togi, and the women of Sujarupa resumed their normal demure behaviour, but I felt that I had been shown a glimpse of quite a different side of their nature, one rarely given free expression".

It must be noted that Indian women have developed the art of concealing the extrovert side of their nature. From their external behaviour it is difficult to fathom their psyche. One must patiently go deeper into the analysis of their behaviour pattern. It is firmly asserted that they are neither treacherous nor evil. There has, however, developed some complexity in their behaviour promoted by the sadistic attitudes of the men and suppressed feelings of the women for, the ages.

In all the normal human beings, both the attitudes of dominance and submission may be found. Both are necessary for survival. In women, submission is overt, while in the men, dominance is external. But covertly, neither the domination in women nor the submission in men is completely lost. Women learn to submit in order to dominate, and men learn to dominate in order to submit. Thus it may be wrong to contend that the Indian world is absolutely a male world. It is true that men have the economic power but this is what the women desire. Until they learn to desire overtly their own freedom and independence the situation regarding their status and position is not going to change. Here is then a challenge for those who plan for women education in our country. They have to plan, for a different cultural training than that which is prevalent today.

We may again repeat that domination and submission are a universal parts of nature. When one is confronted by physical danger, the instinct of self-preservation leads him to choose either to fight or flee. Some animals play possum" and pretend they are dead until their predator leaves. Others attack ferociously. Pardweshi made an attempt to fight. Women after her learned to be more careful and played possum. They took flight in the inner dorms of their psyche and wage a battle in which their unconscious played the part of warrior who fought not with weapons of destruction, but with the weapons of seduction and devotion. If the Indian women are satisfied with the situation as described above then why bother to change it? If she is dominant in her own way why consider her the weaker sex? To find satisfactory answers to these questions the following consequences of her above described behaviour pattern must be taken into consideration. The most important consequence is that the development of the psyche of the Indian woman takes place in the direction of creating a split personality. The person who is responsible to subdue her becomes her passion. She becomes too ritualistic, superstitious and superficial. She becomes too modest and looses all her initiative in taking decisions. Her life becomes one, of rigidity and ignorance.

She curbs independent thinking not only in herself but also in her daughter and other female relatives. She develops intolerance to any deviant member of her own sex. She becomes ruthless with her dependent relatives, particularly towards those women who are either divorced or widows.

Indian men respect motherhood in their women folk while women seem to want to turn their husbands into little boys so that they can "mother" them. The women want their men to be completely dependent on them to fulfil their needs. This type of behaviour pattern may be at the root of Indians lapses in taking bold decisions in the hours of crises and in the development of the "killer instinct" in the competitive games and competitive enterprises. They very often lose control even in the win-win situations.

The subordination of the Indian women served the purpose of securing for them the protection they needed so that they might avoid hardships for themselves and their children. Aileen Ross writes:

> "The attitude of Hindu women to this subordinate position has not often been understood by Western observers, for they have seldom seen it in the context of the total family setting. Bachmann interprets the satisfaction, which the Hindu women did, in fact, derive from her seemingly 'low' position. He describes Kasturbai, Gandhi's wife: 'Whoever knows her is bound to believe that the self-surrender of the widow which led to the custom of self-immolation on the funeral pyre, must in certain cases have been quite voluntary".

The Indian women are considered downtrodden, but to a great extent they are exercising their own will to this effect. They must now understand through proper education and training that the subordination might have been prudent in the past and the tension relieving in the present, but it is no longer necessary for the Indian women to submit to it. They must reflect upon on to what they desire and develop enough strength to achieve their goals of life. They must purge out old orthodox traditions and adapt to the modern world. It is satisfying to note that quite a few modern educated women are taking initiative in achieving their economic independence and in the free exercise of their will power. They are showing their excellence in very diverse fields. There are at present almost all the avenues of work or activities in which they are competing with men and achieving success. No doubt there are still a large number of women who are living the life of drudgery and toil mostly because of lack of initiative on their part and due to their ignorance. Hence the educational system in this country is facing the gigantic task of emancipation and empowerment of such women.

Eleanor Maccoby and Carol Jacklin (1974) reviewed and integrated the extensive research literature on psychological sex differences, reading through some 2,000 books and articles in the process. Most of these studies were comparisons of male and female behaviour in infancy and childhood, rather than in adulthood. On the basis of their review, they concluded that many of the differences that are commonly believed to exist between males and females are in fact myths. For example, there is no good evidence that boys are more independent, ambitious or achievement oriented than girls or that girls are more nurturant, sociable or suggestible than boys are. On the whole Maccoby and Jacklin conclude that male and female are much more similar to one another than they are different, and they share the same fundamental needs, emotions and abilities.

If many of the stereotypical differences between the sexes are myths, then why are they perpetuated? The main reason for the perpetuation of the myths seems to be the different opportunities that society provides for men and women. In fact, as children grow up, boys undoubtedly become more politically and professionally ambitious than girls, and girls become more interested in taking care of children. The differences that we observe probably result from social values and opportunities, rather than from basic psychological differences.

Our expectations about what men and women should do and what they should like are called sex roles. Boys are encouraged to be ambitious and assertive and discouraged from expressing their weaknesses or their tender feelings. Girls on the other hand learn to play a more submissive and dependent role. They are taught to be well-behaved and co-operative and to act as if they have no aggressive impulses at all. Girls are also expected to be tender and nurturing. These expectations are effectively communicated to the sons and daughters. This communication is sometimes done directly by suggesting the desired behaviour to the child and by rewarding the child for performing it. In addition, once the child learns his or her sex which all children do by age three, the child invariably wants to demonstrate that he or she can behave like a member in good standing of that sex.

Gender Equality

As we are marching towards 21st century, the growing age of computer technology, the psychologists and sociologists are coming to the conclusion that traditional sex roles are in need of change. They have come to believe that by putting people in slots labelled 'male' and 'female' and shaping them to fit the slots we are limiting their full development as human beings. Instead they propose that each child should be treated as a total person; without regard for the traditional notions of what a boy or girl should be.

It may, however, also be noted that as the idea of breaking down traditional roles has gained force, there has also been a great deal of opposition to it. It is argued that sex roles are based on biological differences that have evolved over the course of millions of years and, therefore, should not be tempered with. In his book Sexual Suicide, George Gilder (1973) writes:

> "When reforming the roles of men and women, we must always be careful to avoid gibberish-patterns of activity that so violates the inner constitution of the species that they cannot be integrated with our irreducible human natures"

Gilder's warning 'may have some validity, but recent research findings reduce the force of his arguments. Maccoby and Jacklin emphasise that psychological differences between men and women are small, and they are based on only a slight degree of biological predispositions. Considerable change in sex roles could be accomplished by changing our values and expectations, without negation of our biological nature.

A second argument against sex-role changes is the notion that if boys and girls do not develop the pattern of traits that are appropriate for their sex, they may become confused about their sexual identity and thereby run the risk of serious maladjustment.

But recent research provides little cause for such alarm. Virtually all girls and boys learn without much trouble which sex they belong to and they do this by the time they are three years old. The extensive sex-role training that follows is not necessary to develop a stable sexual identity. In addition, highly 'masculine' males and highly 'feminine' females are not better adjusted or healthier than people who are less highly sex-typed.

Sandra Bern (1975) has called the ability to behave in ways, traditionally associated with both sexes Psychological androgyny. An androgynous person is one who combines 'masculine' and 'feminine' behaviours. Bern has, measured androgyny by asking students how often various adjectives are descriptive of themselves. Some of the adjectives were traditionally masculine, as for example, ambitious, self-reliant, and independent. Some were traditionally feminine like affectionate, gentle, sensitive. Subjects were categorised as androgynous if they indicated that they are about equally well-described by masculine and feminine traits. Bern found that androgynous students of both sexes behaved more effectively in a variety of laboratory situations than students who were highly masculine or highly feminine. The androgynous men and women could be independent and assertive when they needed to be men or women. They were also responsive in appropriate situations. They were able to behave in a more flexible and humane manner.

The above finding has very significant implications for schooling. Some schools keeping in mind the value of androgynous personality have started to provide work experiences for boys and girls in order to develop the dignity of labour in them and to accommodate reciprocal roles. Some co-educational institutions have introduced cooking, homecraft and embroidery for both boys and girls in their curriculum. They are providing the same type of curriculum for both boys and girls. It is desirable that almost all the schools should provide such a curriculum, which do not discriminate between the two sexes.

In spite of various measures, which have been taken for ameliorating the conditions of the Indian women there is still much scope for reforms. Unless such customs, traditions, rituals and values and attitudes which view and treat women as inferior beings and less desirable than men are discarded and changed, the status and position of the Indian women are not going to improve. This change can be brought about through equalitarian, formal and informal education. Education must prepare both the sexes for becoming all that they can be without any discrimination or prejudice.

The Downtrodden

We have described the socio-psychological factors which are influencing the education of the Indian women. In considering Indian women we have kept in our frame of reference a Hindu middle class woman. But Indian society is a very stratified one.

There are many castes, classes and religions. The women belonging to upper and lower castes, rich and poor classes and Hindus, Muslims and Christians have their own specific problems even though as women they suffer from all those limitations with which the average woman of Hindu middle class suffers. In the present and the next chapters we are paying special attention to the problems concerning education of Dalit women and the women of the minority communities specially the Muslim women.

We are using the term Dalit women for all those women who are either put in the category of Harijans or Schedule Castes. These women suffer from many types of social disadvantages. Some of them were considered, untouchable while in the case of most of them the food touched by them was considered as defiled by the caste Hindus. Many of these indignities have now been sought to be abolished by the legal measures, but still their lot is far from satisfaction. One of the important reasons for this state of affairs is the woeful neglect of their education. Their ignorance is the major threat to their existence. Why has their education suffered ? What were the factors are still existing which have pushed them into a miserable existence? What factors which are putting hindrances in their respectable right of living? The thesis of this book is that these factors have to be searched out in the socio-psychological make-up of the women, particularly in relation to their education.

The Dalits have been put at the lowest level in the caste hierarchy of the Hindus. They were required to serve the higher castes. We are not entering into any discussion here as how and why this happened. This has already been a subject of a large number of investigations and discussions. Our concern here is that how this has affected the psyche of Dalits as well as the upper castes.

The Dalits were constantly reminded that they were the objects of hatred and their salvation lied in the service of the upper castes. This was done sometimes by persuasion but most of the times by force by the Brahamanical order of the Hindu society. They were told that they must have committed some heinous crimes or evil actions in their past life and hence they are born as "untouchables". This developed in them a feeling of inferiority complex and they began to consider themselves as the inferior specimen of the mankind. This feeling was much more aggravated among the females of the Dalits since they were considered inferior to their own men. The Dalit women accepted their lower status and position and started believing that it was fated that they involve themselves in doing menial tasks. Since these tasks required no education or training they developed a mentality that education is meant for the upper and richer castes and not for them. They thus never made an attempt to send their children to the schools. Also the higher castes did not allow Dalit children to sit with their own children in the schools and there were no schools exclusively set up for Dalit children.

The literacy rate in India according to the census of 1991 was 52.11 per cent. The percentage of male literacy was 63.86 while that of female was 39.42 only. According to the census report of 1981 the general female literacy percentage was 24.82. The literacy percentage of scheduled caste females was as low as 10.93 and of scheduled tribe females was 8.04 (Census was not conducted in Assam and no castes were scheduled by the President of India for Nagaland, A and N Islands and Laskhadweep and no tribes were scheduled in Haryana, Jammu and Kashmir, Punjab, Chandigarh, Delhi and Pondicherry). These figures show that the education of the Dalit women was totally neglected.

The Dalit women were mostly working in the unorganised sector. In the organised sector their percentage Was quite low. There were only two scheduled caste women in Indian Foreign Services in 1987 while the number of male scheduled castes was 65. The male scheduled tribes number was 30 while that of the females was 5 only. Similar was the case in most of the other Central services. In all the Central services while the total number of the women employed was 994 in the year 1987 only 31 were scheduled caste women and 31 scheduled tribe women.

The employment prospects for Dalit women in the organised sector are very few. These women neither have the educational, nor technical qualifications and nor have contacts or social connections. They have also to face discrimination from two directions. One is that they are women and the second that they belong to low strata of the society. Hence in spite of the reservations for schedule castes and backward classes the benefit do not reach up to them. Hence most of the Dalit women in the urban areas are self-employed in the areas like hawking, scrap collection, domestic help, petty trade, etc. The women have to undertake such employment for their survival and for supporting their families. The income from such jobs is very meagre and also has uncertainties. There is no security also in these types of activities. Some Dalit women are also employed in wage employment activities. These activities include construction labour, earthwork, petty manufacturing activities like beedi making or candle making etc. They are employed by some traders in these activities and are being paid very low wages. In the rural areas the Dalit women are engaged for labour in agriculture and agro-based industries.

From the brief account of the education and employment of the Dalit women it may be evident that in spite of more than 50 years of our independence they are in miserable plight. It is, therefore, necessary for the government as well as the general public that serious efforts are made towards their betterment. We can tackle this problem only when we make all out efforts for their education. One way to do it is to open more and more schools for them and give them incentives like free tuition, dress and mid-day meals. But this is a very simple solution. The women may still not go to attend the school. The majority of the Dalit households will not send their girls of school going age to the schools as this may mean the loss of income for the family as these girls might have been employed in some type of wage earning work or these girls might be busy in looking after their younger siblings, etc. when their parents have left for work. If we wish to educate them and provide help in their social and economic progress we must understand their psychology and the sociological problems which they face.

Various Angles

The Dalit women suffer from extensive inferiority complex. The indignities that they have suffered in the past have left such a deep mark on their psyhe that they had started considering themselves as persons meant to lead a miserable life. This complex has not been altered till the present times. Hardly they take interest in raising their pattern of life. The Dalit leaders have recently made very powerful efforts to bring changes in their thinking. Mayawati and Phoolan Devi are the present day examples of such leaders. But still there is a long way to go before the mentality of Dalit women as the scum of the society is going to change. The efforts of social workers and political leaders are undermined from time to time by the atrocities being committed on them by the upper caste and affluent members of the society. The tradition bound society in India do not relish that the Dalit women should think themselves as equal to them. They are prepared to commit all sorts of acts of aggression on them if they express any desire to achieve equality with the higher caste women.

The daily newspapers are full of incidents describing rapes, murders, and beatings of both the Dalit males and females. These have two types of reactions. One is that the Dalit leaders raise Dalit Sena and try to retaliate by attacking the citadels of the upper castes and the seconds that they take it as a matter of their fate. Both are wrong approaches. The Second approach increases caste tensions without offering any solution. The other approach of it being their fate is the pessimistic outlook that throws them back to square one. A better approach is to educate them in terms of their importance. They should not feel marginalised. It is the duty of their leaders to educate them in terms of their importance in the present day social and political order.

One of the factors responsible for their poor economic condition is the large number of children, which they produce. They do not realise that more children mean more mouths to feed. Unfortunately the Dalit leadership has failed to develop among Dalit women the value of family planning. The syndrome of what is fated will happen need to be altered. We may call such a syndrome as "fatelinked proverty syndrome". Unless the Dalit women are prepared to discard this syndrome their plight will remain the same.

As we have already pointed out the Dalit women's low status and position is due to their poverty and involvement in menial tasks. To improve their lot it is necessary that they should get better education and training. Now no task may be taken as menial. The technology has created a situation in which even the most menial task can be performed with machines. The handling of machines is the task of the technologists. The technologists are those who have got training in the handling of the machines. Thus the women are to be trained in handling machines and in the use of gadgets. One example may be given to clarify the issue raised here. We all know that Barber or Nai caste was considered among the low castes. His job was hair cutting, etc. Today this role has been taken up by the so called beauticians or by the owners of "air conditioned hair cutting saloons." The hair grooming is no more considered as a low task. Similar is the case with cooking. Now Chef is an honourable member of the society. The change has been brought about by the introduction of the specialised training being associated with these professions.

The Dalit women's aspirations and the motivations have to be increased manifolds. For this the social workers have to strive hard. The politicians cannot perform this task because they only want to keep their leadership intact or to get Dalit votes in the election. They have a vested interest in keeping the electorate ignorant and keeping it in the state in which it is so that these leaders can always exploit it by arousing its emotions for caste or class struggle. The enlightened electorate may question their leadership and may ask them to be accountable to the electorate. Only the leaders gain by creating hatred among different castes and classes. We may say that all the leaders are not like this. There are many selfless workers. It is to them that an appeal to bring a change in the psychology of the Dalits should be made.

The role of teachers in bringing attitudinal changes among the Dalit women cannot be ignored. Education does not mean simply learning the language or some other subjects. Real education is that which has a bearing on a better personal and social life of that individual who is getting education. It is, therefore, very important that those teachers are appointed in the schools where the Dalit children are studying who are dedicated to the task of freeing the Dalits from the syndrome of linked poverty.

5

Status in Society

Patriarchy looms large in feminist debate. It implies that power is imperative in gender relation, in producing and maintaining gender relations.

The basic value of the term patriarchy and importance of its use by women is that it denotes a structural system of male domination. In doing so, it contrasts with the ways of looking at women both in the academic social science and in the traditional left movement.

The term 'patriarchy' has double meaning: 'rule of men' and 'rule of the father', the latter been its literal meaning. Its original use was to describe a specific type of male-dominated family - the large household of a patriarch, which included women, junior men, children, slaves and domestic servants, all under the rule of this dominant male. The term patriarchy has not been as universally accepted by the academic feminists as it has been by the women's movement. Rubin Gayle wants to reserve its use for the traditionally extended patriarchal family because she feels that it implies male domination as inevitable. She argues for using the term 'sex-gender' system on the grounds that these can bring equilibrium or perhaps even show aspects of female dominance. Barrett Michels also objects that the term implies a system of male dominance that is completely historical and external to economic systems such as capitalism.

Difference in terminology does not solve the problem of giving an adequate analysis of Patriarchy.

Focussing on the concept as used by the feminist theorists would be the first step. In analysing the development of the concept of patriarchy, it is useful to keep in mind the fallacies discussed in Barrett's recent book Women's Oppression Today.

(a) Dualism - which sees patriarchy and capitalism as separate parallel systems without comprehending their relation and interaction.

(b) Biologism - biological differences are highlighted between men and women to explain social differences.

(c) Functionalism - (or reductionism, economism) which explains particular structures of female oppression in terms of their use for capitalism or any other general structure of oppression.

It is to avoid this characteristic fault of Marxist analysis that feminists originally developed such concepts as patriarchy.

"The difficulty in avoiding these fallacies is that they all have seen in one way - more than a grain of truth. Patriarchy is not fully identical with the capitalist mode of production; gender differences or patriarchal structures do have atleast some biological base, and they do serve functions for economic structures. The problem is to develop an analysis, which can integrate all these facts without going to the extreme."

The origins of the concept can be traced back to the women's movement of the 19th century and Marxism. Einstein maintains that women like Mary Wollenstonecraft, Elisabeth Lady Canton or Harriet Mill, understood in their own fragmented way that men have power as men in a society organised into sexual spheres. But while they spoke of power in caste terms, they were only beginning to understand the structure of power enforced upon them through sexual division of labour in society. These feminists tended to accept the different 'sexual spheres' of men and women even while they argued for equal rights. They argued that motherhood was a basic reason why women needed more power and independence.

These feminists in their own way challenged the patriarchal structure, but could not develop a theory of patriarchy.

Leftist Angle

In The German Ideology, Marx and Engles had incorporated crucial insights about women. Engel's major contribution was to bequeath to the working class movement a conceptualisation that women were not naturally second sex, that they were in fact exploited within an oppressive family structure; and, that this exploitative system was historically created and would historically disappear. Though he used the term father-right, this was essentially a conceptualisation of Patriarchy.

Contemporary feminist theories of Patriarchy emerged primarily in reaction to and in confrontation with the mechanical materialist form of Marxism which developed. This was because it was within the Marxist tradition that concepts such as Patriarchy were retained in however inadequate a form. It has had a theory of patriarchy, though it is inadequate. It has avoided biologism and retained the notion of a separate, male dominated family/ reproduction Systems.

Radical feminism has sought to replace economic class struggle with a notion of sexual class struggle without re-examining Marxism or really attempting to develop a total social theory.

Male Dominance

Radical feminists see patriarchy as the 'rule of men.' It is represented in Kate Millet's Sexual Politics and Shulasmith Firestones' The Dialectic of sex, published in 1970. Both books see patriarchy as a broad system of the power of men over women, particularly over their sexual functions, and see it as historically preceding and more, fundamental than class division. As Kate Millet maintains.

"Our society is a patriarchy. The fact is evident at once if we recall that the military, the industry, technology universities, science, political offices, finance, in short every avenue of power within the society including coercive power, is in male hands."

Mackinnon Catherine argues that gender in society is determined by sexuality and not vice versa.

Sexuality is to feminism what work is to Marxism-that which is one's own, yet most taken away. The moulding, direction and expression of sexuality organises society into two sexes - women and men, - which underlines the totality of social relations.

Millet Firestone, Catherine and the whole movement behind them have drawn our attention to the pursuance of sexual domination, and the role of force and male violence as a major social historical reality.

Marxist feminism, through domestic labour debate, brought out a new conceptualisation of patriarchy. Discussion on domestic labour made it clear that traditional Marxism could be called inadequate not only because it made social and cultural (or sexual) oppressions simply a reflection of the economic oppression, but because it had too narrow a conception of the 'economic' itself.

Socialist Angle

Those who took up the theory of patriarchy from this point of view are all consciously socialist feminists because they began from a partial acceptance of Marxism, an awareness of class oppression and a concern for revolutionary change. At the same time as they took up the feminist awareness of Marxism's inadequacies and the new issues brought forward in women's, movement on the one hand, they criticise traditional Marxists focus on economic class struggle. On the other hand, insights of the radical feminists and the domestic/labour debate, which included both sexual psychological-cultural issues and a new version of economic, tended at first to take a dualistic approach, looking at male and female roles as conditioned by a set of dichotomies, wage labour/domestic labour Public/private productive/reproductive etc. Zillah Eisenstien's work best typified this dualism.

Socialist feminists historical materialism is not defined in terms of relations of production without understanding its connection to the relations that arise from women's sexuality - the relations of reproduction. And the ideological formulation of these relations is the Key. The stress on ideology was new both in comparison to the radical feminists, who had emphasised sex and force, as well as the Marxists domestic labour debates, who had talked only of a particular kind of labour. It apparently comes out of Marxist tradition, but not simply out of a Marxism that relegated women to the superstructure, but out of a Marxism that was itself in the process of developing towards a new stress on cultural-ideological factor. However, these two elements were not really integrated in Eisenstein's theory. It gave a name to structures and relations of male domination and asserted their importance along with class relations in understanding society.

Many theorists have moved in the direction of defining women's labour as a special kind of labour, and patriarchy in terms of male control of that labour.

We can usefully define patriarchy as a set of social relations among men, which has a material base and which, though hierarchical, establishes or creates interest to dominate women. The material base on which patriarchy rests lies most fundamentally in men's control over women's labour power. Characteristic of this approach is that it not only adds reproduction to the concept of production, but also very often makes it basic.

It is significant that nearly all versions of 'women's labour' or 'production of life' approaches to patriarchy involve a two-tier structure of exploitation with male hierarchy at the top, structured by the exploitation of women.

Theoretical View

The 'ideological theory' of patriarchy locates its essential features in the ideological-psychological cultural sphere. Juliet Mitchell's Psychoanalysis and Feminism and Gayle Rubin's Traffic in Women, were both published in 1975. They base their theory by interpreting the work of well-known anthropologist Levi-Strauss and founder of psychoanalysis Sigmund Fraud.

This approach comes to recognise the importance and of early socialisation and of sexual relation between human beings in the construction of personality and at the same time in showing their social base and not taking them as something simply biological and natural. The advantage of this perspective is that it gives a notion of a 'deep structure' at a psychological-ideological level, which can then interact with the economic system of production to produce the concrete forms of "male control of women's sexuality, fertility and labour."

By the early 1980s, patriarchy was no longer a central concept in feminist theoretical discourse. Doubts about its usage and usefulness had emerged. There were four major problems with Patriarchy:

First, it lacked precise definition and the bases of patriarchal control. Mary Wollenstonecraft and Weber located patriarchy in the control of "fathers over household organisation and production", thereby controlling the labour of the household members. Gayle had tried to limit the concept to a certain historical form of control by fathers. Patriarchy should be reserved for a specific sex-gender system: the form of male dominance described in the nomad societies of old testament. Later, feminists have, however, retained the concept for many forms of male domination. Michelle lodges it in 'kinship system'. As to the basic, some seek it in biology, some base it in the cultural and ideological sphere. A third position embraces some form of economic materialism.

The second group of objections raised against in and relates to its persistent universalism, Rowbothom and Barrett maintain that it is not useful to extend the concept because of its extreme variance in expression of role dominance.

Third objection relates to charge of essentialism. Patriarchy assumes pre-given sexual characteristics of men and women. Often this means reverting to biological essence, which contradicts the ideas of second wave feminism. This maintains that gender is separable from biological sex and is constructed by social relations at large. Eisenstein maintains that assuming internal essence of gender can also lead to some very politically reactionary positions.

A fourth objection has been the matter of dualism. Black and ethnic feminists talk about racism being another system of oppression.

A final question is — is patriarchy a system, a set of structured social relations or is it about individual men oppressing individual women?

R Coward has pointed out, in the past historical variety in forms of gender relations colluded in keeping forms of power and domination hidden, and this prevented certain questions. The problems remained regarding explanation of hierarchy between the sexes, and also how to deliver a historically specific account at the same time.

Several theorists, while rejecting container concepts like 'patriarchy' and oppression, have retained the basic ideas of both concepts that 'power' is involved in the production and maintenance of "gender asymmetry". American political scientist Nancy Harstock, who was the first to re-examine power from a feminist perspective, pointed out that feminists, aware of women having always been the object of domination, tended to avoid power, in this way they tacitly reproduced the idea that power is masculine. Examining the power theories, she affirms that power is a gender concept.

Politics has been refined by feminist literature in the context of gender and patriarchy. The elements of patriarchy are very visible in the perception of the political role and status of women.

Political Factor

Politics has been defined variously, but there is a common thread running through all of them, that is inevitable in any society. It is about representation, policy position and power with government as its arena. Miller maintains that it is the activity which aims at bringing government to bear in a particular direction to secure particular results. The definition of politics in recent years has, widened considerably from merely denoting the area of formal government in its widest sense, including all processes directly or indirectly associated with it and in which, in a democracy every citizen has a share.

The concept of politics in terms of objectives and activities has evolved much further than this. Theorists have now accepted that movements, protests, and struggles are legitimate expressions of political behaviour. The political sphere, thus, includes the "spheres, in social relations," where power relations are generated, institutionalised and used to encourage, control or move people's behaviour, attitudes, beliefs in a specified direction to control and regulate the distribution of resources.

This broader definition was drawn up by a group of women scholars and activists, who participated in the UNESCO seminar in Lisbon in 1983. In 1985, this definition was endorsed by a non-aligned ministerial level conference on Role of Women in Development in 1985.

Feminist scholars have been very concerned about what constitutes politics-that it is basically "male activity". Feminist scholars have challenged the dominant hypothesis of the discipline of political science that politics is confined to public sphere. They are critical of the "sexual definition" of politics and of the manner is which the discipline of political science perpetuates this definition. Traditional politics legitimises women's exclusion or absence from power spheres and also, depoticises and, thus, devalues women's concerns. Feminists, therefore, question the rational behind the rigidly dichotomies 'public-private' spheres of activities, and assignment of the spheres on the basis of gender. Traditionally, political science has been built on the recorded knowledge of what has been basically male activities in a sphere designated as public. Feminist scholars have been critical of male Has in research, which accepts male as the norm.

The feminists argue for a redefinition of politics. An important feature of the feminist efforts has been to proclaim the political nature of private life, and the relation between the sexes which has brought traditional politics into question. It has forced the authorities to take account of problems hitherto regarded as belonging to private life. Suggestions have been put forward to bring politics to home rather than trying to bring women to political structures.

Women's political behaviour and their activities in the political arena are severely conditioned by the considerations of gender and patriarchy, Gender could be understood in terms of sociocultural norms, which decide the spheres of action of both the male and female gender. A preconceived notion of the nature and attributes of men and women operate in the society. Culture affects women's political behaviour by depriving them of the self-esteem necessary for political leadership. In a culture, which values the male more highly than the female, women may never acquire the confidence and autonomy required to seek power and wield it effectively. This observation made by Jeene J Kirkpatrict on American women can very aptly be applied in almost all societies. The cultural factor sees the personality of women as the principle cause for the scarcity of women in politics. Culture decides role choices. The transition from the roles of housewife and mother to the role of political decision-maker is not easy and has not been frequently attempted. The roles of housewife, mother, law-makers etc., do not have what Eulau and Spranger have called professional convergence. The traditional role system does make it difficult for women to begin a political career before middle age; to change her place of residence, to develop the skills and acquire the experience needed for political career.

Kirkpatrick refutes the established relationship between power, politics and maleness. According to her, female psychology is no more a necessary disqualification for politics. She maintains that in the ultimate analysis, to many radical feminists "culture, ideology social structure is conspiracy, the enemies are males, and females are the most oppressed political caste in history."

Patriarchy as a concept implies that power is operative in gender relations and in maintaining the status quo some way or other. It is a structural system of male domination over the female, and this relationship is a political relationship. Thus, to Kate Millet, "our society is a patriarchy". Hartman Heidi maintains, the personal is political means for radical feminists that the original and basic class division is between the sexes, and that the motive force in history is the striving of man for power and domination over women.

It is with this backdrop that an attempt has been made to study and assess the participation of Indian women in Politics - in its structures and in its processes and also in sociopolitical movements. The next chapter will present a synoptic view of the political environment in India: the criminalisation of politics through the use of money and muscle power, which affects the entry of women in politics in a very negative way.

6

Position of Authority

This chapter aims at a definition of the term 'political participation' from the vantage point of women's studies, its various manifestations and components, significance in terms of its effectiveness and limitations.

The concept of political participation is closely involved with the concept of power. Since politics is a study of an exercise in power, any political participation should mean a participation in this exercise of power, the power to effectively influence decision-making processes and policies, to reverse the existing situation wherever they are disadvantageous and to bring about the necessary social changes. Hence, political participation Is much more than a physical participation in formal Institutions and structures, though physical participation in formal political institutions is very much necessary for itself and as a means for influencing decisions. Direct and visible participation helps to enlarge freedom of the social group and accelerate the pace of its advancement, but this is not enough. Even an enlarged participation by way of numbers may not lead to the advancement of the cause of that social group. It is, hence, untenable to argue that a substantial increase in the representation of women will automatically lead to greater promotion of women's interests. Further, it is one thing for more women to hold political positions and it is another thing for them to use such positions and power for women's aids. This would also imply that it is lack of sufficient representation of women in various positions at present, which is responsible for their low status or share in the development. It is very much the reverse. A sexual division of labour, the exclusion of women from certain positions and levels of power and their poor representation at decision-making machineries are themselves the result of their poor status.

There are further instances of women when put in positions of power have been the first ones to cut off policies and schemes specially helpful for women. One also finds there is no correlation between extent of participation in formal institutions and the extent of development of women in society. There have been instances where the socially backward regions in India have sent more women into Assemblies, where women have gone in greater numbers to vote (as in Utter Pradesh). In fact, the first woman Chief Minister as well as the first woman Prime Minister in India belonged to this state, even though from the point of view of all development indicators for women, Utter Pradesh is one of the lowest.

It is thus necessary to ask the question as to whose benefit is this participation directed and what impact has this participation made on the policies and the system over a period. For effecting this impact, it is equally necessary to assess as to the levels at which this participation is taking place. There number is not enough; it has to be situated at levels which are significant and effective for exercising power. Massive mobilisation and numerically impressive participation in political processes, formal or informal, are not goals in themselves. They are a means and a strategy for achieving something more, which the group can do, only when its participation touches at the structure of politics itself. One has to therefore identify the broader processes of the political structure and the way power is arranged in a particular society. The ideology of the state, the interrelationship between the important components in its structure, like class, caste and gender, and its basic development goals are essential in understanding the repercussions of participation. Often, a vastly expanded participation and wide mobilisation of a socially weak community - in this context women has led to the strengthening of the present pattern of development rather than directing this pattern to their own development. Even values like equality (constitutional, political and economic), rights (property, access to resources) etc. may be meaningful only when women possess and exercise them for bringing about a change in their own position as well as of the society; otherwise they will merely add up to strengthening and reinforcing the existing social system by operating within the framework of patriarchy. Values like equality and rights, and concepts like participation and mobilisation need to constantly keep before them the objective of the client group. Above all, it should be related to and tested against another equally important value justice.

Any assessment of the political participation of women in India, then, has to start by asking questions like: Whether such participation has led to bringing about or moving towards improving the quality of life for them or simply making it more liveable for women? Whether such participation, by women, either as individuals or as group, has meant developing alternate strategies for development as well as structures of power? Whether political interventions, which women seek to make, start with women as points of departure or merely help women to infiltrate systematically in the existing hierarchies of power, thereby lending themselves to becoming women performers or even worse, careerists? If increasing political participation has to have any meaning for women, such participation should be based on a widespread and well orchestrated mobilisation of women on the central Issue of women's oppression and subordinate status in society and family.

Any analysis of political participation of women in India, hence, would have to combine a few components like (a) the extent, level and nature of women's participation in the political processes of India, by way of both formal and informal institutions; (b) the impact and significance of such participation for women's rights and living conditions, and, (c) types of feminist issues that were raised in the course of this participation.

With the above three criteria in view, one can assess the nature and extent of women's participation in some of the significant formal and informal processes of Indian politics. The Freedom Struggle, peasant and trade union movements, electoral and legislative institutions, the local self government (Panchayat Raj system) and administrative and judicial functioning are some of these formal processes wherein participation of women can be evaluated. There are also institutions like political parties; interest and lobby groups; and, regional, linguistic, religious and casteist, movements where women are participating increasingly. Finally, it is the women's movement, with various women's groups and organisations.

This chapter cannot aim to examine all of these. To illustrate the main argument of this chapter on how to assess participation of women, Let's take up a few examples.

Past Experience

The Freedom Struggle in India is one of the few liberation movements in the world, where women had participated in great number. Ever since the formation of the Indian National Congress In 1885, the participation of women in its activities grew steadily, but slowly. The years of social reforms for women from the second quarter of the 19th century, had helped to make them come forward and participate in many ways, both directly and indirectly, formally and informally, with support and backup or many which are now been unrecognised. The huge increase in women's participation following the clarion call of Mahatma Gandhi is, however well documented.

What was the impact of such participation on society, family and on women themselves? The mobilisation of women in large numbers weakened the bondage of traditions and helped them to develop a perspective on wider sociopolitical problems. Their close link with the national movement helped them acquire the right to political participation, to franchise and to other constitutional rights. There developed a tacit acceptance of women occupying various positions, both in the political and professional spheres. It gave them the space, as well as the power to claim rights and question its noncompliance. It thus, helped in bringing about significant changes in the way of thinking and attitude to life of women. Women were initiated in politicisation, and the effect of it could be seen in the gradual but a definite change in the bringing up of the next generation of girls.

The Effects

The net gain in the process was a heightened political awareness, and a much greater social consciousness among women. There were, of course, very few instances of women having defied the family to join in the nationalist movement, or of having given up her traditional values and roles. But the fact that many women, of all classes and walks of life, even housewives and the uneducated joined picketing, moved from house to house collecting clothes and donations, courted arrest and were imprisoned in distant jails, showed that there was nothing which could really prevent them from moving beyond traditional roles. The prevailing political environment and values, seem to have accepted and even positively encouraged such activities on the part of women. The Freedom Movement and Indian women's widespread participation in it, thus, brought out a conducive climate for perceptible changes in many areas. Women's education and participation in work outside home and in the income generation, were some of the changes which come about. The nationalist movement under Gandhi stressed on the simple ways of living, giving up of ostentation in daily lives as well as marriages, in eating habits as well as in women's relief from daily chores so as to give time to picketing, spinning, etc. These broader changes, undoubtedly, led to a changed attitude towards life and women's position. Marriages became simple; dowry system got weakened; education of girls went up; potentialities of girls were identified, tapped and encouraged; widow remarriages and singleness of girls definitely showed an upward trend. More and more women gave up purdah.

The impact of women's participation was immediate and visible on the Congress leadership. Gandhi and Nehru recognised the women's valuable contribution to the nationalist movement, and felt the need for improving their situation. Gandhi said, "I am uncompromising in the matter of woman's rights ...she should labour under no legal disability not suffered by man".

The liberal egalitarian legacy of the Indian National Movement, in turn, had led to the Constitution of free India granting a position of equality to women by way of political rights. The provision of Fundamental Rights to women as equal citizens of India, it was believed then, would automatically provide a status of equality in actual political life. It was assumed that such a constitutional provision would take care of the various issues that had been bedevilling women for centuries and pave the way for their development much in the same way as it was viewed earlier that women's upliftment would come once freedom was achieved.

However from the point of view of women's studies, it would be interesting to see the impact of women's participation and contribution on (a) cultural institutions in society, whether it could break some of the shackles on women and mitigate the social oppression by way of illiteracy, economic dependency, social movement, etc; (b) on the family and its patriarchal structure and values. Did women's role and contribution increase their status in the family to one of equality? Did the nationalist movement then, and the policies and programmes of independent India reflect the recognition of women's contribution and potentialities? While Gandhi's clarion call to women helped them to come out of the four walls, of their houses and join the ranks of soldiers for freedom, he could not deliver much to women by way of rights or policies. His economic policies for women by way of charkha or spinning wheel, did not find a place in the future economic plans. It is only of late that such questions are being pursued. Studies on women in the Freedom Struggle are gradually moving away from women in history to one of women's history.

There is also the question as to how far has this promoted a feminist consciousness in them - whether the women were able to perceive and analyse their own position and work to promote their own rights, within or outside the context of India s freedom. The struggle against a common enemy (the British rule) seemed to have diverted the women by and large, from their own specific oppression. The questions of women's rights within the family, protest against their traditional roles as wives and mothers, against the traditional power relations within the family or to the male defined values etc., did not seem to have figured in a big way. Freedom Movement was born, the movement did not seem to feel concerned with the women's rights issues so as to face them squarely.

This also leaves us with another nagging doubt - 'did this (if so, how far) massive participation of women make any impact on the Indian nationalist movement itself'? Did it affect the stances of the leaders, as well as bring forth any type of policy decisions or programmes for women? Obviously, the concern for women's rights and social position did not pervade the whole of national movement nor did it have any impact on their policies and perspectives. Those like Gandhi and Nehru who recognised women's valuable contribution to the nationalist movement, believed in the need for improving their small proportion.

Nothing really happened or was undertaken for emancipating the women from their various disabilities. There was never any such well articulated organised campaign for women's emancipation, in the same way as there was for Harijan reforms or communal equality. Not that much success could be achieved in those areas either but at least it led to much social awareness. This was evident from the fact that when (soon after Independence) the resurrected report of the BN Rau Committee on the Draft of Hindu Code called the Hindu Law Bill was placed before the Constituent Assembly, it was opposed by many traditionalists in the assembly Apparently, the Fundamental Rights and the equality that Congress had talked about, related only to the political spheres - not to the private and familial spheres. It took more than seven years before the Parliament could finally adopt one small portion of the original draft, viz. with regard to marriage, divorce and maintenance. One had to be happy with the mere inclusion of the Uniform Civil Code in Article 44 of the Directive Principles of State Policy of the Constitution. Obviously, the voice of women was not loud enough to shake the leadership nor their participation in the decision-making was strong enough to demand their rights effectively.

Active Role

In any modern political system, elections occupy the most central place. The nature, periodicity and rate of participation by the masses in elections, is viewed as the touchstone for the representative character of democracy, and hence, democracy itself. Almost all nations in the world have adopted universal adult suffrage, wherein every adult, without any additional qualification or conditions, has the right to vote in general elections held periodically. How regular are these elections? What is the percentage of participation in voting by the people? How organised or peaceful the polls are? These, in turn, indicate the health and strength of democracy.

Elections being a forum for and method in self-government and democracy, occupy a significant place in drawing the attention of the nation to the problems and needs of the disadvantaged sectors. The party manifestoes, campaigns, individual candidate's promises, track records and future course of action, are indicative of the national concerns, as well as, mandates for action. As the instrument that brings into being the national Parliament and state

Assemblies, the outcome of elections in terms of parties and individuals are significant for the adaptation of policies and measures for women's development.

Democracy does not, and cannot operate by proxy. Every citizen, conscious of his and the national movement's development, and aware of the value and utility of the vote to fetch the same, needs to correlate this right with development. This, he can do only by exercising this right (or by participating) in elections. The participatory theory of democracy believes that direct participation in decision making would be the ideal of citizens ruling themselves in a modern state whose size and population are large, whose problems are complex, and the art of governing almost a managerial technique, the next best would be a representative democracy. It is then that a psephologist worries about the voting percentage of the population in general, and of the depressed sections in particular. The proper selection of a correct party/ candidate in an election is vital, if this representative democracy has to function in the interest of a majority of the population, which are depressed and disadvantaged.

Many studies believed that women are not independent voters; (ii) that a majority of them are illiterate; (iii) that a majority of them make their choice on the basis of suggestions given by male members of the family husband and sons; (iv) that women lack information and political awareness; and (v) women were not politically conscious. However, these studies defined the words political participation very narrowly. Despite these limitations, one way make a general analysis of the voting pattern of women. A quick glance at their participation in elections over the past four decades will confirm the initial hopes placed by the founders of the Constitution. The extent, nature and level of Indian women's participation is much greater than in many other countries developed or developing, except possibly in the countries that were going through radical revolutionary wars. A certain cultural background as well as the freedom struggle could be the main reasons for this. This participation has been more or less expanding steadily over the years, through the various elections-by way of voting, as candidates and participation in campaigning etc. The gap in the turnout between men and women is getting more and more narrowed. The number of women getting elected to the representative bodies is slowly increasing.

This increase in the turnout of women voters, particularly of the lower class and castes, may be attributed, to a high degree of mobilisation rather than of one's own political consciousness. In India, one can talk in general of high level of awareness of the value to vote which is possessed and cast eagerly by the poor and the Scheduled Castes at times very pragmatically and rationally. They are politically sensitive, well aware of their interests and even the political issues. But this awareness, in order to be translated into a political exercise like voting needs tremendous mobilisation. This is all the more in the case of women as poverty and daily work, household chores and care, patriarchal and family norms, act as great disincentives. Distance of booths, possibility of violence, health and other factors further discourage them. The linkage between the 'personal' and 'public' is missing; and women do not feel automatically impelled.

Recognising the significance of the women voters many political parties have, of late, been exerting themselves to devise various methods. Mobilisation in the past have been mainly at the time of decisions in the form of adhoc promises made on populistic and opportunistic short-term basis, rather than on long-term goals of a social change for women.

To the extent there was any correlation between the campaign promises and voting support, it also reflected on the low impact that the women's movement had made in educating their lot, as well as in making a dent on the patriarchal politicians. The Congress Party too, was not far behind. In 1984, much of the victory of Congress (1) could be attributed to a sympathy vote by women for the young Prime Minister and against the slaying of the women Prime Minister Indira Gandhi on a woman-to-woman basis.

The increase in the number of women voters since independence and their eager participation in voting, has made almost all political parties pay special attention to organising themselves, campaigning among themselves, and choosing them to contest elections. Definitely in the earlier years such campaigning among women and soliciting their votes were done rather casually. More recently, the parties have organised regular party forums, cells and front organisations, specially for women. These women's cells not only mobilise and campaign among women, and seek their support and membership for party issues during elections as well as normal period, but also quite often take up issues concerning women. Of late, parties are also taking stand on women's issues, organise rallies and demonstrations, pass resolutions, lobby with and pressurise the government for specific policies. Women are participating in them in great numbers and have even courted arrest on issues like sati, Muslim Women's Right to Maintenance, rape incidents, violence, police excesses on women etc.

Party Politics

But in this context, there are many important questions to ask. In view of the extent of the recognition of the need for women's support, both for image building as well as electoral successes, how many women have been able to occupy important positions in the party? There have been many important political personalities among women at the helm of various parties. There have been a number of women who were members of the highest executive committees of their parties and have functioned as office bearers. The Congress Party, particularly, has taken care to give representation to women among its office-bearers. In fact, it has almost become axiomatic in India that the highest decision-making bodies of the various parties need to have definitely at least one or two women members. It is, however, necessary to ask the question whether it is a mere tokenism. Such representation by being very limited in number, as well as often occupied by weak and colourless personalities, does become more a symbolism rather than real power wielding. There are, of course, some exception to this.

Despite the increase, the number of women contesting the elections still constitute only one to 2 per cent. Even where seats are reserved as in the Panchayats, they do not come forward so easily. Out of these contestants, the ones who get elected constitute still smaller percentage. While those who belong to the major political parties stand a better chance of success, the non-party candidates and those who belong to minor political parties, are hardly successful. Despite this, many women contest as independents. This perhaps implies that political parties are, by and large reluctant to choose women as candidates, the maximum number of candidates being from the Congress Party. But even this party allotted only 3 per cent of seats in 1977 to women. Obviously, this is much more in the nature of a tokenism rather than an acceptance of women's equality or capability. Often women candidates are viewed as depriving men in their chances. Even the small number of women who contest, gain their candidates by their birth and close relationship with already established party leaders. Almost all the women who figure in electoral politics are invariably someone's wife, daughter, daughter-in-law or in other close relations. There are exceptions only among the Left parties, where a few of them can claim as having worked with the working class. Most of these women, thus, come from urban, middle class, with educated elite, background and cannot claim a stage-by-stage growth or participation in their political career. Apparently, there is no correlation between female population's voting percentage and their number in the elected assemblies. The subordinated position of the 'ordinary' women in families, their routine and normal duties of looking after the family, bringing up children, performing both the unpaid and paid work, do not allow them much scope to participate freely in public-political activities. To this must be added the economic factor. Elections in India as in all other modern democracies, has become very complicated, violent, dirty and expensive, inviting thereby very many legitimate and not so legitimate ways of finding and managing them. Women cannot obviously fit into this matrix of election. The participation costs in formal politics is at present too high for women. Political participation of women, by the conventional and formal yardstick, thus is low, and lower than men of even weaker sections. In the case of Scheduled Castes and Tribes, due to reservation of constituencies, the number of representatives is proportionate to the population. But it is ironic, if not cruel that only one of these seats had gone to woman. No study has yet been undertaken on an all India basis, on the nature and extent of women's participation in the legislative business. In the early years after Independence, the Parliament did witness many women like Renuka Ray participating vigorously in the Hindu Code Bill, etc. More recently, many women members of Parliament (MPs) belonging to different parties are drawing attention to issues like atrocities against women, women's rights, social crimes like sati, dowry, rape, etc. Still by and large, such participation is confined repeatedly to few women. A majority of them are silent on many issues, particularly on the general, political concerns. On the whole, it looks like those who are good and articulate and participate often. Others who are dormant, are invisible and silent on most of the issues. Political parties must exercise more care in choosing the correct type of women who are knowledgeable and can represent the majority of the poor and rural women. More presence of women in Parliament, even if of a greater number, will mean very little by way of women's development.

The above two processes have been taken up merely to point out some of the possible dangers involved in analysing the participation or pleading for increased participation of women in political developments and institutions. This is not attempted in order to discourage such pleas nor in a mood of cynicism nor negativism. The visible participation of more and more women in the public sphere, their greater representation at the decision-making and managerial level, are definitely important for more than one reason. Apart from their own possible contribution to women's development with a degree of empathy and understanding, they also would be able to project and sensitise fellow workers, politicians and executives on women's perspectives, and help adopt mid-term corrections in policies and their implementation. It acts further as role models for younger and other women with political and personal ambitions. May be it is too much to expect from every woman to have cultivated a perspective on "correct" women's studies on every issue, but one can hope at least some women to have images or acquire it in the course.

As women's studies are gaining deeper roots in India and as women's development is getting increasing attention, it is prudent that the women's studies scholars take stock of some of the developments and attempt conceptual clarification.

Decision Making

Women's participation in decision-making process is vital for the betterment of their human right conditions. If real democracy has to be sustained, the women, comprising about half of the world's population have to be incorporated at different levels and different processes of decision-making. This fact was realised at the UN convention on the political rights of women in 1952. All congresses worldwide emphasised the need for political participation of women. They discussed and planned strategies to achieve this objective. Significant deliberations on women's empowerment were made in: (a) World Plan of Action in 1975, in Meidco, (b) The Copenhagen Programme of Action 1980; (c) World Conference on the UN Decade of Women in Nairobi (1985); and, (d) the World Congress of Women in Beijing (1995). Women's involvement in decision-making processes at different levels was necessary for them to acquire confidence.

When analysing the woman factor in decision-making, the foremost consideration would be to find out whether women have taken key decisions or just helped in taking a decision. The next step would be to identify the internal and external situations in which they could take key political decisions, and third, the interaction processes followed by such decision makers. Moreover, the analysis should throw light on the formal as well as non-formal structures in decision-making system on central, state and local levels, wherein women performed their roles as key or non-key decision-makers.

Thus decision-making positions acquired by women would give a general idea of the vertical as well as horizontal mobility of women to power position. The study by its very nature generally becomes a study of elite women in decision-making positions. In this study, the key decision-makers are actors- who could convert decisions into political action or one, who possessed efficacy or who had impact upon the political system in some way or the other.

It is true that women in top power positions in politics were no Indicators regarding the social, economic or political status of the women masses. But they indicated the span of mobility in recruitment process and gender toleration in a political system. This kind of study would help in understanding the elite structure in a society which in its turn would depend upon the political culture prevailing at that time.

Symbols of Women Power

The universe in this study is within the Indian context and limited to those women only, who were or are key or non-key political actors in the decision-making process, and whose efficacy could be assessed on the basis of the results of their performance.

Indira Gandhi. As Indira Gandhi was one of the strongest political leader in the world, this paper intends to start with her and then proceed to few other women who joined the political arena after her. These had been either chief ministers or held key party posts. Nevertheless, all of them have affected political scene in their respective states or at the national level. When this study was being completed, BJP led coalition had already taken over power at the Centre. The women's reservation bill could not be introduced in Parliament because some members in the opposition had scuttled it.

Indira Gandhi's environmental interest revealed her as one of the first true planetary leaders. Maurice F Strong, executive coordinator, United Nations Office for Emergency Operation in Africa, wrote about her: "She was the first leader of any great nation to appreciate that the concerns for environment which has been so dramatically manifested in the late 1960s and early 1970s in industrialised societies had a profound relevance to developing countries. At that time, most of the developing world regarded the emergence of the environmental issue as a preoccupation of the rich, which threatened to divert attention and resources from the development needs of the poor, but Indira Gandhi saw the indispensable need to force an alliance between environmental and development concerns in meeting these needs."[1]

Maurice F Strong held that Indira Gandhi's ideas were the single key to the sources of Stockholm conference on environment in June 1972.

Indira Gandhi's impact on India's political system was such that it became unrecognisable and totally different from the Nehru period. Under Jawaharlal Nehru's style of politics, there was a system of checks and balances between conflicting regional interests and powerful party bosses. The dominant political leaders were accommodated by the federal structure of the Indian Constitution. This gave strength to India to weather the turbulent formative years. The Shastri government also followed the Nehruvian line.

The Indian political system was confronted with most serious internal crisis during the latter period of Indira Gandhi's regime. Well accepted peaceful procedures and peaceful means for resolving internal conflict were shattered. Fragmented political culture and battered accommodative attitude became the features of the Indian political system. The systemic and structural failures became obvious. She had personalised and centralised Indian politics. Indira Gandhi was intolerant of political personalities who showed signs of entering into competition with her. She dismissed non-congress ministries in the different states and imposed her confidents as chief ministers in the Congress ruled states.

The structure of the Congress party changed qualitatively. There was enormous centralisation of power in the office of the Prime Minister's secretariat. The personalisation and centralisation of political authority made a dent in the capacity of the system to accommodate regional demands.

The political system was affected by Indira Gandhi's decisions in such a way that the system went on working under its inertia. Terrorism raised its head in Punjab and Kashmir. Democracy declined. The institutions of party parliament and judiciary were twisted to make her more secure in her decision-making position. The style became authoritarian and the Indian political culture broke off its moral moorings. In 1969, when the Congress was split, the political culture scenario changed basically. All political parties in India were affected by Indira Gandhi's decision to divide the historic Congress Party reducing it to a collection of subservient sycophants.

Indira Gandhi went on with her populist image, by propagating the concepts of a committed bureaucracy and a committed judiciary. She showed scant respect to the Constitution of India. Inspite of the fact that the Shah Commission report denied any threat to law and order in the country, Indira Gandhi declared Emergency in 1975. She claimed that Emergency was a necessity for preserving law and order in the nation. The probity of the civil service was impaired and press came under attack. The electronic media was misused and suppersession of an army general was considered necessary.

There was no place for Nehru's style of consensus during Indira Gandhi's regime. She stressed on cohesion. The syndicate in Congress was delegitionised by her tirade against it. The breaking of consensus resulted into opposition agitational politics and the government had to become repressive.

Populism came to be established as an important element of politics. It meant direct appeal to the masses. Consequently the intermediate structure and the elites were ignored. With the Sanjay Gandhi factor, musclemen and local mafia came to form the new infrastructure of politics.

Rajni Kothari had observed that "now, it is clear that almost the entire Institutional order (not just the Congress system) has very nearly broken down. The system had under gone a series of changes." The new model of politics had been as follows:-

(i) Displacement of a cabinet system of government.

(ii) The abrogation of parliamentary system by first permitting a brute use of party majority by the executive wing, and then under mining the simpler mechanics, let alone the spirit of election mandates by frequent recourse to defections and toppling of duly constituted governments.

(iii) The erosion of the federal framework by recourse to similar practices engineered from the very apex of the system.

(iv) The undermining of judicial independence and probity by executive manipulation of the concept of parliamentary supremacy.

(v) The uncalled for use of presidential powers.

Indira Gandhi had few equals in recent history in the art of power wielding. Her rapport with common people was extraordinary. After Mahatma Gandhi and Nehru, she had been the most charismatic leader in India. She could bypass all the stalwarts of her party as well as the most fiery leaders in the opposition. Even when she was out of power the she enjoyed the same popularity among the masses. Her dynamism was unmatched and she was the only woman Prime Minister to be assassinated. The

Congress syndicate was totally disillusioned with its scheme about her, that is, to use her as a sophisticated totem for the Congress.

Indira Gandhi was a bold key decision-maker and her decisions resulting into Important actions, had great impact on the Indian political system, with its processes and its culture.. As mentioned before, she personalised and centralised politics in India. By her decisions she eroded the federal system in India.

Indira Gandhi went on with her concept of 'committed judiciary'. It was during her regime that India witnessed Emergency for the first time. She displaced the cabinet system and abrogated the parliamentary system. During her regime, the constitutional system of India became Prime Ministerial system. Many important constitutional amendments were passed by Parliament without any debates.

After Indira Gandhi, some women leaders in states had made their strong impacts on state politics as well as on national politics. Keeping in mind the time frame for this chapter, after studying Indira Gandhi's role in decision-making process as key actor, I have taken current examples like Sonia Gandhi, Mamta Banerji, Jayalalitha, Mayawati and Rabri Devi. The former two were leaders of a national party. The others belong to regional parties and have adorned the chair of chief ministers in their respective states. Except Rabri Devi all the others have been dynamic and active in politics. Their decisions and styles have left impacts on national parties, state politics and party politics.

The Late, 1980s and 1990s have witnessed the emergence of women political leaders who have influenced political decision-making at the national and state level. Jayalalitha emerged as a powerful Chief Minister of Tamil Nadu after the death of M G Ramchandra. The, 1990s saw the emergence of Mamta Banerji in Bengal representing initially the Congress (I). She has steadily consolidated her position and could not be contained within the fold of the Congress Party. In 1998, she broke away and founded the Trinamul Congress. The year 1998 also witnessed the emergence of Sonia Gandhi as the prime decision-maker of the Congress party. She also exerted pressure on the government at the Centre. Mayawati made her presence felt in the politics of Uttar Pradesh with her Bahujan Samaj Party. Aggressive, and to some extent very articulated in her speeches and actions, she has emerged as a very strong leader of the Dalits.

The Sonia-Mamta-Jayalalitha trio is affecting the course of political events. They affected structure of their respective parties and influenced them. The trio also challenged the Vajpayee government on several occasions. Mayawati, who was the Chief Minister of Uttar Pradesh twice, showed her persistence in the state politics and also as a leader of the Dalits. Rabri Devi is a puppet installed as Chief Minister of Bihar, the second-most populated state of India. Her installation developed certain serious constitutional and political trends in the politics of Bihar.

Sonia Gandhi. After a long silence, Sonia Gandhi decided to campaign for Congress (I). She started her first four campaign meetings in south India on January 16, 1998, and created an excitement among the Congress workers. She made a dramatic entry on the central stage at the Netaji Indoor Stadium, on August 9, 1998, where the Congress plenary session was being held. A virtual riot broke out as scrambled the members by to take a glimpse of her. She sat down on the floor, the place for All India Congress Committee (AICC) delegates. When Congress president Sitaram Keshri rose to speak, he was hooted down. He came down to Sonia, dropped his Gandhi cap at her feet and beseeched her to join the leaders on the dais. In 1993, P V Narasiniha Rao, also had to face similar treatment and he had to invite her to the dais. At that time she had refused. The message was clear that the Nehru-Gandhi family and Sonia herself had greater appeal among the party workers. Ultimately, she displaced Sitaram Kesri from presidentship of the Congress.

Another occasion when the sycophancy regarding Nehru-Gandhi family had become more obvious was during the golden Jubilee celebrations of Indian Independence on August 15, 1997. Sonia was given place of pride in the Central Hall, in the front row with Congress president Sitaram Kesri and the BJP president L K Advani. Other members of the Nehru-Gandhi family, Priyanka Gandhi and her husband Robert Vadhera were seated in the row just behind her. No other Congress leader has been able to pull as large a crowd as Sonia because of the Gandhi family factor.

Some old Congress men who joined other parties were of the opinion that Sonia Gandhi entered politics essentially to keep a hold on the Congress (1) as a political vehicle for her children.

The way the dynastic principle worked in Sonia's own estimation, could be assessed by her own prologue in Rajiv by Sonia Gandhi. She wrote: "We had both observed the world of politics from a distance. We had come to understand the critical line that distinguishes ambition from a sense of purpose." She remained non-political for a long time. But when Sanjay Gandhi met a violent death, Indira Gandhi turned to her elder son so that the dynastic principle could go on working. Sonia claimed that she "fought like a tigress" against this decision, but she respected her mother-in-law. "I understood Rajiv's duty to her. At the same time, I was angry and resentful towards a system which, as I saw it, demanded him as a sacrificial lamb. It would crush him and destroy him - of that I was absolutely certain." After Rajiv Gandhi was killed, she said at Sriperumbudur that she put aside her Inclination to remain as a "private person" and stepped forward in the sanctified family tradition of duty before personal considerations.

Congress had been a party as well as a process because it was the principal carrier of India nationalism. More over, "the dynamics of electoral competition at the local level created a broad convergence of political interest between particular sections. This under wrote the consolidation of an electorate between social classes, which dominated the realm of representative politics... The key to the Congress success was its ability to remain awake to local political situations... But the social factions deserted the party. One of the reason was dynastic political succession which ensures the survival of neither commitment nor vision. The Congress organisation, which was the key to its ability to recruit loyalties at the local level, is today in shambles. The decline began in Rajiv Gandhi's regime. Organisational elections were never conducted for about more than seven years. There was lack of local leader, who could create durable alliance. The electoral appeal of the Congress depended solely on the charms of the Nehru-Gandhi family. When Sonia became president of the Congress (I), she emphasised on reorganising party. On July 28, 1998, she led a Congress rally and marched to Rashtrapati Bhawan against "price rise and the all round failure of the BJP government." It seemed that she was taking pro-active steps to succeed in competitive politics. She marshalled support for the candidature of P M Sayeed for the post of deputy speaker of the Lok Sabha. These actions showed that after emphasising on strengthening organisational machinery, she appeared to have switched suddenly to a policy of bold initiatives. BJP deferred the decision on the election of deputy speaker and withdrew its candidate Rita Verma. BJP virtually admitted defeat. After playing this game, Sonia announced the prospect of assuming responsibilities of power. It was a dramatic change in the position of the Congress (I) president. Sonia earlier virtually rejected a call by Chandra Shekhar to bring down EWP. The reason behind the aggressive policy could be to retain her popularity among the party workers. Before scandal had tainted the name of her family, Sonia has been calling for transparency in the Bofors crisis so that the Nehru-Gandhi family's name was steer-cleared. But the CBI affidavit before the Delhi High Court candidly declared that "investigation had shown that the families of the then Prime Minister of India (Rajiv Gandhi) and Ottavio Quottrocchi were on very intimate terms with each other and they used to meet frequently. Quattrocchi and his family had free access to the Prime Minister's house." A E Services of Ottario Quottrocchi entered into negotiations to cheat "because the two parties to the agreement conspired to deceive the Government of India, and dishonestly induced it to part with money to the tune of US$ 7.34 million," says the CBI affidavit.

Sonia could not chart out a political strategy at Panchmarhi Congress (1) session to revive the party and even clarify its ideological positions on many questions.

There is no doubt that Sonia has rejuvenated the dying Congress party, to a certain extent. She is gaining popularity, and this became evident when the Central Election Committee (CEC) of Congress decided to complete the selection of candidates by January 11, 1998. There were disputes between various groups and for the final list all sought Sonia Gandhi's guidance in the matter. Sonia war, not the president of the Congress at that time. She was waiting to take over the organisation, which she did later. Her entry into active politics helped the Congress (1) in its electoral battle against other political parties. But it exacerbated factional conflict within the Congress party itself.

Though belated, Sonia decided to come to the aid of a dispirited party, which was rapidly declining. She made difference to the outcome of the contest, and was able to produce another hung Parliament. The effect of her entry into electoral politics for the 12th Lok Sabha, lifted spirits within the Congress party, and attracted a noticeable degree of curious mass voters. BJP alone could not get majority and with "friends" it had to form another shaky coalition government at the Centre. Sonia controlled the drift away from Congress.

However, Sonia Gandhi has steadily consolidated her position not only as the head of the party, but also as a formidable player in the decision-making process at the national level. On January 12, 1999, at a function at the Ramkrishna Mission in Delhi she spoke strongly against conversion of Hindus, while just a week ago she visited Gujarat to express her solidarity with the Christians there.

The Congress party had been earlier in support of the reservation bill for women, and Sonia Gandhi had also announced her decision to implement 33 per cent reservation for women in her own party hierarchy. She had inducted four women - Mohsina Kidwai, Yanga Patai, Ambika Soni and Laxmi Devi - in the party working committee in as reported to have been effected in the last week of January in the Hindustan Times of January 29, 1999. Simultaneously, she also made a statement maintaining that the bill advocating for 33 per cent reservation would ensure only the entry of affluent women in the Lok Sabha and Rajya Sabha. On February 8, she lambasted the BJP government at the Centre for Misgovernance, while there was trouble brewing in the Congress led Orissa government, after the killing of an Australian Christian missionary along with his two young sons. After much discussion Sonia Gandhi took the decision that Chief Minister J B Patnaik be replaced. By taking this tough stand she sent out a loud message to the BJP government and Congress itself. She did what the BJP could not do in Gujarat after her clear enunciation that the BJP and its front organisation have no monopoly over the Hindus or Hinduism. After visiting Tirupati, she chose Haridwar as her next venue to address partymen in Uttar Pradesh. By urging Congressmen to fight against communal and castist forces she has taken the battle not only to the territory of its principal enemy - the BJP but also to the other two strong parties in Uttar Pradesh the BSP and the samajwadi Party.

After the massacre of Dalits in Narayanpur, Bihar, on February 10, 1999, she expressed "deep shock and abhorrence." At another massacre of Dalits in Bihar within a fortnight while stating that "any government which is helpless in presenting such henious acts forfeits its moral authority to govern." She reenacted the visit of her mother -in-law in Belchi in 1978, by going to Narayanpur on February 13, 1999. It seemed to ring bells of warning for the Rabri government. However, the Congress party remained non-committal on President's rule in Bihar. Now Sonia Gandhi has very clearly stated that the Congress will oppose the ratification of President's rule motion in the Lok Sabha and Rajya Sabha. The

Bihar Pradesh Congress Committee reacted sharply to the party high-command's decision, and requested Sonia Gandhi to reconsider her decision. Many senior leaders of the Bihar Congress Committee resigned in protest.

The months of March and April of 1999 have been hectic for political turnovers. Sonia Gandhi has changed her attitude several times. The dismissal of navy admiral Vishnoo Bhagwat triggered off a controversy with the opposition parties rapping the government for reinstatement of the admiral. Personal insults were hurled at George Fernandes by all opposition parties, Congress and AIADMK leading the process. Towards the middle and end of March 1999, Sonia Gandhi categorically rejected the Left offer on alternative government at a meeting in Calcutta. She maintained that the BJP led ruling coalition will collapse on its own. She promptly remarked to newsmen that the question of forming a govenment with the help of the Left parties does not arise. She also remarked that there was no need to talk to Mamta Banerji but for Jayalalitta, she remarked. "why not, we can talk to her'.

Sonia Gandhi still denies the plot to dislodge Atal government on April 10, 1999. Speaking at a huge meeting in Karimnagar, she maintained that the Vajpayee government was itself digging its grave. The Congress was ready to shoulder constitutional responsibility of forming government at the Centre if and when situation arises. She also rapped the government for its reluctance to set up a joint Parliamentary committee (JPC) to probe into the corruption charges against people in high government position. She recalled that the same party had earlier demanded setting up of a JPC to probe into the Bofors gun deal based on a report broadcast by a foreign radio station. Earlier on April 7th she denied that she was having talks with Jayalalitha.

The Vajpayee government, fell on April 17, 1999, by the lowest margin of just one vote as the BSP leader Mayawati cast her vote while one day earlier she had given indications that BSP will abstain from voting in the Lok Sabha. Immediately efforts were made for the formation of an alternative government. The Congress being the second largest party claimed to form the government. Sonia Gandhi met President Narayanan on April 20. The spokesperson of Congress party Arjun Singh remarked, "we will have letters of support from all parties that voted against the Vajpayee government." He also maintained that the Congress will establish its majority and an alternate government will be formed by Sonia Gandhi. Sonia had meeting with other opposition party leaders including Jayalalitha, RJM leaders and Laloo Prasad Yadav. Mulayam Singh Yadav dealt a severe blow to the plans of Sonia Gandhi when he refused to support the government led by her. Despite hectic efforts Sonia Gandhi was unable to produce the list of 272. Mrs. Sonia rejected the requests for sharing of power with other parties. Earlier, she had told the President that the Congress will form minority government with outside support. Samajwadi Party, RSP and Forward Block categorically opposed the plan for a Congress minority government. Sonia Gandhi was able to produce a list of only 239 MPs. As a result, the President had to dissolve the Lok Sabha. Fresh elections was declared by the Election Commissioner K P S Gill.

Sonia Gandhi after much speculation met Jayalalitha at a tea party, organised by Subramanium Swamy. The coming together of these two leaders was termed as a 'political earthquake.' Thereafter, they met several times. But ultimately the plans misfired and Jayalalitha finally packed her bags and left for Chennai on April 27, 1999.

Sonia Gandhi played the key role in toppling the Vajpayee government and the next general elections will be a testing ground for her acumen, charisma and manipulations. She has been able to rejuvenate the Congress party.

BJP has become vocal charging Sonia Gandhi as an alien. But, Advani speaking in Bhubaneshwar on May 12, 1999, did admit that Sonia is now an Indian citizen. Waves of resentment were also brewing within the Congress party. Sharad Pawar, Tarik

Anwar and P A Sangma submitted a letter to the Party President on May 15 questioning the legitimacy of her candidature for prime ministership. However, these three leaders were expelled from the party. Sonia Gandhi responded by giving in her resignation for the post of party president. Leaders like Pranab Mukherjee and Madhav Rao Scindia tried to perused her to take back her resignation, but Sonia was adamant. However, she presided over the AICC session held on May 25th and emerged stronger than before. Later, she took back her resignation and emerged as the undisputed leader of the Congress party. Sheela Dikshit played an important role in bringing together the party members. Speaking at the AICC session, Sonia Gandhi appealed to the 15,000 delegates to teach a lesson to those who had questioned her patriotism. In a typical Indira Gandhi style she did not compromise, and finally emerged as a very strong political decision-maker.

Mamta Banerji. Like Sonia Gandhi, Mamta Banerji was also instrumental in pulling down Sitaram Kesari from the presidentship. Mamta Baneiji is a firebrand leader. She protested against alleged rigging in the election of delegates who were to elect the Congress president. election to the post of the Congress president was being held for the first time after 47 years. Mamta split vertically the Congress (1) in West Bengal on August 9, 1997. She declared the formation of a new state wing of the party and christened it the Trinamul (grassroots) Congress. Mamta boycotted the AICC plenary session held in Calcutta. She addressed a huge rally of the Trinamul Congress at the same time, and said that the new wing was needed "to save the party from fake leadership, and launch an uncompromising fight against the niling CPI(M)."

She claimed that she still belonged to the Congress. Her Trinamul Congress was the real Congress. She would use the same flag, the tricolour. She also claimed that it was she who represented the real Congress in West Bengal. She bitterly criticised the Congress president Sitaram Keshari, and alleged that he had reduced Congress (1) into a signboard organisation. She formalised the infrastructure of the Trinamul Congress, three days after the plenary session of the Congress (I) in Calcutta. Mamta announced the names of conveners of parallel district committee, heads of organisation and 116 - member steering committee. Mamta also formed 'Save Bengal Front'. She urged like mined parties to be its constituents. She left her post as the West Bengal Congress president, for one of her loyalists. Many thought that Mamta would face disciplinary action for the formation of Trinamul Congress, holding a rally parallel to the Congress (I) plenary session by boycotting it. But nothing happened. Central leaders were unable to make her desist from holding the parallel rally. The party high command decided to ignore her and isolate her. Mamta set up a parallel party office and announced that her supporters would not be accountable to the AICC or the Pradesh Congress - Committee. She said, "we looked towards Delhi for far too long. From now on we will fight our own battle".

The advent of the Trinamul Congress was seen to end the politics of polarisation between the Left Front and the Congress (I). One of the senior state Congress (1) leaders conceded that the presence of the Trinamul Congress had changed political equations. Congress (I) feared that Mamta's party would eat into its traditional support base in West Bengal. It received jolt when former Union Minister Ajit Panja and Krishna Bose joined the Trinamul Congress.

Mamta did approve of the BJP candidate Rita Verma for deputy speakership. Though her Trinamul Congress gave its support to the BJP led collition, she joined the opposition on the opening day of the monsoon session of Parliament. She alongwith her partymen, accused the government of failure to control prices. She demanded that to check price rise, the government should ensure better delivery of essentials through the public distribution system to check prices. She also expressed disappointment with the government because it failed to introduce the bill for women's reservation in Parliament.

Mamta had entered the coordination committee of BJP and its allies with some reluctance. On the issue of rising prices of essential commodities, she resigned from the coordination committee. After much persuasion, she accepted Vajpayee's offer to join the Cabinet at the Centre, but she again put up a bargain - she wanted the railways portfolio for her party MP. Talks broke down on this issue. In a dramatic development after the visit of George Fernandes and Pramod Mahajan, a joint rally was held in Calcutta on February 10, 1999, where a mellowed Mamta did welcome and felicitate Fernandes and Mahajan after they had assured Mamta that most of the demands in the package for Bengal will be considered and fulfilled by the Centre.

Mamta was very critical of the communal killings and attacks on Christians in January and demanded the resignation of Home Minister LK Advani on January 28, 1999. She also trained her guns on Murli Manohar Joshi, another BJP hardliner. She reacted against the inclusion of Joshi in the three-member cabinet team on a fact-finding mission on the murder of an Australian missionary and his sons in Keonjhar, Orissa. Earlier Mamta had joined hands with the Congress demanding ban on Bajrang Dal. She had taken a mellow stand towards the Vajpayee government throughout the months of March and April 1999. She was impassioned in the Sabha during the no-trust motion against the government. She pledged her party's support to Atalji's government. But the Vajpayee government was edged out by just one vote. After hectic consultations between both the government and the opposition, Mamta agreed to a joint election, alliance in the new elections, but also reiterated that Trinamul Congress will have its own symbol and manifest.

Jayalalitha. The famous actor of Tamil cinema, the founder of AIADMK party and its symbol of two leaves was M G Ram Chandran. He was also the Chief Minister of Tamil Nadu.

Jayalalitha was also the Chief Minister of Tamil Nadu. But she faced an electoral route in 1996. A revolt broke out in her party, AIADMK. She was secretary of her party. Many top leaders left her faction. As a result, she was defeated. The deputy general secretary Thirunavukkarasu led a faction against her. Jayalalitha expelled him from the party and the latter expelled her from his faction.

Jayalalitha was a former film actress and a follower of M G Ramchandran. When she assumed chief ministership of Tamil Nadu, it was alleged that during that period three of her associates acquired assets worth more than Rs 66.65 crore, according to the chargesheet filed by officers of the Directorate of Vigilance and Anti-corruption (DVAC) in a case relating to Jayalalitha!s wealth. It was alleged to be disproportionate to her known sources of wealth.

The chargesheet ment on June 4, 1997 before the special court-III judge P Anbazhagan named Jayalalitha as the first accused. Other accused were her 'surrogate sister' Sasikala Natrajan and Sasikala's sister-in-law J I Thirunavukkarasu Lavarsi. Jayalalitha had publicly renounced her relationship with Sasikala and with her foster son Sudhakan.

Besides the crisis created by corruption charges, Tamil magazine Dine Manu and a Tamil biweekly Junior Vikatan published a colour photograph of Jayalalitha with a group of people, which they claimed included 'Dhanu' the human bomb, who assassinated Prime Minister Rajiv Gandhi alongwith Sivarajan, the leader of the LTrE assassination squad. Since it was photograph of other persons totally unconnected with the murder of Rajiv Gandhi, the sensation flopped. It was a case of sheer media irresponsibility. But Jaylalitha had to go through humiliating experience.

Jaylalitha's party became the principal ally of the BJP led government in 1998. She kept on harping on her demand for the dismissal of the Karunanidhi government in Tamil Nadu on the grounds of failure of governance. On Cauvery issue, the AIADMK warned Prime Minister Vajpayee of "disastrous consequences" if his government did not notify immediately the scheme on Cauvery water in the official gazette and table it in parliament. According to her, there was no possibility of a compromise between Tamil Nadu and Karnataka.

The AIADMK chose to celebrate the 90th birth-anniversary of Annadurai. She was isolated from other Tamil parties, and also from BJP in these celebrations. Her speech was carefully worded and was contered around three themes. First, was her justification for her repeated threats of reviewing support to the BJP led government. Second, was meant to be a warning to her allies at the Centre and in the state against treating AIADMK unfairly. And the third, was condemning the "anarchic DMK rule" in Tamil Nadu. She indicated to EVP that in a mixed vegetable dish, no single vegetable was important. The AIADMK was as important as the vessel in which the dish could be prepared." Jayalalitha tried to grab BJP attentions by alleging Karunanidhi's indifference towards maintenance of temples in the state, for which she had launched schemes when she was the Chief Minister in Tamil Nadu. Despite all these she was eager to retain her links with BJP.

Jayalalltha consciously put pressure on BJP led government at the Centre. Despite, all allegations of corruption, she is still a very popular political figure. Vajpayee had to tread carefully where Jaylalitha was concerned. No wonder, Jaswant Singh had to rush to Chennai quite often to pacify Jayalalitha and restore her good humour. At the meeting of the coordination committee of BJP and the allies, a common statement was released stating that the allies should not criticise the government in public, Jaylalitha had her reservations and refused to sign the statement. George Fernandes rushed to Chennai to appease Jayalalitha on February 2, 1999, but the 45 minutes talk could not bear any fruit. It has been evident that Jaylalitha had openly criticised the Vajpayee government on several occasions, and threatened to withdraw support of her party. She had maintained a belligerant stand towards the Vajpayee government. She pushed the government to the wall by demanding that George Fernandes be sacked from the Union government. She wanted to know why the defence minister was being shielded the Prime Minister when serious charges had been made against him by a naval chief. As a prelude to putting out of the BJP led coalition, Jayalalitha withdrew her two ministers from the government after the Union Cabinet rejected outrightly all her three demands on the Vishnu Bhagwat issue. She also held talks with other political leaders to explore the "formation of a government that livers rather than promises and does not discriminate on grounds of religion, caste or region." The government on April 7, 1999, signalled that its ties with AIADMK have been apart and attacked Jayalalitha that she could enter to a deal with the Congress to dismiss the Karunanidhi ministry and seek withdrawal of corruption cases against her. Ultimately, on April 9. 1999. AIADMK withdrew from the coordination panel. By April 12, Jayalalitha was all set to withdraw support from the Vajpayee government. She declared that withdrawal of support to the Vajpayee government was inevitable as there was "no room for any repprochement". She also admitted that it was a wrong decision to support the government, and that one year had been wasted. Later, she met Congress president Sonia Gandhi. To a querry by a newsperson that whether she was Prime Ministerial candidate, the AIADMK leader remarked, "I am not ruling out anything."

Earlier, in the last week of March Jayalalitha announced the reservation of 33 per cent party post's for women, and she promptly packed her party's hierarchy with 48 women joint district secretaries.

It was termed as a "political earthquake" when Jayalalitha and Sonia Gandhi met over a tea party arranged by Subramanian Swamy. They ultimately unseated the government. A very uncharitable comment became the headline of major newspapers, which was 'two women send Atal packing'.

Mayawati. Mayawati is one of the most dynamic Dalit leaders. She was earlier the general secretary of the Bahujan Samajvadi Party. She donned the chair of Chief Minister of Uttar Pradesh twice. First time she was the Chief Minister in 1995 with the outside support of BJP. Second time she became the Chief

Minister in 1997, when BJP was a constituent of the her government. She is also presently the Chief Minister of Uttar Pradesh.

Mayawati is shrewd and assertive. Ideologically, she proclaims that she was against Manuwad. At a rally of the United Front government and its constituent partners in Lucknow against Mayawati, the erstwhile Prime Minister Deve Gawda supported the Samajwadi party's stand against Mayawati. They had alleged that the Schedule Castes and Schedule Tribes Acts were being misused. It had alleged oppression of Samajwadi Party workers. Mayawati Issued counter waring to the UF at the centre, to hold back attempts to topple her government. Against the allegation of this act being misused, Mayawati justified her "casteist" action for enlarging her support base.

During her first Chief Ministership in 1995, Mayawati found that BJP was not unhappy with the government. It supported from outside and created no hurdles. She retorted to the remarks of Mulayam Singh that BSP was communal because it had formed alliance with BJP for her second Chief Ministership. She, however ignored Samajwadi Party's remarks, accusing that Mulayarn Singh or indulge in communalism only when it suited his purpose. When the daughter of a Dalit was helped by BJP to come to the position of Chief Minister Mulayam, finds communal forces behind. He had no problems about joining BJP in 1989 to become Chief Minister himself.

Mayawati has been an opportunist like other politicians. Before forming the coalition with BJP, she had agreed to this "grand alliance" arrangement. But even then she had insisted to take up her chance first. Her condition for agreeing to remain in coalition with BJP was that they would have to agree to her being the Chief Minister first. The volatile Mayawati is perhaps the only woman Chief Minister, who confronted physical assault allegedly by "Samajwadi goons" at the state guest house in June, 1995.

As regards her style of functioning, one of the Samajwadi Party leaders, leaders, Beni Prasad Verma, in his speech addressed to a ray, compared Mayawati with Hitler. Soon after the elections in 1997, Bahujan Party had made it clear that it would join hands with any force that would make Mayawati, Chief Minister. BSP secured not only the Chief Ministership but also half the ministerial positions although it had only 66 MLAs compared to 173 MIAs of BJP. BSP was sure that power position would help it to grow. In the issue of the expansion of the ministry on March 27, 1997, Mayawati asserted that there was no need for it and left out many senior leaders of BJP. The allocation of portfolio also met with rough weather. Mayawati kept home, finance, health and planning. The CPM politbureau member Prakash Karat said that everybody knew Mayawati's style. Transfers and postings on a large-scale started even before the government had begun functioning. He remarked that the real problems of the people would be neglected. Farmers would face difficulties, many public sector undertaking could be shut down, workers would be deprived of their jobs and growing crime would be the major problem in the state. However, BJP complained that It was not consulted in majority of transfers and postings. It also alleged that Mayawati had been misusing the SC/ST Prevention of Atrocities Act against the upper castes.

According to a report of Venketesh Ram Krishna, Mayawati held that "the job of identifying and appointing loyal officers in key posts is of utmost importance for the government and it is being carried out smoothly."

Mayawati government's handling of law and order did not seem sound - there were communal, caste and sectional clashes. There were allegations and counter allegations, too. The Samajwadi Party alleged that the government arrests their workers under the Scheduled Castes and Scheduled Tribes (Prevention of Atrocities) Act and Goonda and Gangsters Act. These two acts had became the bone of contention among the coalition partners.

When the BJP government was formed under Kalyan Singh, it instituted a vigilance inquiry against bureaucrats considered close to Mayawati and reinstated officers suspended by Mayawati.

Kalyan Singh transferred 184 senior bureaucrats in the first 15 days of his government.

BSP demanded a mechanism for regular consultation at the state level, like the one at the national level. Mayawati also complained that Kalyan Singh's measures were against Scheduled Castes and Scheduled Tribes and an anti-Dalit mood was created in the state.

In the last week of May 1997, the Union Home Minister Indrajeet Gupta and Chief Minister Mayawati exchanged letters over law and order situation in Uttar Pradesh. Mayawati, however, denied any deterioration of law and order situation in the state. She personally directed administrative actions to be taken against senior officials, particularly in the police department. Senior bureaucrats described these actions as "self defeating frenzy". The Union home minister disapproved these so called "corrective" steps. It was alleged that the "punishment transfers" were made against those who had expressed views before the media against the state administration. According to Mayawati, these actions violated discipline of the police and brought disrepute to the administration.

One of the BSP ministers, whose women welfare department was taken away from him and was given the portfolio of culture and youth affairs, revolted and resigned. He also accused Mayawati of taking bribe during her regime.

Mayawati won the Lok Sabha elections of 1998. She is still very vocal and critical of the Vajpayee government. At the state level, she continuously rapped at the BJP led Kalyan Singh government. She is undoubtedly a force to reckon with in the politics of Uttar Pradesh. She still is the undisputed leader of the Dalits and if strategies are planned with some care, and her harsh tongue is checked a little, she can form a strong political front of Dalits.

Mayawati did it again. After promising to abstain from voting in the Lok Sabha on no-confidence motion against the Vajpayee government. she cast her vote in favour of the motion and thus, her one vote toppled the government on April 26, 1999.

Rabri Devi. A great writer has said that some are born great, and upon some greatness is thrust. In a similar strain it could be said that (in Bihar) some are born leaders, and upon some leadership is thrust. It could be appropriately applied to Rabri Devi - the Chief Minister of Bihar. Her Chief Ministership is an example of family principle of succession. It was adopted for keeping Bihar under the freedom of the Rashtriya Janata Dal (RJD) supremo Laloo Prasad. The dynastic principle had been applied earlier also with Indira Gandhi and Rajiv Gandhi, and now on Sonia Gandhi by the sycophancy of the congressmen to maintain the influence of Nehru-Gandhi dynasty. Sonia came out of nonpolitical "private life," and as suggested in her own writings, she jumped to national politics for family's sake. But she waited for the appropriate moment. Her intention seems to preserve her hold on the Congress party as a vehicle for her son and daughter. In Bihar Rabri was suddenly made Chief Minister. In her case, it seemed to be Laloo's intention to keep RJD as a vehicle for his next generation. He did every thing hurriedly. He made a travesty of the principles of doctrine of responsibility in the cabinet system of the government, by appointing his wife Rabri Devi as the Bihar Chief Minister. He had resigned because he was facing corruption charges before a CBI-designated court. He surrendered on July 30, 1997. Laloo Prasad also violated the principle of probity and accountability in public life by appointing his wife as Chief Minister. As he was alleged to be a "trained" Chief Minister, the person who had to replace him should have been a person distant or independent of him, but this did not happen. The requirements of accountability and responsibility were put on the shelf.

In the appointment of Rabri Devi as Chief Minister, a high voltage drama in a very short period was played. Laloo Prasad, RJD legislators and Rajyapal Kidwai played the main roles in this drama. The people of Bihar were unable to believe the news that Rabri Devi was appointed the Chief Minister and sworn in within hours after the resignation of her husband from the post. On July 30, Laloo Prasad was remanded to judicial custody after he surrendered before the CBI designated court. He resigned as Chief Minister on July 25, 1997 after the court issued an arrest warrant against him. He proposed the name of his wife as his successor at a hurriedly convened meeting of RJD legislative party.

The Rabri episode ensured proxy rule by Laloo who had said in jail, "being in jail does not mean I am a rotten egg. Several leaders had called on me and others will come." It was alleged that many Bihar officials met him regularly and received orders from when he came out of jail, he accompanied Rabri Devi everywhere and acted as an extra constitutional authority on behalf of her. It was alleged that Sitaram Kesri and I K Gujral had approved of Laloo's decision regarding installing his wife as Chief Minister.

Rabri Devi has no formal education and no interest or experience in active politics. When she became the Chief Minister of Bihar, she was neither a member of the Legislative Assembly nor the Legislative Council. She perhaps had never thought of such a windfall. Laloo had said that when his party legislators had unanimously elected her as a new leader, she was not ready to accept the new assignment. "It was only after a great deal of persuasion, that I prepared her for the changed situation."

The Governor of Bihar, Shree Sunder Singh Bhandari, gave Rabri Devi 15 days time to prove her majority in the Assembly. Before surrendering to the court, Laloo ensured and made his wife's position secured. He arranged for his wife to seek vote of confidence on July 28. She won the vote by a huge margin. She won confidence by winning 194 votes against 110.

To consolidate Rabri's position, Laloo made her to appoint a jumbo ministry of 32 cabinet ministers and 44 minister of state. She became a target of controversy and butt of jokes by many. The CPI(M) leader Harkishan Singh Surjeet emphasised Laloo's decision as an insult to those who elected him. BJP and Samta Party were furious, but Kesri ordered his party's Bihar MLAs to ensure Rabri's accession to office. Rabri could not make speeches. The television focussed upon her everywhere, but barring very few occasions, no one could hear her voice. In the first week of October 1997. She had to face a tricky situation created by the non-gazetted secretariat employees. Ministers and senior government servants were not permitted by the employees to attend their offices. It is said that she shut down the secretariat for four days and then the employees agreed to negotiate with her.

In month of September 1998, the Rabri regime was threatened by the Centre's recommendation to the President of India for the promulgation of Article 356 in Bihar for non-governance and detracting law and order. Every one knows that she is a puppet because she had not been trained in the art of politics. But gradually, she seemed to be maturing in carrying herself with confidence in public functions. The Rabri government was saved in 1998 as the President disagreed to promulgate Act 356. The Shankarbegha carnage at Narayanpur on the eve of Republic Day also threatened the Rabri government; it came under severe attack from all comers. The cabinet advised the President, to dismiss the Bihar government and promulgate Presidents rule. Ultimately, the Rabri government was dismissed on February 12, 1999, and President's rule was promulgated in Bihar for the seventh time in a sudden development, the governor of Bihar, Shree Sunder Singh Bhandari was recalled to Delhi. Laloo Yadav continued attacking the BJP government. He received support from the Left parties. Sonia Gandhi did not comment on the justification or otherwise of President's Rule. Meanwhile, the pressures on BJP government mounted and the President's rule in Bihar was ended on March 8, 1999. The RJD government under Rabri came back to power again. A radiant Rabri Devi once again took oath as Chief Minister on March 9, 1999 and submitted a list of 164 members to the governor. Bhandari was sent to Gujarat as governor on March 13, 1999, and Chief Justice B M Lal was made the acting governor of Bihar on March 16. The RJD hailed his appointment but very soon there started a rift between the governor and the Rabri government.

In Legislatures

At the legislative levels of the Centre and the states, women have not been given much importance as political actors.

Though there has been a substantial increase in voting participation by women, have not fared as contestants in national elections or state elections. They could never occupy more than 8 per cent seats in Parliament, and more than 10 per cent in state assemblies. In the Council of Ministers, the highest percentage of women had been 12.96 per cent in 1962.

With regard to the efficacy of women legislators in decision-making, there have been some studies in India as well as in Bihar. In R K Verma's study on rural political leadership, the writer held that women legislators had been contributing to the new models in 'developing national politics' of India. A Ph.D. thesis by Prabhawati, presented to the Magadh University in 1994 came to the conclusion that the representation of women in Lok Sabha was never substantial. In one of his studies, S M Sayeed was of the view that in near future because of social, cultural and practical reasons, female representation in legislatures would not increase.

The suggestions made in one of Dahelrup Drude's studies (1986) with regard to 'critical mass' theory becomes relevant here. In the context of study of women in the Scandinavian countries, she held that, when two factors combined in any political system women became 'critical mass' that is, politically strong. This happened (i) when women got at least 25 to 30 per cent seats in the legislatures, and, (ii) when support to women legislators from outside was given by strong women movement.

In the Indian political system, women in legislatures could not become a 'critical mass' because they were only 8 per cent in Lok Sabha and 10 per cent in state assemblies, and there were not sufficiently strong political women movements in India to support them.

In the legislative process, women legislators do not seem to have much impact. Recently, on the 81st constitution Amendment Bill seeking reservations of one-third seats in Parliament and state legislatures for women, they could not be effective. Though women MPs had been united inspite of their diverse political allegience and ideologies, the bill could not be passed.

Though they differed ideologically, women from different parties had come together to support the bill. There were some prominent women among them like Ratanmala, Savanoor and Uma Bharati, who had supported the stand taken by Sharad Yadav and the Muslim league, MPs that there should be sub-quota within the quota for the women of the backward castes and the minority communities.

The former Prime Minister I K Gujaral had inducted in his cabinet the most vocal women like Renuka Chowdhury, Jayanti Natrajan, and Kamla Sinha. Different impressions were created by this act of the Prime Minister. One view was that Prime Minister Gujral wished to correct the impression created by Sharad Yadav that Janata Dal did not intend to give space to women. The other view was that Gujral took this step to put a constraint upon them in raising a hue and cry over the women's reservation bill. Gita Mukherjee (CPI) refused any cabinet post because she wished to remain outside so that she could fight for the reservation bill for women. Thus, he had included five women in his cabinet; all of them were placed in the second rank.

There were some controversy from the very beginning among the women MPs on the formation of the committee on empowerment of women to be chaired by Gita Mukherjee of CPI. It held its first meeting on the May 6. 1997. Margret Alva (Congress) was apprehensive that this committee would put hurdles in passing the 81st Constitution Amendment Bill 1996. According to Alva, there was no need for it because the joint committee had already discussed the bill in detail. The new empowerment of women committee would now review the bill and It would be scuttled.

The quota system became a goal in itself and created its own momentum. The original purpose was lost. Now sub-quota within quota would bring disaster upon the society. Quota for women in the Panchayats would, let us hope, gradually brings more and more women into the political field.

Madhu Kishwar in her two articles 'Not a gender war' and 'a Flawed measure' in The Hindustan Times, Patna, had discussed about the provisions of the reservation bill along with other related matters. She had pointed out that the lottery system of gender-based reservations proposed in the 81st amendment bill meant that fresh set of constituencies would be earmarked for women at every elections. It would mean that the women would not be able to develop stable relationship with their constituences. That would be true for men also who would not like this scheme. Secondly, when once the bill was passed, the men would not like that women should be allowed to contest general constituencies. Third, in the Scheduled Castes and Scheduled Tribes constituencies, which were permanent, the male would not give space to women. Quota system would ensure that women would contest only women and never men. This would mean "a sure way to perpetually ghettoies women's politics". To add to all these harmful effects of the reservation bill, in another, it would be impossible for a woman to get elected twice to the legislatures in Centre or in states, because the same constituencies would not be likely to be reserved twice in succession.

The suggestion for multiseat constituencies should be considered seriously. These constituencies could be clustered together to make one. These would be represented by three people, one of whom must be a woman. The first two seats would go to the two candidates who polled the highest number of votes - man or woman. The third seat would to the woman who polled highest number of votes among the rest of the women candidates not elected on either of the two general seats in the constituencies.

After the fall of the Gujarat government and the installation of Vajpayee government in March 1998, preparations were on for introduction of women's reservation bill in the Lok Sabha. All major parties had included the issue of women's reservation in their election manifestoes. However, there was so much rumpus in the Lok Sabha that the bill could not even he placed on the table. Copies of the bill were destroyed by Laloo Yadav and Mulayarn Singh Yadav, Sarad Yadav was also against the introduction of the bill. He maintained that the bill would be beneficial only to educated elite women.

The attitude adopted by most of the male MPs cutting across party lines was an expression of their fear and anxiety over the loss of more than 180 seats in the Lok Sabha, if 33 per cent seats were reserved for women.

At the grass root level institutions, the 73rd Amendment to the Constitution did provide 33 per cent reservation for women in Panchayati Raj institutions (PRIs). It has produced very good results in Bengal, Maharashtra and Karnataka, but in Bihar, elections to PRIs have not been held even once in the last six years, since the passage of the amendment.

Some organisations like the People's Union for Civil liberties, Rashtriya Lok Samiti, Nav Bharat Jagriti Kendra and Jan Jagaran Kendra, Prayas, Catholic Centre and Xavier's Institute of Social Service came into existence for mobilising women, besides other programmes. Except Prayas, all these groups were part of wider national movement.

Apart from these organisations and action groups in which women are involved politically, socially, and economically, Bihar had witnessed the rise and growth of several woman organisation during the pre-Independence days. One such organisation was the Mahila Charkha Samiti, known as Mahila Charkha Class in its initial days. Several great personalities like Gandhiji, Rajendra Babu, Jay Prakash Narain and Prabhawati Ji were associated with it and were involved in its activities.

Another important women's agency was the All India Women's Conference, already mentioned before, which in its earlier days was known as Women's India Association. At the Centre in Delhi, Margret E Cousins, the secretary of Women's India Association, made concerted efforts to establish the present All India Women's Conference. Its branches were gradually established in different states.

Another old and important women's organisation in Bihar had been the Bihar Council of Women. Working women had also organised themselves under the leadership of Lakshmi Menon. The Centre for Women Development studies (CWDS) was started a few decades ago in Bihar by the encouragement and initiative of Veena Mazumdar. This organisation is quite active in the tribal belt with its social and economic programmes. There are some other NGOs like Aditi, which are also involved in women's field.

In Political Parties

Maciver defined political party as "an association organised in support of some principle or the policy, which by constitutional means endeavours to make the determinant of the government". This definition focussed attention on the associated and the organised aspects of a political party, while brining about the rationale for its existence in terms of some guiding principle or policy and linking the same to political power as exercised by the government. Political parties are the closely connected with government, and thus, in decision-making position. The parties furnish the government with personnel.

In order to socialise the masses effectively, every political party must have competent leadership. Party workers or cadres must establish contacts with the people on a regular basis so as to aggregate and articulate their interests, educate them politically, and thereby, secure their support for the party. The party officers and workers aim at imbibing the ordinary members with the party spirit, imparting party ideologies and motivating them to be active in implementation of party programmes.

Since recruitment by political parties encourage circulation of elites, it infuses new blood to keep the party vibrant. Their neglect of women would not augur well either for the parties or the women, who formed half of the body politics.

Political parties in India have shown neglect of women in recruiting them for party posts like presidents, secretaries, treasures, spokesperson or whips at the Centre, state or local levels. The Congress party, as compared with any other party, has been most liberal towards women in their recruitment policies. But even then women members never exceeded 10 per cent limit. Even the Left parties did not find women very much fit for their tickets in elections of posts. It was only EVP who found in Sushama Swaraj party spokesperson. Though the number of women in politics has increased, their appearance into the ranks the politically active or key decision-makers or non-key decision-makers is still very low, if not nil.

There might be several reasons for acquiring less decision-making positions in a political party by women. Besides their socialisation or political culture in the society, one very important reason was that the party system in India itself is in shambles. They have no proper organisations or proper offices or definable ideologies or identifiable issues and long-term programmes. They seem to be interested only in seeking chairs for the sake of collecting benefits and privileges accruing from different positions. In such chaotic situation, even if women entered decision-making apparatuses of the party, they would have bleak future. They would affect very little - either the party system or the political system as a whole.

The role of, specially the mainstream political parties is very important. They have to be sensitise to provide space to women in their decision-making forum. Merely reservation of seats for women might not be much successful in creating a 'critical mass' in the legislature.

Women in politics have not been held in esteem and with respect by political parties as has been disclosed in a study Bhog by well known Journalist Vikas Kumar Jha. The writer has narrated the sad story of many women party workers, who were lured into the organisation by politicians as "workers". He alleged that "women political workers" had been exploited by the male politicians for satisfying their lust. The writer of Bhog includes fake characters also in his study of Indian politics in order to establish his point. Vikas, in his earlier work, had thrown light on corruption in politics and a brief history of the country. In Bhog, Vikas has probed and made efforts to determine women's status in politics.

Political parties have gradually recognised the importance of including women's issue in their election manifestoes as witnessed during 91, 96 and 98 general elections. But neither in 96 nor in 98 the parties gave enough tickets to women. It has not gone beyond 10 per cent by any party. Women were given decision-making positions of the secondary level except Kanti Singh in Deve Gowda Ministry, some good vocal members in Gujaral Ministry like Renuka Chowdhury.

Indira Gandhi has been the lone example of a potent political decision-maker. At the planetary level, she was the first to strongly formulate a guideline for the prevention and presentation of environment. At the national level, she was a powerful and effective Prime Minister. She left her father Nehru way back in the game of real politics. She almost replaced the parliamentary form of government by a Prime Ministerial form of government. It is often remarked that she was the only 'male' is her Cabinet. She ruled her party and government as an autocrat never witnessed before.

After Indira Gandhi, several other women politicians have emerged exerting considerable influence on the formulation of national and state level politics. Mamta Banerji exerted pressure on Congress party, even broke away from the party to formulate a new party which to her was the 'real' Congress party in West

Bengal. She dictated terms to Vajpayee government regularly. The year 1998 saw the emergence of Sonia Gandhi as a leader with ample influence and political clout. To certain extent she has revived the Congress party. Then there is Jayalalitha, a very strong and popular leader of Tamil Nadu. Then there is Mayawati, the undisputed Dalit leader and an important decision-make in Uttar Pradesh politics.

The years 1998-99 witnessed the crucial role played by women leaders of the likes of Sonia Gandhi, Jayalalitha, Mamta Banerji and Mayawati. While Sonia Gandhi succeeded to a certain exact in pumping new blood in the otherwise anaemic Congress party, Jayalalitha and Mamta Banerji put pressures on the Vajpayee government from its very inception. Jayalalitha continued threatening the government that she would withdraw. When the Vishnu Bhagwat issue flew up, Jayalalitha ultimately decided to withdraw the support of her 18 MPs on the issue of formation of JPC. The final act was performed by Mayawati when she voted against the government. These four women leaders brought down the Vajpayee government. Obviously in 1998 and early 1999, Indian political scenario was virtually dominated by these women leaders. The coming years will be a testing ground for these women leaders.

7

Electoral Politics

The process of election is the main wheel of a democratic system. With the prevalence of indirect democracy in almost all the democratic countries of the world, it assumes great importance as a mechanism for choosing representatives for elective offices by means of votes by the people. By voting, we constitute the government and choose our law-makers and law-executors. It is not only primarily a legitimising instrument for those in, authority and for their governance, it is a positive right of the people, through which they decide the destiny of their political system.

The total population of any country does not constitute a homogeneous group. Similarly, our society is plural and consists of vârious well-organised groups and communities with different interests and needs competing for a share in political power through the mechanism of elections. Not each group has equal access to power in a democratic polity despite the popular myth of equality for all. There are minorities identified on the basis of religion, race and ethnicity all over the globe. Women do not constitute a minority in numbers as they constitute nearly 50 per cent of the total population of any country, but practically have a minor position and only a marginal access to polity due to gender bias.

Feminists have thrown up gender as the most potent, significant and enormously useful analytical concept. The feminist scholarship places gender, the sociocultural manifestation of being a man or woman as the focus of study in research. Gender is defined as the social construction of relations between women and men and among various groups of women or men. Sex is defined as the biological similarities and differences between and among men, and women.

Gender and patriarchy combine together to push women to the periphery of politics. Politics is regarded strictly as a male preserve. Rationality, self-discipline, competition, aggression, orderliness, universality to mention a few, are the priced qualities in political parlance. On the contrary, irrationality, indiscipline, particularity, submissiveness impulsiveness are some of the qualities associated with feminine nature. The result is the distancing of women from everything political. Women are perceived as part of the social structure and not as part of the "power" phenomenon, which Seinon De Behaviour calls as "being rather than doing".This socio-cultural perspective in addition to mass-scale illiteracy and poverty of Indian women prevents them from a meaningful involvement in the political process.

Women's right to vote and to stand for elections has only been a legal reality for about 100 years globally. Although men vote was not extended initially to all classes and races, generally their universal enfranchisement preceeded women. It was first adopted by the European countries, the Americas and Australia. The end of World War II in 1945 brought former colonial countries in Asia and Africa to grant women's suffrage, and the trend has continued worldwide, with South Africa enfranchising black women and men as late as 1994.

Although the right to stand for elections, to be a candidate and to be elected follows in theory from the right to vote. Earlier several countries had granted suffrage only. Women's right to vote was restricted to male candidates only. Canada granted women the unrestricted right to vote in 1950, but not until 10 years later did they gain the right to be candidates. Conversely, some countries put women's right to be elected as their first political right. USA, Norway, the Netherlands, and Guyana, for example, allowed women to run for office and to be elected by an all male electorate. Kuwait disallows women both voting and candidates rights while extending them to men, and four others. Saudi Arabia. Qatar, Oman and Somalia - deny them to both genders. Since Finland adopted both these fundamental democratic rights in 1906, over 95 per cent of the countries of the world have followed suit by the end of the 20th century.

The Constitution of India from 1950, guarantees equal opportunity for participation in politics to both men and women. Women were given this right equally with men in recognition and as a 'token' of appreciation by the national leaders for the massive role played by them in the freedom struggle. The Preamble to the Constitution of India resolves to secure to all its citizens. Justice, social and economic and political; Liberty of thought, expression. belief, faith and worship; Equality of status and opportunity; and to promote among them all, fraternity, assuming the dignity of all individuals and the unity of the nation. Article 14 of the Constitution ensures 'equality before law" and Article 15 prohibits discrimination" interalia of sex among other things.

The gradual transfer of power from the British to Indian hands gave women experience in participation in democratic process. The Government of India Act of 1935 extended the franchise to more than 6 million women, a great improvement on the earlier figure of 3,15,000 under the act of 1919. But for this franchise right, women did have to wage a grim battle. Lord Lothian, the head of the franchise committee after meeting the women's delegation led by Sarojini Naidu, remarked that "they were very firm in their demand for equality as a basis of the new Indian Constitution". As early as 1930, a meeting of the representatives of women's organisations had demanded immediate acceptance of adult franchise without sex discrimination. Though rejected by the British government, the Karachi session of the Indian National Congress in 1931 accepted these demands and committed Itself to women's political equality regardless of their status and qualifications.

In 1937 elections, eight women were elected from general constituencies and 42 from reserved constituencies. The Constituent Assembly set up for the drafting of the Constitution of free India in October 1946 had among its members, Sarojini Naidu, Durgabai Deshmukh, Renuka and Hansa Mehta among other notables.

Power of Vote

India has experienced 12 general elections to date. It has not been possible for election analysts to decide which particular way the women have voted, but their votes have undoubtedly been Included in this "on course" corrective voting for giving a fresh lease of power to the elected parliamentary form of government.

With the rising number of electorate, the percentage of women voters has also registered a steady rise constantly from 37; 1 per cent in 1952 to 69.70 per cent in 1971. However, in 1977 the difference was 9.7 per cent to increase further to 10.77 per cent in 1977 and 10.94 per cent in 1980. In 1984, women had polled a higher percentage of votes to fall again steadily in 1989. Since then, however, there has been a discernable fall from 69.70 per cent to 55.85 per cent in 1977 and 51.22 per cent in 1980. The year 1984 was a 'watershed' when the percentage of women voters went upto 68.17 per cent to fall again in 1989 to 43.90 per cent and 47.42 per cent in 1991. In the 1996 Lok Sabha, elections the total number of women voters in the country was 28,03,69,086, while that of male voters was 30,98,15,776.7 There was a slight improvement in 1998 elections.

As compared to the total voter turnout, the figures for female voters have always been less by approximately 6 per cent. Looking at the trends in female voting, similar fluctuations as in total voting are evident. In 1967, the percentage of female votes was 55.48 per cent marking a decrease of 6.33 per cent. This decrease is somewhat equal to the fall in total voting percentage, which shows that in comparative terms, women's voting did not depict a discouraging trend.

A better comparative assessment can be had by looking at the difference in the percentage of male and female voters. This difference has always been unfavourable to women. In, 1991, the percentage difference was 27 per cent but in 1996 it narrowed down to 5.14 per cent.

The general inferences are that women have shown a gradual increase in the exercise of their franchise, and this increase has been proportionate to the increase in total voter turnout. In 1971 elections, there was decrease in the percentage of voters in general. The difference between male and female voters was 11.85 per cent. The low turnout was due to various factors operating at that time. The split within the Congress Party; election being held one year earlier due to the dissolution of Lok Sabha, etc. Both these factors proved detrimental to the mobilisation of voters in the 1971 election. However, the fact that the difference between male and female voting did not widen with the total fall in mobilisation shows that the female voters were more mobilised than their male counterparts while the total voter turnout increased only by 0.50 per cent (54.76 per cent.to 55.35 per cent), the increase in female voter turn out was 2.52 per cent (46.64 per cent to 49.15 per cent). In 1974 and 1980, there was no improvement, rather a decreasing trend was visible with tremendous increase in 1984, when women's vote percentage was 68.17 per cent nearly 5 per cent higher than the percentage of male votes. It fell drastically is 1989, 1991, 1996 and 1998.

Another interesting feature is that states have been more or less steadily maintaining a consistent record of either maximum or minimum mobilisation of women as voters. While the states of Kerala and Tamil Nadu have maintained their position as maximum mobilisers of women, Orissa and Madhya Pradesh have been equally persistent in leading the list of minimum mobilisers of women. The difference between the maximum and minimum mobilisation of women has always remained high. The states of Kerala,

Tamil Nadu, Maharashtra, Andhra Pradesh and Gujarat in the southern and western regions have shown a relatively higher degree of electoral participation by women. The states in the northern region with exception of Punjab and Haryana in the west and West Bengal in the east have shown a persistent trend of low mobilisation. Orissa, Madhya Pradesh, Bihar, Uttar Pradesh, Rajasthan, Assam, Himachal Pradesh, Jammu and Kashmir present a dismal picture of persistently low mobilisation in absolute terms, and particularly in relation to men with percentage difference actually increasing in Madhya Pradesh. Except for Bihar and Uttar Pradesh the states with low mobilisation have been those which were late in participating in the Independence struggle. Socially extensive and severe restrictions on women's activities outside the family have been prevalent in these states. Economically they are poor with comparatively less urbanisation and industrialisation. Female literacy also has been lowest in these states. These are some of the factors that account for low political consciousness and less enthusiasm for the exercise of franchise rights among women.

The states and Union territories showing greater mobilisation of women socially and politically, are not backward and economically they are not deficient. Most of them being coastal areas they were the first to be exposed to the Western culture of the Dutch, Portuguese and the British colonisers. Places such as Delhi and Chandigarh, though not falling into the above category, have a cosmopolitan cultural outlook, an industrial base and urban character. The social structures of these states and Union territories are not very rigid and male dominated. On the contrary, a state like Kerala has a maternal society, which ensures a relatively dominant place to women.

Inspite of regional imbalances, the mobilisation of women voters is not depressing. But it is also not a factor which should lull us into satisfaction as regards women's political participation. Way back in the 1970s the committee on the Status of Women in India in its report had commented, "women's participation in the political process has increased both in elections and in their readiness to express their views on issues directly concerning their day-to-day life, their ability to produce an impact on the political process has been negligible." It still holds true even after the passage of two decades.

The increase in the turnout of women voters, particularly of the lower castes and classes may be attributed to a high degree to mobilisation, rather than their own political consciousness. The Scheduled Castes and other poor and backward communities are aware of the importance of their vote, but this awareness about the Issues affecting them needs tremendous mobilisation in order to be translated into a political exercise like voting preferences with regard to women who have many disincentives such as poverty, daily work, violence, health and patriarchal family norms.

The parties have recognised the significance of women voters, and have been exerting themselves to devise various methods. Mostly adhoc promises are made to women during election campaigns. Moreover, there was any correlation between the camping promises and voting support. It also reflected on the low impact that the women's movement had helped in educating the women as well as in making a dent on the patriarchal politicians (92). In 1984, much of the victory of the Congress could be attributed to a sympathy vote by womenfolk against the slaying of Prime Minister Indira Gandhi on a woman-to-woman basis (92).

Key Players

The number of women candidates contesting for the Lok Sabha has been extremely discouraging. It has not been much above 5 per cent of the total number of male candidates. The number of women contestants in Lok Sabha, however, has increased since 1952 with the exception of 1957 when it came down to 45 from 51. There has been a steady increase in the number in 1991-1996 to fall again in 1998.

The fall in the number of women candidates is not surprising since in this election the total number of candidates was much smaller than in 1996, may be due to the changes made by the Election Commission, and also the unexpectedness of the general elections.

The difference between male and female contestants of the Lok Sabha seats has also shown a declining trend from 1977 onwards—94.17 per cent in 1977 to 93.82 per cent in 1980 and 90.23 per cent in 1984. The differences had increased slightly in 1991 and 1996.

The actual number of seats contested by women has been less than the number of women contestants since some of the seats were contested by more than one women.

The number of seats in the first to five general elections were 6, 5, 5, 5, 9, respectively. The number and percentage of the successful women candidates increased in 1957 from 19 to 25 and from 37 per cent to 62 per cent. Since then there has been a steady decline. In 1971 only 21 were successful out of a total of 86. In 1971, a sudden spurt in the number of independent women candidates from 10 in 1967 to 31 in 1971- added to the total number. At the same time independent candidates performed very poorly-only one succeeded, and thus the overall percentage fell from 42.4 to 25.9, an all time low. The number of contestants rose steadily from 1980 onwards from 142 in 1980 to 599 in 1996 to fall again in 1998. In the 11th Lok Sabha elections about 2/3 of the total 599 female candidates were independents. Experience has shown that women have rarely been successful as independents. Party build up and support is necessary for women to win elections. In the 1991 elections, a relatively mobile candidate Rita Verma from Dhanbad in Bihar won due to the massive support of BJP. Not exactly similar, but such experiences have been often repeated. The election of Alka Nath (1976) from Chindwara in Madhya Pradesh is another such example.

Statewise: The number of women contesting for Lok Sabha in the states and Union territories has roughly been in accordance with, though not in proportion, to the total number allocated to them. The maximum number of women have entered the race in Uttar Pradesh except in 1951 and 1971 when Bihar, the next biggest state in terms of Lok Sabha seats, took the lead by one number. In the elections of 1996, Uttar Pradesh had returned 10 women to the Lok Sabha, the largest contingent from one state. Some of the Union territories such as Delhi, Goa, Daman and Diu and Madhya Pradesh have put up greater percentage. Madhya Pradesh needs special mention, since it has shown a poor turnout of voters.

The number of women candidates in various states and Union Territories shows wide fluctuations from one election to another. It has fluctuated in Uttar Pradesh, but in Bihar and Madhya Pradesh, the number has gradually gone up. In Kerala, it remained constant at one for the first three elections, then marked a slight increase to three in 1967 and four in 1971. In Orissa, no woman contested in the first three elections, but in 1967 one and in 1971, two women contested. In the Union Territories along with Jammu & Kashmir, Haryana and Mysore may be clubbed into one category, as the number of women contestants in them for all five general elections was either nil or just one.

The number of successful candidates has naturally been greater in Uttar Pradesh, Bihar, Madhya Pradesh and Andhra Pradesh; where the number of contestants has also been greater. Orissa, Haryana, Goa, Daman and Due and Manipur are the states and Union territories where women contested but were not returned to Lok Sabha in the first five general elections. In 1996, Haryana returned one, but Manipur, Assam, Arunachal Pradesh, Mizoram, Nagaland, Sikkim, Tamil Nadu, Jammu and Kashmir Kerala, Maharashtra, Meghalaya, Himachal Pradesh did not return a single contestant to Lok Sabha.

The number of contesting or elected women candidates for Lok Sabha in a particular, state or Union territory does not appear to be decisively related with the literacy among women in that area. Laxmi N Menon, while analysing the first general elections, inferred that the number of women candidates was in inverse proportion to the percentage of literacy among them. The electoral history of different states over the years does not project a consistent pattern of correlation between female literacy and their candidature. Literacy is not a single variable in this respect, and it influences the number of contestants, but only in combination with other factors. The social ethos and taboos prevailing in the state or in a particular constituency visa-vis women's role in politics did influence the success or otherwise of its female contestants, but only in a small way. What mattered most were the personality of the contestants, including their family background and involvement in politics, local conditions, campaign strategy and the political party to which the candidates belong.

The maximum number of female candidates have been fielded by the Congress Party from 25 in 1957 to 49 in 1996. However, it has remained much below its stipulated target of 15 per cent of the total candidates. CPI and erstwhile Praja Socialist Party have been fielding female candidates from the very beginning, but the number has been small. In the 1996 elections, CPI(M) put up five female candidates and CPI fielded four. Smaller, unrecognised parties have shown continuous fluctuations.

As in number, the Congress has also covered the maximum area. Congress women candidates have appeared in most of the states during Lok Sabha elections except in 1971 when they were confined to states and one Union territory. Madhya Pradesh has always secured maximum tickets for women except in 1971. The largest number of independent candidates has come from Uttar Pradesh, Bihar and Rajasthan. The rest of the parties have put up women candidates largely in their strongholds - BJP in Uttar Pradesh, CPM in Kerala and West Bengal and erstwhile SSP in Bihar and Uttar Pradesh. Madhya Pradesh has also been favoured by most of these parties in terms of putting up a women candidate. The average of women contestants to Lok Sabha per seat is 0.30 per cent. Average share among contestants is 3.2 per cent and the success ratio is 28.5 per cent.

Notwithstanding a few exceptions, the women contestants have been found poorly in articulate, in overall perspective and the issues pertaining to the particular contests. They have heavily depended upon either the party machine or the hands of loyal men workers in conducting their respective election campaigns, and after taken recourse to emotional and sentimental appeals to establish rapport with the voters. In 1989, 29 women were elected to Lok Sabha while in 1991 the number was 33 and in 1996 it was 38. In 1998, it increased to 40.

The Parliamentarians

From 1952 to 1967, the percentage of women who contested and won was much higher than the men - 45.09, 65.05, 52.30; and for males it was 25.50, 39.54 and 25.95. In 1971, there was a sharp fall to 24.41 per cent from 46.96, rose slightly to 27 per cent in 77 to fall again to 19.71 per cent in 1980. It improved slightly to 25.6 per cent in 1984. Since there has been a steady decline in the percentage, successful women candidates in relation to the number of female contestants ... 43.6 percent in 1989, 12.00 per cent in 1991 and 6.88 per cent in 1996. In 1998 it was 72 per cent.

The percentage of women in the Lok Sabha in relation to the total number of seats has been very low, from 4.4 per cent in 1952 it increased slightly in 1957 (5.4 per cent) in 1962 (6.7 per cent), 1967 (5.9 per cent) to fall again to 4.2 per cent in 1971, 3.4 per cent (the lowest) in 1977 to increase slightly to 8.1 per cent in 1984 to fall again to 5.2 per cent in 1989. There has been a slight improvement in 1991, 1996 and 1998.

It is ironical that although the success rate of female contestant has invariably been higher in relation to males, they are still a very small percentage of the total number of contestants and so their presence in the Lok Sabha is small, not even 9 per cent. The difference between male and female contestants is very high, hence, the gap is very wide. Therefore, although the number of female contestants has increased over the years, it is still a very small percentage of the total, and thus, despite their high success rate their presence in the Lok Sabha is negligible.

The presence of women in the Rajya Sabha is much better. Till 1996, while women were only 6 per cent is Lok Sabha, on an average the percentage of women MPs in the RaJya Sabha has been 10.3 per cent. However, it has to be noted that women also of through nominations to the RaJya Sabha. Many of them have not fought electoral battles.

Many factors are responsible for this state of affairs, the ideology of the Gandhi-Nehru era has totally disappeared. Elections have become very costly and expensive and most of the female aspirants cannot muster enough funds for fighting elections. Added to these are the extreme criminalisation of politics, excessive use of muscle and money power. Politics is a dirty game and many women do not wish to enter it. The support of political parties could do wonders, but all major political parties are reluctant to put up female candidates despite the high rate of their success in elections. For example in the 1998 elections in Bihar, BJP had put-up two female candidates and both won.

It is true that women suffer from economic dependency, illiteracy and, a particular image of the self-nurtured through the socialisation process, and these factors, also influence their entry into the election process. The gender bias of the political parties adds to it. With the backing of a strong party, a woman candidate can also win elections. Rita Verma has won thrice since 1991 on EUP ticket from Bihar. Same was the case of Alka Nath from Madhya Pradesh.

The fact remains that unless in Dehlerup's word, they become a 'critical mass', that is, by having 30 per cent to 40 per cent seats in the House, things are not going to change.

In States

In the period from 1952-57, the percentage of women in states' Legislative Assemblies has certainly not impressive. Delhi has an average of 5-9 per cent women representatives. Next comes Madhya Pradesh with an average of 5.1 per cent. The lowest average is found in Nagaland with 0.5 per cent. The average of women contestants per seat is 0.19 per cent. The 6 per cent of share among contestants is 2.8. The average success ratio of women contestants is 21.0 per cent.

The Influence

In spite of mafia politics, money and muscle power, Indian women have come on the political agenda of the country through the technique of collective action consciousness raising programmes, petitioning and lobbying. Many struggles in Karnataka did result in the implementation of a 30 per cent reservation for women at the local and state level in early and mid-80s. Thus, all is not lost. Glimmering of hope can be seen in the determined efforts made by women of progressive social organisations and movement to challenge vested interests (caste, class and gender) and make a determined bid for power.

Women issues and demands have found a place in election manifestoes of almost all the parties in the 1990s.' The demand for 33 per cent reservation for women was taken account of in the 1991 election manifestoes, but not complied with in 1996 elections. The bill for 33 per cent reservation for women in the Lok Sabha and the state legislature was placed before the Lok Sabha as the 86th Amendment to the Constitution in September 1996, but could not be passed. Male members cutting across party lines joined hands in ridiculing the bill, despite intense lobbying by women MPs of all parties and their threat to boycott the Lok Sabha session until the bill is passed, the Bill has yet to see the light of the day. In the 1998 elections, all Parties-from Congress to BJP to RJD pledged the implementation of 33 per cent reservation to women. There is a strong demand both from inside Lok Sabha and outside by women activists to implement the demand by passing the women's reservation bill immediately. As Pramila Dandvate had remarked in one of her interviews to the *Hindustan Times* in December 1996 that the male MPs are afraid of losing 1/3 seats in the Lok Sabha, and what it would do to their patriarchal authority and control over the Lok Sabha proceeding. The bill could not be even placed on the table in 1998 under the Vajpayee government. The Samajwadi Party and RJD chief Mulayam Singh and Laloo Prasad Yadav displayed utter disregard for parliamentary decorum. Document was torn into shred this is how women are made to remain in the margin of politics. Due to their scarce representation in Lok Sabha, their voice can hardly be hard. They are often pushed to the wall and gradually become a silent minority.

Women's movement had till recently taken an indifferent interest in election process, but with the debate on reservation of seats for women in the legislative bodies, some interest has been created which is reflected in the mobilisation of women's group during election campaign, etc. Some groups in Pune made a united front that is the Stree Mukti Andolan Sampark Samiti. The Krantikari Mahila Sangathan (KMS) of Pune has been actively involved in electoral politics. It has put up candidates independently or jointly with political parties like the Republican Party of India, Janata Dal or with Social Action Group as in Mumbai. This organisation, which came into existence in the early 1980s, has grown considerably and has branches in other cities outside Pune. It is involved at two levels contesting elections at grassroot level, and participating in election campaign for raising consciousness.

There are many women's groups in Ahmedabad, Pune and Bangalore, which have prepared women's manifestoes. They conduct exposure programmes on 'Know the Candidate' and leaflets concerning women's issues such as exposing a candidate who has a criminal involvement in murder, rape or molestation cases.

In Bangalore, Vemochana, a women's group campaign against such candidates, who have committed violence against women, by organising street meetings, writing in news-papers and issuing leaflets, as a result of its campaign, many a candidate lost elections. The campaign against the gang rape of a

Kasthakari Sangathana activist by CPI (M) Cadres resulted in the CPI(M) candidate losing his Lok Sabha election.

The Nari Samata Manch, another feminist group in Pune, though small in size, has also tried to address itself to the issue of electoral politics. Putting up candidates for elections is beyond their capacity, but they considered it important to mobilise and educate women voters.

Nevertheless, the issue is of grave concern for democratic politics all over the world. Worldwide the representation of women in single or lower national assemblies in 1997 including authoritarian and long standing democratic countries - was 11.6 per cent. The range was from 0 per cent in Comoras, Djbouti, Kiribati, Micronesia, Palan, Papua New Guinea and Tonga to 40.4 per cent in Sweden in 1997.

At the United Nations Fourth World Conference on women, a commitment to achieve women's equal representation in parliaments and other governmental bodies was made by unanimous vote on September 15, 1995. One hundred and eighty eight nations participated in the conference held at Beijing in China. The delegates not only pledged to seek equality in governmental decision making for women, but also specified in their plan of action how nations might achieve it. These included governmental review of electoral systems and adjustment or reforms of them and positive-affirmative action by political parties to nominate and elect women. Following up on the United Nation's Universal Declaration of Human Rights, which specifies that every citizen has the right to participate in the government, the Beijing Conference adopted this statement "Women's rights are human rights." Therefore, women are entitled as a matter of simple justice and democracy, the delegates stated, to all political rights now afforded to men.

At the Beijing Conference stress was laid on two factors- electoral reforms and positive/affirmative action by political parties.

Balance of Power

In long-standing democracies, proportional representation has been repeatedly documented as the most significant factor among contextual variables, explaining women's election to Parliament (Rule 1981, 1987, 1994 Norris 1985, 1997). Wilma Rule through her studies has derived the correlation between proportional representation (PR) and women's election to Parliament. Her study revealed that the party list proportional representation countries were generally higher regarding women's recruitment to legislatures of single member plurality/majority countries. She maintains of a 10 candidate constituency gives a women a greater chance for party nomination than does a lower magnitude of three or more. It allow the electorate to choose on an open party list. The preference vote has been used successfully in Finland and Denmark.

Rule gives her observations on updated percentage of women's parliamentary representation in long-standing democracies in 1993 and 1997, and remarks that there has been an upward swing. The three major explanations are: (i) Political party quotas or goals to nominate an increased percentage of women to Parliament in PR countries; (ii) Laws requiring that a proportion (quota) of women be placed on party list in PR countries; and, (iii) Electoral system change from single member plurality to proportional representation. The first measure was adopted just by Denmark, Finland, Norway and Sweden with great success in the 1980s. The same happened in Spain in 1996 elections and in Great Britain in 1997 elections. The second strategy was adopted in Italy after the 1992 elections. A new election law provided that 1/4 of Italian Parliament was to be elected from party list and the remainder from single member districts. In 1994 elections the success of women on party list was 33 per cent but it was only 9 per cent in the case of single member constituency election. The third approach resulted in New Zealand rank as the sixth highest nation in women's parliamentary representation among long-standing democracies by 1997.

There is an urgent need of electoral reforms in India. The above mentioned strategies, which yielded very good results in long-standing democracies, could be tested in this country too.

The proportional representation facilitates quicker change than a single member majority/plurality system. It is easier for a political party to add women to its list for 10 constituencies averaging ten contestants. Then it is to change 100 single member majority or plurality constituencies from male to female representatives.

The laws requiring a quota of women to be nominated on party list provide that women's name be positioned so that they could be elected if their party won sufficient votes in the election.

Election laws may be changed to provide for proportional representation in place of single member constituency.

Positive action in the form of laws to ensure proper representation of women in Parliaments have been proposed by nine developing countries, which have a majority/ plurality system. A bill for providing 33 per cent reservation to women in the Lok Sabha and state Legislative Assemblies in India was introduced in the Lok Sabha in September 1996 and 1998, but despite much publicity debates and discussions, It has still to see the light of the day.

Dehlerup Dirude (1986) has Suggested several measures which when adopted could assists in augmenting women's place in political life. This included changing electoral laws (for Instance, proportional election system tended to be more favourable to women than election system with single member constituencies) women's political parties (successful use In Iceland in 1983) and public campaigns to bring more women into Politics. Political Parties should evolve a system of Yevolving funds to finance women contestants.

The most important is to sensitise political parties towards gender issues. Laws should be made to make it obligatory for Political Parties to nominate a percentage of women in their list of contestants. If the 1996 and 1998 elections are any Pointer. Political Parties in India have failed miserably on this score despite their commitments as reflected in their Party manifestoes in 1991, 1996 and 1998 elections. The Opposition directed towards the 33 per cent reservation bill for women by almost any major political Parties reflects the male antagonism towards the entry of women in politics.

It becomes imperative for liberal democratic governments on the one hand to go ahead with electoral reforms and seriously provide for their implementation and on the other hand. it becomes a responsibility of women's organisations and movement to exert pressure for the same especially in the wake of the Beijing Conference of 1995. According to Bernis Lot "Power generates power and powerlessness generates powerlessness. Because the society is patriarchal where men hold power more power will always be given to men, and women will be made powerless incapable, on the margin. This is a reminder to the fact that women under representation in legislative bodies all over the globe with the possible exception of Norclic and Scandenevian countries is a matter of grave concern for the future of democracy. Also the Status of women's rights. The right to political participation is a human right.

8

Institution of Panchayati Raj

It is global a experience that in the formulation of policies and programmes for national and international goals, women banning a few, have seldom played an effective role. They have been marginals in politics and political decision making process. In 1988, the average percentage of women represented in national parliaments worldwide stood at 14.6 per cent. What is more, it is decreasing considerably per cent. True, women in almost all the countries have de jure right to participate in political decision-making, but in fact they continue to be, under represented and marginal in political decision-making bodies at all levels. How can there be, then, equality in political decision-making? The urgent need of the hour at this juncture is to find a way to increase the number of women in the politically representative bodies. In a democratic polity, it is expected that the processes and decisions reflect the will of the people and represent the interests of all the various groups and formations in the population of the country. It rarely happens. The decision, in fact, are made by the powerful in the society for furthering their self interests of various groups. Women form the largest minority group, almost 50 per cent of any country's population, but are hardly visible in the area of politics, They are so scarce, their voices can hardly be heard. They are the silent minority unheard and unseen. But democracy does not and cannot operate by proxy. Every citizen needs to take part in the political activities and perform the political duties. Women have to take processes to ensure the democratic nature of the policy and for this they have to be present in political bodies.

It is easier seen than done. Politics is an exercise of power and, denotes the functioning of a whole array policies of public institutions and forms, which are involved in moulding the lives of people by way of decisions, which influence their interpersonal relationships. Thus, politics throughout the ages has been constructed and moulded on the basis of those norms which have been identified though loosely, as masculine. Rationality, self discipline, competition, aggression, orderliness, universality to mention a few, are the priced qualities in political parlance. On the contrary, irrationality, Indiscipline, particularity, submissiveness, impulsiveness are some of the qualities associated with the feminine nature. The result is the distancing of women from every thing political. Women are perceived as part of the social structure and not as part of power phenomenon. Simon de Behaviour calls as "being rather than doing". The male-public and female private dichotomy in social perception has been found to be the greatest hindrance in the way of women's access to power and political decision-making, even in highly developed countries like the Nordic ones. "Democracy was still unfinished, since women constituted a minority in politics (as Drude ' Dahlerup remarks in The Unfinished Democracy: Women in Nordic Politics). It is even more true in the countries where cultural norms and traditions still restrict women to the private sphere of action. Politics is not for them. It is strictly "public" and male dominated sphere of action.

It would be apt here to discuss and define politics in a slightly wider perspective. An important feature of the feminist efforts has been to proclaim the political nature of private life, and the relation between the sexes which has brought traditional politics into question and has forced the authorities to take account of problems hitherto regarded as belonging to private life. It is now a well recognised proposition in women's studies/movement viz. that all spheres of lives involving any relationship is political; that millions of women are silently (and not always very successfully) waging a struggle against the patriarchal and feudal forces that seek to confine and contain them. It is not lack of consciousness of her human and political rights, but the vicious circle into which she is placed from the very beginning of her life. This struggle against patriarchy in its myriad forms is a prolonged and complex one, and it needs effective participation in politics in a visible and appreciable number at effective levels and in meaningful positions.

This brings us to a theoretical discussion of what a sizeable number of women can do in the political bodies. Drude Dahlerup maintains that it makes a big difference whether women constitute a small minority or a large minority, although still a minority. She developed a theory of the 'critical mass' in which she maintains that if women's number rose to 25-30 or higher, these women reached a critical 'mass' which permitted them to intervene and benefit from the support of women colleagues in what was 'nevertheless' still a male-dominated body.8 She considers support from outside by a strong feminest movement as a necessary requirement towards effectiveness of women's participation in the decision-making representative bodies. She quoted the developments in her own country where women now constituted approximately 25 per cent of all elected members of parliament and local councils. It is the same with other Nordic countries.

Various strategies have been suggested for augmenting women's place in political bodies, such as changing the electoral laws (for instance proportional election systems tended to be more favourable to women than election systems with single member districts) women's political parties (the successful use of these in Iceland in 1983 was noted), and public campaigns, organisational structure of political life.

Another important method is fixing a quota for women at all levels of political decision-making bodies. This question of quota, in order to Increase women's presence in political life was being discussed in Denmark and was applied in Norway in public commissions. With this theoretical backdrop, let us come to the Indian scene.

The Constitution of India guarantees gender equality in all spheres of life including political. Thus Indian women (at least in law) have equal rights of political participation along with men. They can vote in elections, can fight elections and get elected to legislative bodies right from the federal to the grassroots level. They can hold executive, and leadership Positions at various levels. So it is that India can boast of a very strong leadership. In the Primeministership of Indira Gandhi for more than one-and a-half decade, besides a number of powerful chief ministers and governors. However; nothing much has happened for the masses of Indian women in the last four decades. There has been some mobilisation of women voters in the last two decades, especially during the Women's Decade (1975-85). The political parties to some extent have started to recognise the potential of women as a Vote bank. As regards their candidature for elections, the number has risen constantly, but the percentage of women getting elected to Parliament has declined. A raincheck on the election data to Lok Sabha reveals that women's percentage in the lower house has never exceeded 8 per cent.

Why is it so? There is the argument about a particular style of socialisation process for women, their generally weak economic position, lack of education especially in developing countries like India, and above all the danger of violence hanging over women In all spheres of life, and especially in the areas of politics. The political culture which is predominantly masculine, determines the attitude of political parties towards women, tolerates a few weak women, but is very hostile towards the entry of women in a viable and strong position in politics.

Can we leave things as they are? The question of participation of women in politics and the political process has been debated in Parliament many times. There is the human rights argument that as 50 per cent of the population comprises women, it was unjust that women were under represented in Parliament. The existing conflict of interests between women and men was a determining reason for women's entry in politics. Men would simply be unwilling or less capable to represent women's interests in politics adequately.

Despite the guarantee of constitutional equality, women have not been able to get equal treatment or opportunity because they are not present in the institutions and process relevant for It. Hence the need to get into these processes and institutions, again and entry into the functioning of the status and share control over the apparatus of state. This alone would lead to preserve and promote equality and justice, and bring about the necessary policy changes and social restructuring so as to usher in a humane and suitable social order.

So, this brings us back to the question of strategy, and one important strategy would be to fix a quota for women in all political decision-making bodies, atleast for sometime to come. This might mean, at least for a while, a certain compromise on the quality of participation. Fixing of 'quotas' or 'reservation' of seats for women would open up a possible entry point for them in politics, and this is necessary because it cannot be denied that a handful of women in legislative bodies cannot make their voice strong enough to be heard. How do they, then, equally share in the decision making and policy formulations?

It is precisely at this point that the 73rd Amendment to the Constitution of India, known 'as Panchayati Raj Amendment Act 1992, could have very important implications for women's political participation. This Act, although related to only the grassroots level Institution 'nevertheless provides for 33 per cent reservation for women in local bodies, both at the deliberative and leadership positions.

It has not happened suddenly, India has witnessed a long-drawn debate on reservation for the various minorities and backward communities such as the Scheduled Castes and Scheduled Tribes and women. Although, reservation for the first two categories was provided by the Constitution, reservation for women has been rough weather from the very beginning. Reservation for women in all the elected bodies from the Centre to the local level has been a fiercely debated issue, and it began in the Constituent Assembly itself. One section of the women's movement had at that time suggested continued reservation of seats on the line of Government of India Act 1935. Women members in the Constituent Assembly, however, rejected this as against the principle of social equality. Much later, the Committee on the Status of Women in India (CSWI) decided to maintain the same position, through two members submitted a dissent note. A group of the social scientists consulted by the committee strongly advocated reservation for women, especially at the panchayat (grassroots) level. The arguments given in favour of reservation for women in the legislative bodies at the state and central level are :

(i) That the declining trend in women's representation was the result of the reluctance of political parties to sponsor women candidates which, however, offers real obstacles in making the few legislators act as spokesperson for women's rights and opportunities.

(ii) That in a situation of political parties reflecting the established values of a mal dominated society, certain structural changes in the sociopolitical set up were necessary to make room for desirable social change; otherwise losing faith in the political process to change their condition of life, women might 'opt out' of the political system and become either passive partners or rebels.

(iii) That a system of reservation of a proportion of seats for women in elected bodies would pave the path for a fairer deal to nearly half the population in the various units of government; and,

(iv) That, a system of reservation could increase the women legislators sense of responsibility and concern for women specific-problems, and this would lead to increasing mobilisation of women both in the electorates and within the political parties. Social scientists associated with the committee also hold the view that improvements in the political status of women constituted an integral aspect of the overall problem of socioeconomic change and broadening the 'political elite structure. It was pointed out very forcefully that a 30 per cent reservation of seats in the legislative bodies will alter the very character of our legislature and will compel the political parties to change their strategies and tactics and induce them to give women their due.

'There was opposition on this issue from the side of the representatives of the political parties and most women legislators. The 'Towards Equality' committee rejected the suggestion for a system of reservation for women to state assemblies and parliament. However, it recommended "statutory women's panchayats at the village level to ensure greater participation by women in the political process as an integral part of the Panchayati Raj structures. The recommendation was passed on to state governments, received mostly negative response and was, therefore, buried within the government. Some states, however, began a gradual process of induction of more women in, the panchayats, as they began steps to entrust more powers and responsibilities to the panchayats.

The most daring was the Karnataka zila parishads, taluk panchayat, mandal panchayats and Nyaya Panchayat Act of 1983 which provided for 25 per cent seats being reserved for women.

The National Perspective Plan (1988) proposed 30 per cent reservation to all elective bodies to be filled, at least in the initial years, by nomination or co-option. The debate organised by the nation women's organisations refused the proposal for reservation in the state assemblies or Parliament but recommended 30 per cent reservation for women in Panchayati Raj institutions "with due precautions to ensure representation of the weaker sections of women, especially Dalits and tribals. The women's organisations were, however, emphatic on the need for elections to ensure the emergence of a new leadership from grassroots."

The 64th Amendment Bill introduced by Rajiv Gandhi was a step further in this direction. The 22nd Amendment in 1990 proposed one-third reservation for women in the Panchayati bodies with an additional provision of one-third among the reserved categories of Scheduled Castes and Scheduled Tribes and among office-bearers. Ultimately, the 73rd Amendment was passed by the parliament on December 22, 1992 providing for 33 per cent reservation of seats for women in Panchayati bodies. It was ratified by half the states by April 1993. Undoubtedly, this Act is most significant for the reservation provided to women along with the Scheduled Castes and Scheduled Tribes. If fully utilised as many as 7.95 lakh women including those belonging to Schedule Castes and Tribes can become panches and sarpanches (member and chairperson) in the Panchayat. Following are the provisions of the Act :

1. Not less than one-third of the seats will be reserved for women (including the Schedule Castes and Tribes) and these may be allotted by rotation to different constituencies of the panchayat.

2. In the seats reserved for Schedule Castes and Scheduled Tribes not less than one-third of total number of such seats to be reserved for women.

3. Not less than one-third of the total number of seats for the offices of the chairperson at each level would be reserved for women. This would be rotated among different panchayats at each level.

In addition, there are certain general features which could be taken advantage of by women, such as direct elections for membership and sarpanch (president) posts, at the local as well as the intermediary (block) level.

The duration in the case of such panchayats in operation would be five years from the date of its first meeting. Elections would be direct and held compulsorily every five years. For women it is significant in doing away with the old practice of co-option and replacing it with direct election, assuring that it would not become a stronghold and prerogative of women of rich and influential families.

The reaction of the states as expected have been varied. While states like Orissa and West Bengal did not even wait for the 73rd Amendment and amended their acts in 1991 and 1992 and held elections in 1992-93 electing about 25,000 women in each state of these bodies, the state of Tamil Nadu taking advantage of some loopholes may not genuinely implement the provisions because the ruling party is not is favour. Punjab held elections promptly after the amendment. Going by the old practice of co-opting women and Schedule Castes, it has avoided a true election for another five years.

The Panchayati Raj system has operated differently in various states of India. In the particular context of women's representation, a good number of states showed adequate representation as in Maharashtra, Kerala, Himachal Pradesh, Andhra Pradesh, but the proportion varied. Only in the first two states mentioned above where was the reservation up to 30 per cent. In Orissa it was 33 per cent. In West Bengal, the government has not been too keen on reservation. Elections every five years have been held since 1978. The latest elections were held in May 1993. This election was held on the basis of 1992 Act, which gave one-third membership to women, to be filled up by election. In 1993 elections, the total number reserved seats for women was 25,460, and many more, about 41,000 women got elected. Orissa and West Bengal amended their acts before the Panchayati Raj Act was passed by the Parliament in 1992. Elections in Orissa in 1992 brought 22,000 women to Panchayat Raj institutions.

The recent Panchayati Raj Institutions (PRIs) Act does have the potential to include women in a very good proportion to male at the grassroots level political institutions. Presence of 33 per cent women is likely to affect and influence the political processes of decision-making and policy formulations at this level. It will not only enable them to give a women's angle to the decision and policy formulation activity. It will also awaken them to the problems facing the community as whole. It will enable a journey from the private to the public sphere of activity. It will train cadre of women political activists for partaking in the affairs of state and federal politics. Total sharing and equality in decision making may not happen for years to come, but Panchayati Raj Institutions (PRIs) showed a path towards that goal. When women armed with physical presence of a sizeable proportion reach the position of a 'critical mass', their voices cannot be ignored. They have to be heard. No longer can they be ignored. It could be a road to women's political empowerment. However, for a wider representation effective sharing in power process, this needs to be extended to representative bodies right up to the federal level. Wider representation will not ensure instant quality. It will take time and practice. Moreover many studies have already proved that democracy, even while being the best form of government need not be the best government, that men as much as women are guilty of devaluating its quality all over the world. The experience of Orissa and West Bengal testify that women are capable of efficient political performance given the chance.

However, a word of caution is necessary at this juncture. Women's effective participation at the grassroots through the panchayat system will not become a reality unless women are made aware of the realities and are properly trained for their new role. Reservation alone cannot deliver the goods. It will still be a weak need to rely on, in tackling attitudinal, social and structural barricades. Nevertheless, by getting this one gate opened, women's movement can (and must) flood the rural side with the potentialities and political contribution of women. This will need much intervention by way of action and other inputs.

Political education is the first step. For political education there will have to be two types of target groups. Wherever women have already entered the Panchayati Raj institutions through election or otherwise, these women need to be politically educated and informed. Such education should not be confined only to creating awareness among women of their powers, rights and functions but also about Indian polity, the nature of its democracy and constitution, policies and programmes for women and other weaker sections. For the general women it would mean mobilising them for voting in the elections, standing for elections, and even campaigning and questioning the candidates, both male and female.

Political information: For education, information on issues such as current political developments and trends, legislations, policies and plans is the basic step, information should lead to mobilisation.

Infrastructure

1. For election - Possibility of creating a special fund or efforts for raising resources to help women for fighting elections. Election being fought on party lines, are becoming more and more expensive, corrupt and violent even at the grassroots level. Could women's organisations help the women candidates to raise funds for fighting election?

2. Need for the formulation of one a few models of curriculum development, and of designing a syllabi that would include the different areas in constitutional, political, socioeconomic, social rights and issues, as well as governmental policies, programmes and procedures.

3. Some type of political literacy manual which in brief, precise, easy/readable and commonly understandable style explains the various provisions for (general and women specific) rights, governmental policies, judicial judgements, non-governmental social actions, etc.

4. For sustained political education there is need for an organisation working at site, if not every village atleast in a cluster of villages. Existing women's organisations in the villages and NGOs working in a particular area can be trained, to act as trainers provided they have the inclination, correct and strong approach to feminist issues and women's rights and are somewhat natural towards political parties.

5. Formation of resource centres with full time social activists could help by emerging as forums for information, dissemination, discussions, reading materials and even counselling services. The social activists with the necessary skill in political understanding, raising resources and networking may organise various activities like group discussions, awareness camps lectures, by visiting scholars/social activists and politicians.

As elections are increasingly being fought on party lines, political parties need to be sensitised towards women's right of political action by giving them some priority in fighting elections.

The strategy of reservation or quota for women at all levels of political deliberation has immense possibilities but it alone cannot deliver the goods. It has to be backed by a strong women's movement from outside. Even more, the presence of women sensitised women's problems in deliberative and decision-making bodies, will give strength to their voice. With time and proper training, they will not only be, concerned with women's issue, but in all Issues and problems related to the whole society and polity. They will lead to women's angle to issues of war, militarisation, nuclear power widespread violence and what not.

Norms and Traditions

It is true that having been trapped by sociocultural norms and traditions they have been out of the so-called 'public areas' of activities. But this sad tale is not and should not continue any more, politics is as much a women's concern as a man's because it equally affects her life conditions. What is needed is proper mobilisation, awareness generation through political education and training. For this task the government, NGOs, women's organisations, both academic and action oriented, need to join hands in their effort. For a healthy democracy all need to participate in the shaping and sharing of power. If gender prevents half the population from participation in politics, it cannot be a democratic politics. For Indian women, the 73rd Amendment to the Constitution, the Panchayati Raj Act 1992 opens up the door to many possibilities, They have been given a chance, if one goes by the experience of some states. In India, the signals are very positive. The commonly held view that women have to be found for contesting elections has been somewhat disproved in practices so far. In the Orissa elections of 1992, 2,200 won at three levels. This was more than one-third reservation. In 1988 Karnataka elections out of 30,000 women 14,000 won the elections. A state West Bengal saw 59.2 per cent seats going to women in 1993. Thus, besides the reserved seats, women secured seats also from the general quota. Maharashtra presently have nine all women panchayats.

Generation Awareness

What is needed is awareness generation in women, their mobilisation and training for their new political roles. They have to know about themselves, their rights, the nature of their political system, the myriad problems facing the country the political process through which decisions are made and policies formulated. A concerted effort is necessary by all institutions and individuals who care for women, and do not want them to remain political cripples forever, with proper training and guidance. Women could share effectively the political decision-making, at least at the grassroots level. Some day they might effectively hold power at the national level.

9

Legal Support

Laws Enacted

The existing legislations should be reviewed so that equality and social justice can be ensured to women of all communities and creeds. Where this involves amendments to existing personal laws of the minority group, initial efforts should be concentrated on arousing a desire for change from among the members of such minority groups. A vigorous campaign should be made to educate women about their rights, and to generate among all communities, a desire for a common civil code, to be achieved by the end of the UN Decade for Women in 1985.

Legal aid should be organized for women in need with the active assistance of the Bar Councils.

The setting up of family courts should be considered for speedy and effective adjudication in all cases concerning the family. Women, particularly in rural areas, should be protected against harassment.

The practice of dowry should be eradicated. The legislation should be strictly enforced. This is a social evil which requires sustained action not only on the part of government agencies, but also on the part of voluntary organizations and public leaders.

The provisions of the existing Child Marriage Restraint Act should be reviewed. Special attention should be given to streamlining the enforcement machinery and involving local authorities and voluntary organizations in the implementation of the Act. Active public support should be mobilized by governmental agencies, voluntary organizations and public leaders against child marriage, particularly in rural areas. Simultaneously, systematic programmes of education and training should be developed for girls till they marry.

Governmental Action

Education: Education is the greatest known catalytic agent for social change. All out efforts should therefore be made to achieve the goal of universal primary education as early as possible. The ideas of equality between the sexes and participation by women in development should be woven into the fabric of the educational system.

The employment of women teachers should be actively promoted. The existing employment procedures, including those for part-time, employment, should be reviewed and, where necessary, relaxations in age, etc., made so that more women teachers, can be employed and husbands and wives are posted in the same schools or at the same station.

The content of education should be strengthened in terms of both life and work relevance. Attention should be given to vocationalization and diversification of courses which should not only be limited to traditional women's vocations but also give emphasis on the preparation of women for participation in modern sectors of industrial production. Polytechnics (including mini-polytechnics) should be started for girls in the smaller urban centres to provide training facilities in trades crafts which will prompt self-employment.

At the stage of higher education special incentives like, freeships, scholarships, hostel facilities, and book loans should be made available to girls from rural, backward and hilly areas, from backward classes and from poor families. A greater diversification in the courses offered should be made to enhance work opportunities in non-traditional vocations in modern sectors of industrial production.

Adoption of multiple entry in education, non-formal part-time education facilities, condensed courses for education, correspondence courses and courses for continuing education should be made available in a larger measure to women in semi-urban and rural areas, and to working women in urban and semi-urban areas. Adult education and functional literacy programmes should be vigorously pursued through both official and voluntary agencies.

Employment: Equal Remuneration Act, 1976, has been passed, providing for payment of equal remuneration to men and women workers and the prevention of discrimination on grounds of sex. Special steps should therefore be taken to review recruitment, promotion and other personnel practices in all public and private sector undertakings to ensure that there is no discrimination against women candidates. Women apprentices should be taken without discrimination in industries. Representatives of women's voluntary organizations, should be associated, in the machinery set up to ensure adequate participation of women in employment.

Village industries which provide scope for the employment of women should be further promoted-Special training services should be organized and credit, marketing facilities, etc., extended, specially in regard to crafts which can have a ready export market, through modernization of design, etc. Integrated pilot projects to cover training, production and marketing should be started.

The existing requirement procedures and employment conditions should be reviewed to encourage the re-entry of women into the workforce. For this purpose, the provisions relating to maximum age of entry into services should be reviewed. Part-time employment of women should be promoted wherever feasible. Refresher courses and training programmes should be organized for adult women to make them fit for re-employment.

Organizations entrusted by the government with the task of promoting self-employment opportunities should develop special women's entrepreneurial training motivation programmes and provide special assistance to women entrepreneurs and to women's co-operative in terms of credit, licensing, etc.

The existing legislation in regard to maternity benefits should be reviewed. It should simultaneously be ensured that there is no consequent adverse effect on the employment of women.

Health Care, Nutrition and Family Planning: Maternal and child health care facilities should be expanded, particularly in semi-urban and rural areas, and coverage provided to high risk pregnant women. Ante-natal and post-natal clinics should be started in every Primary Health Centre and district hospital.

Nutrition supplementation should be provided to high risk pregnant mothers. Simultaneously, nutrition and health education should be given to girls and to mothers through all available media and institutions (school, hospitals, PHCs, etc.).

Family welfare planning services should be expanded and measures intensified to educate and prepare couples to avail them, specifically in rural, backward and tribal areas. The facilities under the Medical Termination of Pregnancy Act, 1971 should be made available in semi-urban and rural areas and information regarding the provisions disseminated among women, immunization facilities should be gradually extended to all children.

Facilities of Working Women: The establishment of day care centres, creches, and balwadis should be promoted on a large scale in rural, semi-urban and urban areas to help working mothers and active women social workers discharge their duties, and enable the older children to attend school.

Hostel facilities for working women of the lower income groups should be expanded.

Care for the Socially Disadvantaged: Women without any means of support, and the physically handicapped should be provided services for education, training and rehabilitation so that they can become self-reliant. Old age homes should be opened for the aged and the infirm. Special programmes should be developed for unmarried mothers and their children.

The provision of the Suppression of Immoral Traffic Act (1956) should be reviewed to facilitate their more efficient implementation. Comprehensive rehabilitation programmes for victims of immoral traffic and their children should be developed. Special steps should be taken to prevent vulnerable young girls and women from becoming victims of this social evil.

Promotion of Voluntary Effort: The growth of voluntary organizations, especially in rural, backward and tribal areas and in urban slums should be promoted to mobilize public support for different programmes of welfare. Training facilities should be provided on a large scale to voluntary workers. Leadership training programmes, particularly for women from weaker sections, should be developed so that they can function effectively as agents of change. The establishment of Mahila Mandals should be promoted in every village so that they can function as field level agencies for social and economic transformation. Voluntary organizations have critical role in mobilizing public opinion in favour of equality among men and women and eradicating superstitions, social evils and waste.

A vigorous campaign of education and action should be launched in favour of community sanitation and hygiene. Public utility services for women should be expanded wherever called for.

Machinery for Implementation: In order to ensure that the Resolution unanimously passed by the two Houses of Parliament is acted upon and the implementation of the Plan of Action is ensured, it is proposed that:

(i) A Standing Advisory Committee should be set up at the national level which will review the progress every year so that a report is submitted to Parliament annually. The Committee may be called 'The National Committee on Women'.

(ii) To service the above Committee a special bureau should be set up in the Ministry of Education and Social Welfare (Department of Social Welfare). The Bureau will keep in touch with the implementation of the various programmes by the Central Ministries, State Governments and non-official agencies.

(iii) At the State level similar committees should be set up under the chairmanship of the Chief Minister. These Committees should also have adequate administrative support.

Promotion of Literacy

In realization of the importance of education in general and the need for equality in opportunities for the intellectual development of men and women, successive Five-Year Plans have consistently placed special emphasis on the acceleration of women's education. The emphasis with regard to women's education has all along been to equip her for the multiple roles as citizens, housewives, mothers, contributors to family income and builders of the new society. Efforts have been made during the past two decades of planned development to enrol more girls in school; to encourage girls to stay in schools; to continue their education as long as possible; and to provide non-formal education opportunities for women. The Draft Fifth Five-Year Plan has declared that "the outlays for the education of girls will be stepped up.". The fulfilment of the constitutional directive in respect of providing free and compulsory education up to the age of 14 years has been included as one of the components of the Minimum Needs Programme.

These efforts have had a significant impact on the progress of women's education in India. For example, there is a primary school within easy, walking distance from the home of almost all the children. This has resulted in an increase in the enrolment of girls in classes I-V as a percentage of total enrolment in these classes from 28.1 in 1950-51 to 37.6 in 1973-74. In respect of classes I-VIII, IX-XI/ XII and university education also there has been an appreciable increase in the percentage of girls' enrolment to total enrolment, between the years 1950-51 and 1973-74. In fact, girls' enrolment is observed to be growing at a faster rate than those of boys.

Despite these encouraging trends and marked progress made in respect of women's education, the educational status of women is still far from satisfactory for the following reasons:

(a) Literacy among women is generally lower than that among men. According to the 1971 Census data, only 13.4 per cent of women in this age group of 25+ are literate.

(b) Enrolment of girls in classes I to V is only 66.4 per cent of girls in the corresponding age group, i.e., from 6 to 11 years; while in respect of boys the relevant percentage is 100.2.

(c) Drop-out rate is also very high in classes I to V. A recent study has shown that the drop-out rate especially accentuated in the case of girls from rural areas and from the less privileged sections of society, is as heavy as 42.85 per cent between classes I and II.

(d) In classes VI to VIII, percentages of enrolment of girls and boys to the total girls and boys in the relevant age group (i.e., from 11 to 14 years) are 22.2 and 48.3, respectively.

(e) At the secondary stage, i.e., from classes IX to XI the girls enrolled constitute only 12 per cent of girls in the relevant age group 14 to 17 years as against 31 per cent in respect of the enrolment of boys in this age group.

(f) Enrolment of girls in Post-Matric classes constitutes only 2.3 per cent of girls in the concerned age group 17 to 23 years, while the enrolment percentage of boys in this age group is 7.5.

Factors Retarding the Progress of Women's Education: Girls and women in India have thus not been able to take full advantage of the available opportunities/facilities for intellectual development. This is mainly because of several social and cultural factors in addition to various other reasons. Action plans and strategies for women's education should, therefore, aim at neutralizing the effects of the factors which have retarded the progress of women's education in India. With a view to facilitating the formulation of such a plan of action, in what follows, some of the major reasons which have operated against girls/women in taking full advantage of educational opportunities/facilities are listed below:

(a) General indifference to education of girls.

(b) Social resistance arising out of fears and misconceptions that education might alienate girls from traditions and social values and lead to mal-adjustments, conflicts and nonconformism.

(c) Early marriage and social inhibitions against girls pursuing education after marriage.

(d) Prevalence of child labour among girls belonging to weaker sections and the hard domestic chores which some of the unmarried girls - even in the middle-class families - are required to perform.

(e) The prevailing notion that the sole occupation of women is to bear children, look after her husband and children, and thus be restricted to domestic work.

(f) Discrimination effected by employers against women labour in both organized and unorganized sectors in matters of recruitment, training and promotion.

(g) Many girls and their parents find that the school curriculum do not conform adequately to their needs and interests.

(h) Unsuitable and inflexible school timings and inadequate facilities for girls in schools, particularly in the co-educational schools.

Major Objective of Women's Education: It should be recognized here that the general objective of any policy towards women's education cannot be different from those relating to men. However, in view of the social and cultural handicaps that have operated against women in general and in view of the multiple role that women are required to play, the need for a set of objectives specific to women's education is imperative. The following major objectives are, therefore, considered here:

(a) Prepare women to fully participate in socially productive work, fully aware of family planning needs with a view to achieving her full integration with the democratic and developmental efforts of the country.

(b) Help break down overt covert biases against women.

(c) Make women aware of the various legal, social and economic rights, provisions -and privileges available to them and the way they can take advantage of them, for their advancement.

(d) Enable women to be self-reliant to achieve economic independence.

(e) Impart the idea of equality between the sexes and participation by women in development through the educational system.

(f) And above all, to find full expression for her talent, ability and personality and for this purpose, enable her to adopt a discriminating attitude so that she can escape the bonds of superstition and obscurantism.

Action Plans: Action plans here are evolved within the general framework of major objectives mentioned above. In addition, the action plans have taken into consideration other objectives which are specific of educational categories like elementary education, middle stage education, secondary stage education, university education and non-formal education. For the sake of convenience, in what follows, action plans specific of each age group of girls, are all mentioned separately.

Elementary Education-Girls in the Age Group 6-11 years: Girls in this age group constitute the population of girls of primary school going age. Action plans for this age group will need to be in two directions:

(a) To universalize primary education for girls, and

(b) To strive for the retention of girls already enrolled.

Administrative and Structural Measures

(i) State Governments should take note of the habitations without primary schools as indicated by the Third Educational Survey and make arrangements for providing primary school within a distance of 1.5 km of all habitations within next five years.

(ii) Mobile schools should be provided for children of all nomadic tribes, migrant labour and construction workers.

(iii) Girls in this age are often required to look after younger children and attend minor household duties, particularly in the rural areas and among weaker sections of the society. As this is one of the major reasons that holds such girls from attending school, special efforts should be made to enlarge the scope and coverage of pre-school education programmes like Balwadis and Anganwadis, where the older girls can be given practical work experience and child care.

(iv) These pre-school education programmes should, wherever possible, be attached to primary schools or at least located in the vicinity of primary schools, as that would help in cultivating a school going habit right from the childhood.

(v) Supervision and inspection of primary schools should give particular attention to the problem of enrolment of girls, their retention, involvement of the community, etc.

Promotional and Motivational Measures

(vi) Special and sustained persuasive and motivational campaign and organizational drives should be undertaken among regions/communities which have shown markedly a low achievement in girls enrolment. Voluntary organizations at local levels like Mahila Mandals and local bodies should be fully involved in this programme.

(vii) Promotion and support to girls' education should also be tackled through a multipronged programme of incentives both for bringing girls to schools and for retaining them in schools. The incentives can be in the form of mid-day meals, free supply of books and reading materials, scholarships awards, etc. Active collaboration of voluntary organizations may be sought in this regard.

Pedagogical Measures

(viii) The primary teacher training course should undergo a major revision with a view to adequately preparing the teacher for the promotion of girls' education. Emphasis should be more on the use of such non-formal methods of imparting education that would interest and attract more and more girls to attend schools.

Education for Girls in the Age Group 11-14 years: Population of girls in this age group constitutes girls of middle school going age. This group can be divided into three sub-groups:

(a) Girls students attending middle schools;

(b) Girl drop-outs at various stages from classes I to V; and

(c) Girls who have not attended school.

The objectives of education and training are different for each of the sub-groups.

Action Plan: Action plans for education of girls in this age group should be concerned about:

(i) encouraging further enrolment of girls at this stage;

(ii) retention of girls already in middle schools; and

(iii) rendering the curriculum more relevant.

The following action plans are suggested:

(i) The content should be more oriented to the needs of girls in the village communities so that both the parents and the girls see relevance of this education for their own lives. The curriculum of the middle school stage needs to be given a strong work experience orientation, introducing girls to crafts and skills which will be of direct use to them in the family, community and farm, and help them in rural employment and self-employment. It should also introduce girls to scientific knowledge, principles of home-making, family life education, nutrition and diet, environment education and civic education.

(ii) Women Teachers: It is very important for the promotion of girls' education to employ women teachers in schools. Infact, the general view is that women are more suited to be teachers and larger number of teachers should be women, However, the problem may come up in different ways. More number of men may be qualified and trained women may not be in a position to accept employment as full time teachers due to personal problems; women also have difficulties in working in rural areas.. There has to be relaxation from age restrictions. The States may consider reserving a certain number of posts of teachers for women and where there are not adequate number of trained teachers, untrained persons may be recruited and deputed for training. The question of giving posting to husband and wife both of whom are teachers in the same place may be considered.

It may also be worthwhile in those areas which have schools without women teachers, to select educated women in that area and send them for training and appoint them in the schools in that area. Where educated women are not available for posting in a school, local women may be selected and posted as school matas (school mothers) to keep the girl students company and induce parents to send their girls and children to schools. The rules relating to age and qualification of recruitment and service may have to be relaxed in these cases and the deficiency made up through in-service training.

Women should not be discriminated against in matters of recruitment. Selection and recruitment should be made on merit. No qualified meritorious woman candidate should be overlooked. State Governments may contemplate providing for 50 per cent of teachers in schools being women and to look into this aspect while sanctioning grants to institutions.

In single teacher institutions (the exact position will be brought out by the Third Educational Survey), it may be desirable to ensure that where there are two teachers, one of them should be a woman. If locally educated women are available, they can be recruited. Husband wife teams can be posted.

(iii) The primary teacher training course needs to undergo a major revision to adequately prepare the trainees for their special responsibility for the promotion of girls' education in rural areas, especially in adapting the content to suit the needs and interests of girls, in adopting non-formal methodologies and in linking with community and developmental activities.

(iv) Supervision and inspection of schools should be given particular attention to the problem of enrolment of girls, their retention, factors contributing to wastage and stagnation, revision of curriculum, involvement of the community, working conditions of women teachers, etc.

Promotional and Motivational Measures

(v) School tinings should be flexible, as many of the girls in this age group are required to help their mothers in routine domestic chores.

(vi) Adoption of multiple entry and part-time courses is recommended.

(vii) Incentives like mid-day meals, scholarships, free school uniforms, free books and study materials, stipend, awards, etc., should be extended to all girls in the rural areas and slums in the urban areas.

Middle School-Girl Drop-outs

(viii) For school drop-outs of girls, pre-vocational training programmes should be organized on an extensive scale to cover all girls in the rural areas and in the slums of urban areas. The objectives of such training should be to render them self-sufficient in home management, and help them to achieve economic independence. With this in view, such training programmes should include courses in sewing, knitting, cooking, nutrition, minor repairs of the house, motherhood, child care, etc.

Girls who never attended schools

(ix) For the non-student girls in this age group, the objective should be to provide adequate preparation in life through a combined three-year course in general education and vocational training. Vocational training should be on the lines of pre-vocational training mentioned above.

(x) Such training programmes should be extended to all girls in the rural areas. In the urban areas, preference should be given to girls in slum areas and destitute girls.

Education for Girls in the Age Group 14-17 years: Girls in this age group also can be classified into three groups:

(a) Girl students with motivation to attend secondary school;

(b) Girl drop-outs from classes VI to VIII; and

(c) Non-student girls, i.e., students who never attended schools.

Girl Students

The action plans under this category should emphasize more on:

(i) facilitating more girls to pursue education at the secondary stage, and

(ii) strengthening the content in terms of both life and work relevance.

The following action plans are suggested:

Administrative and Structural Measures

(i) Separate girls schools or separate sections should be started where the social/ cultural environment demands them.

(ii) In co-education schools special attention should be given to the provision of adequate toilet, rest and recreation facilities, separately for girls.

(iii) State Governments which have not yet made high school education free for girls should do so on a priority basis.

(iv) Multiple entry system and part-time education may be provided.

Promotional and Motivational Measures

(v) All courses of training in vocational and technical schools at the secondary stage should be open to both boys and girls. There should be no discrimination in this regard.

(vi) Liberal incentives in the form of book allowances, book-bank facilities, etc., should be extended to encourage more girls in rural and backward areas to pursue secondary education.

(vii) Separate hostel facilities should be provided particularly in rural areas and residential scholarships should be offered.

Pedagogical Measures

(viii) The curriculum should be more diversified taking into consideration the various occupational opportunities available to women and the interests and aptitudes of girls.

Girl Drop-outs

(ix) Condensed courses of education started in 1958 were found very useful. Under this scheme women in the age group 13-30 years who have had some schooling are prepared for middle school, matriculation or equivalent examinations within a period of 2 years' duration. The minimum age limit here should be reduced to 15 years. This scheme should be extended to cover all rural areas and weaker sections of the urban community.

(x) The condensed course should be organized for smaller groups, say 5 to 7 persons, using the community resources like girls' high schools and girls' colleges.

(xi) Apart from imparting general education, condensed course should also aim at imparting job-oriented training with the active co-operation of existing vocational training institutions.

(xii) Correspondence courses and self-study programmes may be introduced.

(xiii) Efforts should be made to cover at least about 215 lakh of girls in the age group 15-30 under the condensed courses programme during the Fifth Plan period.

Non-student Girls

(xiv) Fourth Plan introduced a programme of functional literacy with the objective of imparting elementary general education and vocational training-related to the functions performed to men and women in the rural areas who never attended schools. This programme should be expanded to cover all rural areas.

(xv) Apart from imparting general elementary education and knowledge about farming technologies, the curriculum for women should include courses of training in occupational skills like kitchen gardening, food processing, poultry keeping, animal husbandry; and household, arts like cooking nutritional values of foods locally available, sewing, knitting, etc., and motherhood, child care and family planning as also electronics and like fields.

(xvi) Similar programmes should also be designed for girls in this age group and under this category belonging to urban areas.

Education for Girls in the Age Group 17 Years and Above

Education for girls in this age group also can be divided into three groups, as in the case of other age groups:

(a) Education for girls at the higher education stage;

(b) Education for girl drop-outs from the educational system beyond the secondary stage; and

(c) Education for non-student girls - girls who never had any education.

In respect of the last category here, i.e., education for non-student girls, action plans are the same as those concerning non-student girls in the age group 14-17 years. Hence, this category is not dealt with separately here.

Education for Girls at the Higher Education Stage

Action plans in this area should aim at:

(a) Making higher education available to the less privileged sections of the society, particularly girls from the rural areas; and

(b) Making the curriculum more relevant and responsive to the cultural and occupational needs of women.

The following action plans may be taken up for consideration:

Administrative and Structural Measures

(i) The general policy here should be to discourage separate institutions for women and to promote co-educational institutions for women and to promote co-educational facilities. However, in areas where separate institutions are required to promote education of women, they may be permitted on the merits of such cases.

(ii) Vocational counselling and guidance services should be organized in a more meaningful way to help girls in colleges and universities opt for suitable courses relevant to their talent, interests and needs.

Promotional and Motivational Measures

(iii) Incentives like scholarships, freeships, etc., should be provided to enable girls from rural areas to pursue higher education.

(iv) For girls belonging to weaker sections, in addition to free-ships and scholarships, bursaries should also be provided to meet their expenses on food and lodging.

(v) Provision of self-cooking facilities in hostels for girls should also be considered.

(vi) Girls pursuing higher education should be provided easy access to textbooks and other reference material through book-bank facilities.

(vii) Girls should be encouraged to enter professional courses. If necessary, reservation of seats for girls in professional courses may be considered.

Pedagogical Measures

(viii) Diversification of courses at the junior college level and undergraduate level should be undertaken on a priority basis with a view to preparing the girls for the various employment opportunities open to them.

Education for Girl Drop-outs

Girls in this age group drop-out of educational system for various reasons. Marriage is one of the reasons which force girls in this age group to discontinue further formal education. Economic hardship is another reason which forces some girls to drop-out and seek jobs, with a view to supporting their families. Social prejudices and cultural attitudes also force some of the girls to leave the formal educational system. For girls in this category, therefore, the policy should be to extend non-formal educational facilities on a large scale.

The following action plans are suggested:

(i) Facilities for part-time self-study and correspondence courses should be expanded on a large scale to enable working girls and non-working married and unmarried girls to enhance their educational qualifications.

(ii) In addition to course leading to degree/diploma, short courses in specific subjects through summer schools/sessions, ad hoc programmes like seminars, laboratory work, workshop experience, etc., should be organized for working girls, with a view to upgrading their professional skills and qualifications. Facilities for further education not necessarily leading to a degree but for upgradation of knowledge and skills could be provided.

(iii) While the initiative for organizing such programmes should be taken by the Central and State Governments, the employees should also be increasingly involved.

(iv) Pre-examination training facilities should be organized on a large scale for educated women from the rural areas and those belonging to weaker sections with the objective of equipping them to successfully compete in examinations for public jobs.

(v) Entrepreneurship development programmes should be organized separately for educated women in the age group 18-30 years with a minimum of matriculation level of education.

The objective of such training programmes should be:

(a) Make them aware of the various opportunities for self-employment;

(b) Motivate them to take up self-employment;

(c) Impart needed skills/training; and

(d) Promote achievement motivation among them.

Administrative Measures: To make the various action plans successful and to achieve a real breakthrough in women's education, there is an urgent need for a matching and effective administrative set up, both at the central and state levels. With this in view, the following suggestions are made:

(i) In the Union Ministry of Education and Social Welfare, a special unit/cell may be set up to be in charge of women's education to review and initiate follow-up action.

(ii) In each State education department, a senior officer should be placed in charge of girls' education in order that it may receive adequate emphasis, execution and co-ordination.

(iii) As the district is the operational unit for all educational programmes and as the needs of girls vary in extent and kind from area to area within a district, a separate cell for girls' educational – formal and non-formal may be created within the purview of the district educational officer at the district headquarters.

(iv) School supervisory system should be staffed with more women.

(v) A suitable machinery may be set up at the Centre and the States to help in the formulation of plans for women's education - formal and non-formal to monitor, co-ordinate and evaluate progress of women's education from time to time, to create public opinion in favour of women's education, etc.

10

Welfare Schemes

Pt. Jawaharlal Nehru, India's first Prime Minister had once said:

> "We talk about a welfare State and direct our energies towards its realisation. That welfare must be the common property of everyone in India and not the monopoly of the privileged groups as it is today. If I may be allowed to lay greater stress on some, they would be the welfare of children, the status of women and the welfare of the tribal and hilly people in our country. Women in India have a background of history and tradition behind them, which is inspiring. It is true, however, that they have suffered much from various kinds of suppression and all these have to go so that they can play their full part in the life of the nation".
>
> (Foreword to *Social Welfare in India*)

Indian planners have generally seen development as a process comprehending the entire social system. According to the Planning Commission on the First Five-Year Plan:

> Maximum production, full employment, the attainment of economic equality and social justice constitute the accepted

> objective of planning ... plan for development must place balanced emphasis on all these.
>
> Development touches all aspects of Community life and has to be viewed comprehensively. Economic planning thus extends out into extra economic spheres- educational, social and cultural. Second Five-Year Plan.
>
> This broad approach to development was to give shape to the policy of transforming India into a welfare State, as directed by the Constitution.

The overall development process envisages a share in the development generated by the Plan equally for women and men. Since the Constitution stresses the need for promoting with special care the educational and economic interests of the weaker sections of the people, the welfare and development of women received particular attention from the beginning.

The Planning Commission's 'Plans and Prospects for Social Welfare in India', spells out social welfare services as intending to cater for the special need of persons and groups who by reason of some handicaps-social, economic, physical or mental—are unable to avail of or are traditionally denied the amenities and services provided by the community. Women are considered to be handicapped by social customs and social values and therefore social welfare services have specially endeavoured to rehabilitate them.

The Planning Commission defined three major areas under which they have paid special attention to women's development: (a) education, (b) social welfare, and (c) health. The development of education for women has been already discussed. In this Chapter we shall examine the policies, provisions and programmes for women's development, in the fields of social welfare and health including the administrative agencies created by the Government of India to implement the overall policies regarding women's development, in order to assess the achievements in this regard.

The *First Plan* emphasized that, in order to fulfil women's legitimate role in the family and the community, adequate services needed to be promoted for her welfare. Well organized social service departments were needed in the States to initiate comprehensive programmes of women and child welfare. It recognized that the problem of high infant and maternal mortality was mainly due to malnutrition and undertook to develop (a) school feeding schemes for children and creation of nutrition sections in the State Public Health Departments; (b) maternity and child health centres; and (c) family planning.

The *Second Plan* emphasized the need for special attention to problems of women workers, since they were comparatively less organized and suffered from certain social prejudices and physical disabilities. They were also paid less because of the feeling that they were less suited to heavy work and were more vulnerable in situations which produced fatigue. The Plan stated therefore that women should be protected against injurious work, should receive maternity benefit and creches for children. It also suggested speedy implementation of the principle of equal pay for equal work, provision of facilities for training to enable women to compete for higher jobs and expansion of opportunities for part- time employment.

The main thrust of the *Third Plan* as regards social women's development was on the expansion of girls' education' in social welfare, the largest share was provided for expanding rural welfare services and condensed courses of education for adult women. The health programmes for women mainly concentrated on provision of services for maternal and child welfare, health education, nutrition and family planning

The approach in the *Fourth Plan* was a continued emphasis on women's education. As regards social welfare, the approach was to let the voluntary sector operate the bulk of departmental Programmes. Governmental efforts were confined to the provision of institutional services for destitute women and women rescued from prostitution. The basic policy was to promote women's welfare with the family as the base of operation.

The outlay on family planning was stepped up to reduce the birth rate from 40 to 25 per 1000 through mass education and motivation, and with cooperation of voluntary agencies and local leadership. High priority was assigned to immunization of pre-school children and supplementary diet for children and expectant and nursing mothers.

The *Fifth Five-Year Plan* indicated that priority was given to training women in need of care and protection, women from low income families, needy women and dependent children and working women. A programme for functional literacy to endow women with necessary knowledge and skills to perform the functions of the housewife (including child care, nutrition, health care, home economics, etc.) will be launched for the age group 15-45. Special steps will be taken for the Placement of follow-up of successful candidates under the exciting scheme of condensed courses, of education and the socio-economic programmes.

In addition to production-cum-training units, managerial and sales training will be introduced to promote the marketability of goods produced in different units. Under the Health programmes, the primary objective is to provide minimum public health facilities integrated with family planning and nutrition for vulnerable groups, children and pregnant and lactating mothers. The plan emphasizes the need to correct regional imbalances and provide services to meet the minimum needs of the community.

An examination of the Five-Year Plans reveals that in spite of the policy emphasis on welfare or investment in human resources, the share of investment in the social services in terms of the actual allocation has been steadily declining in successive plans. The objectives emphasized in the various plans, as well as the share of allocations indicate that among programmes specifically designed for women's development, the order of priorities up to the Fourth Plan has been education, then health, and lastly other aspects of welfare because it was generally assumed that all other programmes will benefit women indirectly, if not directly.

Plans and Programmes

Programmes for women's welfare and development may be classified as follows :

Programmes under Statutory Obligations: The Suppression of Immoral Traffic in Women and Girls Act, 1956 provides for institutional custody and after-care programmes. The Maternity Benefits Act, 1961 has a provision for leave and cash benefits. Under the protective laws, women in organized industries are entitled to provision of creches and family welfare facilities.

Programmes for Development: Under this category can be included the largest number of programmes which provide essential services and opportunities to women for development, such as education, health, maternity and child welfare, family planning, nutrition, socio-economic training and certain community organizations.

Programmes for Special Group: These vary from State to State. Some special assistance programmes have been initiated to serve groups like widows, the aged and the destitute, in the way of pensions or homes. A programme to provide hostels for working women in urban areas was initiated in the Second Plan, and has been continued over all successive Plans. For girls from backward communities, Scheduled Castes and Scheduled Tribes, there is provision for scholarships, and free residential schooling in Ashram schools.

While there have been additions and shifts in emphasis regarding the concept of women's welfare and development under the various Plans, and in some cases programmes have been expanded or integrated with others under a new nomenclature, the nature and content of the programmes have not changed.

1. Any programme for women's welfare and development must have an integrated approach. In order to prevent any ambiguity in the understanding of what constitutes women's welfare and to prevent the development of policies that sometimes go against the basic objective, we recommend that the Government of India should evolve a National Policy on women's development in the light of the Constitutional Directives and pledges made to the women of this country and to the international community from time to time.

   We also feel that in the absence of a general policy for social development, the weaker sections of society tend to receive inadequate attention. Economic development has sometimes contributed to elimination of social inequalities, but has also aggravated them. Adoption of a policy for social development would clarify matters, and provide a frame of reference for assessment of governmental and voluntary effort in these fields.

2. In view of the need to maintain links between governmental and voluntary and community effort for promotion of women's welfare, and to assist the process of government planning with actual knowledge and experience of the problems and needs of women at different levels, the following steps are recommended:

   (a) Reorganisation of the Central Social Welfare Board as a statutory and autonomous specialized agency for planning, co-ordination and management of welfare and development programmes for women and children.

   (b) Reorganisation of the State Social Welfare (advisory) Boards as statutory autonomous agencies at the State level with similar functions. In addition, the State Boards may also serve as links among the Central agency, the State Government and the local bodies.

Agencies at Work

In pre-independence India, while provisions of health and educational services had been increasingly demanded from the State, social welfare programmes were administered mainly, by voluntary agencies. There was no comprehensive nation-wide programme to provide welfare services. After the attainment of independence, it was felt that social and economic uplift of the masses required Government assistance to strengthen the services rendered by voluntary agencies. The administrative structure inherited from the colonial Government was clearly not equipped for this task. The Central Government therefore created a new agency-the Central Social Welfare Board in 1953 to promote welfare and development services for women, children and other underprivileged groups by providing assistance to voluntary agencies, improving and developing welfare programmes and sponsoring them in areas where they did not exist. Following the creation of the Central Social Welfare Board, the State Government set up, at the request of the Central Social Welfare Board, State Social Welfare (Advisory) Boards for the same purpose. This was necessary, as welfare is a State subject.

Even after creation of these Boards, there is no clear pattern in social administration. The responsibility for planning and administering women's welfare and development is scattered in various departments and other agencies of the government. The federal framework, and the need to involve voluntary or community organization in this task generally results in a three-tier structure of administration, with agencies at the centre, the State and the local level.

Agencies at the Centre: At the Centre, the major responsibility for planning and implementing women's welfare and development programmes rests mainly with the following: (i) Planning Commission; (ii) Ministry of Education and Social Welfare with its two specialized agencies - the Central Social Welfare Board and the National Council for Women's Education; (iii) Ministry of Health and Family Planning; (iv) Ministry of Home Affairs; (v) Ministry of Labour and Employment.

Agencies at the State Level: At the State level, there is no uniform pattern. Programmes for women's and children's welfare and development are administered by a large number of departments. All States have separate departments for Health, Family Planning and Education. With the exception of a few States, the Department of Agriculture and Community Development also is responsible for some women's programmes. In some States, the department of Local-Self-Government is involved in these programmes. Social Welfare departments or directorates as well as Social Welfare (Advisory) boards have been set up in most States. In some cases, they exist independently while in others they have been combined with education, tribal welfare, etc. A few States have set up separate directorate for Women's Education, or Women's Welfare.

The Committee endeavoured to collect information from all Central and State Departments concerning their special programmes for women's welfare and development. 12 Ministries of the Central Government indicated that they have some programmes for women's welfare. 19 States and one Union Territory indicated the existence of similar programmes. The replies were not comprehensive and often did not provide full answers to our questions. Two things, however, clearly emerge from these replies:

(a) These programmes, even when they have common objectives, are supervised and implemented by many Government departments without any effective machinery to coordinate their functions.

(b) Government departments, by and large, are not at all clear in their understanding of what constitutes

> welfare or development for women. Some adopt a comprehensive view, some a very limited one. A few regard improvement of earning power as essential for any development. Most are, however, content to adopt a somewhat charitable approach to welfare and equate it with assistance to women in distressed condition.

Since the major responsibility for social welfare and development lies with the Ministries, of (a) Health and Family Planning and (b) Education and Social Welfare, we have examined them in some detail. The rest are only briefly enumerated.

The Assessment

It was impossible to use quantitative indices to measure progress in the implementation of these programmes. Owing to data particularly in the field of development, programmes specifically meant for women are very few and do not give a total view of governmental effort to improve the condition of women. The general programmes, designed for all sections of the population, do not maintain separate records of allocations or expenditure for women, nor has any attempt been made so far to evaluate their impact.

We were, however, surprised to note that with the exception of the Second Plan, all the others have confined their concern for women's development to only education, health and welfare. Conspicuous by its absence is any reference to the need for generating and improving employment of women. Even the Fifth Plan, which gives highest priority to employment generation, appears to accept the present low representation of women in the labour force as a natural order of things, which will continue unchanged in the years to come. This expectation appears to be in direct contradiction to the Planning Commission's own view, that utilization of idle manpower would be a tremendous force to speed up the process of development. It is also a denial of the Government of India's stated objective of the total involvement of women at all levels of national development.

It is interesting to note that all the agencies engaged in programmes exclusively for women, inevitably attach the highest priority to increasing women's earning power. But since these programmes are classified as welfare and therefore non-productive, they invariably enjoy lower priority.

This ambiguity and confusion springs from traditional middle class attitude regarding women's roles in society. It will continue to affect both planning and administration of women's welfare and development unless the objectives of such policies are clarified and given concrete shape.

Programmes for Health

According to the World Health Organization, health is "a state of complete physical, mental and social well-being and not merely the absence of disease and infirmity." Health is both an important factor in the achievement of status as well as an indicator of social status, particularly for women, whose health is conditioned to a great extent by social attitudes. The health status of women includes their mental and social condition as affected by prevailing norms and attitudes of society in addition to their biological and physiological problems. Societies delineate women's roles partly according to their biological function and partly from prevailing attitudes regarding their physical and mental capacity. These social attitudes also influence the provision and use of preventive and curative health care, including maternal care. The health care facilities offered by a community in the form of medical, particularly maternity services for women, is a significant index of the emphasis that community places on the health of its women. Some studies in both the developed and developing countries have shown a definite link between low status of women and deficiencies in the knowledge and utilization of preventive health services.

In 1957 a study was made of the percentage distribution of ailing males and females both adults and children according to expenditure for treating the illness in six rural communities covering six districts in Maharashtra State with a total population of 37,000. The survey revealed that in the year under study there were 730 ailing females and 513 ailing males in the age group below 15 years. The percentage of males getting medical treatment was higher than females. The study also showed that more adult women had to be content with free or traditional treatment or no treatment as compared to the medical facilities used for the males.

Cultural Norms and Attitudes: The cultural norms that particularly affect women's health are the attitudes to marriage, age of marriage, the value attached to fertility and sex of the child, the pattern of family organization and the ideal role demanded of the women by social conventions. They determine her place within the family, the degree of her access to medical care, education, nutrition, and other accessories of health. In India, marriage is almost a universal function because of cultural and religious influences. The age at marriage and fertility rate have important demographic implications. The largest number of children are born to women who marry at the age of 19 years. Cultural insistence on the marriage of women in the early phase of their child bearing period leads to high fertility rate and each additional child is a burden on the mother, affecting her physical and mental health. Barrenness is regarded as a curse and the woman is always blamed for this. Though the desire for many children may not be, the desire for sons is widespread. The joint family system also has in many ways contributed to high fertility in India. It encourages early marriage and large sized families which appears as a source of collective economic security as well as emotional security.

The lower status of woman is the result of her dependence and lower educational and social position. Tradition idealizes her role as the mother, housewife and the distributor of food. It is customary in all Indian households for the women to serve the family first and then to eat whatever is left. According to our survey, 48.53 per cent of persons stated that in their families males eat first. In families affected by poverty, this generally results in still greater malnutrition for the women. The young girls as they grow up are taught subservience and self-effacement.

The process, therefore, starts at an early age and has very adverse consequences on women's health particularly at the time of pregnancy and child-birth. From their childhood, girls are taught to be uncomplaining and to maintain strict secrecy about their physical troubles. With menstruation, taboos are enforced and restrictions placed on their movement. They are unable to either discuss their health problems, if any, or even visit the doctor. Later as a mother, with children depending on her for care and attention, the woman has a tendency to carry on until ailment overtakes her. Reluctance to visit a doctor, particularly a male doctor, arises out of these restrictions imposed on women from the beginning. Such social attitudes, therefore, lead to a general neglect of women's health and in view of their child bearing role, they are the greatest sufferers as compared to men.

A study of data from particularly the developing countries indicates that other health problems of women-the higher maternal and infant mortality, maternal morbidity, lower expectation of life at birth, malnutrition, mental disorders, suicide rate and certain sex-selective diseases are linked to their status and role in the society. Child bearing and rearing is still the dominant role assigned to most women in developing nations. In the context of low socio-economic status of the bulk of the population, this factor becomes adverse to good health-in the case of women. All the developing nations are faced with rapidly growing population. Inadequate housing sanitation and poor medical facilities adversely affect the vulnerable segment of the community. Maternity, therefore, constitutes a special problem. The bulk of the stress and strain falls in the women who suffer from extremely poor health.

The Symptoms

The indicators of women's health status in India are drawn from two sources: (a)Demographic trends, and (b)Access to health services. They should be examined separately.

Demographic Trends: We have already drawn attention to the adverse and declining sex-ratio, higher mortality rate and lower life expectancy of women. The high birth and fertility rates, beyond doubt, contribute to the low health conditions of women. Starting with 1871, almost every census report has emphasized: (i) The crucial role of female mortality; (ii) The significant contribution of mortality in the age group 15-44 to aggregate female mortality; (iii) The crucial role of neglect of female health in determining female mortality; and (iv) The insignificant role of under numeration to explain the adverse sex-ratio.

Neglect of women was proved by customs like female infanticide then prevalent in certain parts of the country. Child marriage, premature consummation resulting in early childbearing, overwork and malnutrition were cited as other causes of women's poor health. The census of 1931 drew attention to higher female mortality in the age group 5-10, and "at the reproductive age".

The apparently low sex-ratio of deaths (female deaths per thousand male deaths) is actually due to large under-reporting of female deaths as compared to male deaths. The doubtful accuracy of SRS data on age-wise and sex-wise mortality rates has been demonstrated in a recent study. The difference between estimated and reported deaths of females is sometimes said to be as high as 75.69 per cent for rural areas and 59.07 per cent for urban areas in the lowest age group; 46.57 per cent and 35.47 per cent in the age-group 1-19; 58.56 per cent and 37.94 per cent in the 20-49 age group; and 50.2 per cent and 28.54 per cent in the 50+ age-group. This difference in the case of males is consistently lower.

All the available evidence leads us to conclude that female mortality infact is higher for all the three age groups, namely, during infancy, childhood and during the productive age particularly in rural areas. The inference from this is that female mortality is due to the consistent neglect of female health.

It is observed that the maternal mortality rate is high enough to raise the overall death rate for females and accounts for the low sex ratio. It was reported to be 252 per 1,00,000 live births in 1964 for the country as a whole, but for rural areas, it is as high as 573 in 1968. It is unfortunate that no later figures are available for this.

The SRS data for 1968 and 1969 also reflects the same pattern as reported in the various censuses, namely that female mortality continues to be higher in the age groups 0-4 and 15-34.

Factors Contributing to Women's Ill-Health: Recent medical research has tried to identify particular contributory factors to the problem of women's ill-health and higher mortality. Since maternal mortality in India continues to be so high, it is understandable that the bulk of this research has concentrated on this aspect of women's health. The specific factor that has been identified by various studies is firstly pregnancy wastage, caused by abortions and still births. The incidence of this phenomenon has remained constant over the period 1957-68, a period which witnessed intensification of family planning activity. In fact there was even an increase in actual numbers. Such foetal wastage prevails more in low income groups. One study reported that pregnancy wastage of malnourished mothers was 30 per cent as late as in 1972. Still births are reported as constituting 11 per 1,000 live births. Much of this pregnancy loss and prenatal mortality and still births result from premature births, itself a consequence of maternal malnutrition, particularly iron deficiency during pregnancy. Haemoglobin estimations carried out on about 5,000 pregnant women in different parts of the country show that 30 per cent of them are anaemic, i.e., they have haemoglobin levels below 10 per cent. There is evidence that this is largely due to iron deficiency. Premature births have consistently been a very high proportion among the cause of infant deaths.

A second group of causes for both infant and maternal mortality relate to higher birth orders. Frequency of pregnancies causes protein malnutrition of the mothers. As it is, the majority of Indian women are victims of malnutrition. 10-20 per cent of maternal deaths are known to be due to nutritional anemias. This has been borne out by a series of studies of the National Institute of Nutrition.

It has been estimated that if causes of maternal mortality are eliminated female mortality will decline substantially, since pregnancy complications still constitute 16.44 per cent or the second highest contributor to female morbidity. The Bhore Committee had observed that even psychiatric morbidity among Indian women was the result of malnutrition, frequent pregnancies and anaemia. While data on this aspect of women's health is scanty, a WHO Report indicates that psychiatric morbidity is more prevalent among women than men.

All the demographic indicators thus point to a low health status of women. In particular they suggest that child bearing in India, for the majority of women, is more a health hazard than a natural function.

Health for All

The broad objectives of the health programmes so far have been to control and eradicate communicable diseases, to provide curative and preventive health services in rural areas through the establishment of primary health centres in each block, and to augment programmes for the training of medical and para-medical personnel. In the Fifth Plan the main thrust was to improve the deficiencies in building, staff, equipment, drugs and medicines in the primary health centres and to integrate family planning and maternity and child health services. Health is a basic component of the proposed minimum needs programme. Any assessment of the impact of these programmes on the health of women has to take both quantitative and qualitative factors into account. A comparative assessment of available basic medical facilities in selected countries of the world indicates that India's position is more backward than even some of the developing countries.

In spite of the achievements during the last Four Plans figures indicate that medical care remains inaccessible to a large section of the population.

Any increase in personnel or medical facilities is nullified by increase in the population. The quality of the existing health services is reduced by inadequacy of staff, medical supplies and equipment, by overcrowding. In rural areas not even the minimum medical facilities by trained personnel is available in all districts. Distance and inaccessibility remains a major problem, particularly in hilly and difficult areas.

The lowest unit of the Health Service structure or its rural arm is the Primary Health Centre which is supposed to provide integrated and comprehensive curative and preventive health services in rural areas. The Bhore Committee which proposed the setting up of primary health centres had recommended that, to start with, each centre should cater to a population of 40,000 with a 30 bedded hospital to serve four Primary Health Centres. It visualized district level hospitals with a strength of 500 beds. Among other staff, primary health centres were to include four public health nurses, two medical officers, four midwives and four trained dais. Describing these requirements as the irreducible minimum, the Committee had recommended the key importance of developing preventive health services, with 'the country-side as the focal point.'

The Mudaliar Committee reiterated these recommendations, adding further the provision of three specialists in medicine, surgery, obstetrics and gynaecology, and 75 maternity and 50 paediatric beds to each district hospital.

In fact, when the primary health centres were established, the 'irreducible minimum' requirements were not provided. They had to serve a far larger population of 60 to 70,000 with only one lady health visitor and four auxiliary nurse-mid-wives (ANM), six beds and three sub-centres. Each sub-centre was put in charge of one ANM. Their functions were wide, including medical relief, maternity and child-health, control of communicable diseases (including the major national programme of Malaria control), school health, environmental sanitation and health education. By 1961, 2,800 primary health centres had been established.

Though the recommendations of the Mudaliar Committee were not implemented due to shortage of trained personnel and funds, from 1963 family planning services were initiated with additional staff (one woman medical officer, one extension doctor, one ANM, and two family planning workers to supervise four sub-centres). The sub-centres were to cater to a population of approximately ten thousand and were more than doubled in number, but with family planning as their major activity. The emphasis on family planning was strengthened further in 1966 by treating it as a crash programme, providing additional staff, and delinking it from Malaria control activities. In most States, the existing four health assistants were transferred to the family planning side.

Though the number of primary health centres increased from 67 to 5195 and the sub-centres from 17,522 to 32,218, their impact on the health of the rural population has not been substantial. An expert Committee observed that apart from West Bengal and Kerala, where utilization was 50 per cent, in other States like Bihar, Rajasthan, UP, Orissa, Madhya Pradesh and Jammu & Kashmir, the net utilization in primary health centres was hardly between 5-15 per cent. The reasons for this under utilization were: (a) apathy of the staff, (b) the status barrier that separates the doctor and his team from the village population, particularly the lower socio-economic groups, and (c) absence of lady doctors in many centres. Emphasizing the need to improve maternity and child health services, the committee recommended the provision of domiciliary maternity services as essential.

Critics of the present pattern of health services feel that they have deviated from the basic recommendation of the Bhore

Committee, to emphasize preventive services in rural areas as the keystone of public health. Under the present system, the expenditure on curative services is thrice that on preventive services, but most of it is concentrated in urban areas. The 10 per cent of hospital beds meant for the four-fifths of the population living in rural areas are ill-staffed, ill-equipped, and ill-financed. In the sphere of women's health in particular, while all the expert Committees emphasized greater attention to maternity services, the actual position shows wide regional variations in the provision of this crucial service.

According to the estimate of the Study Group on Hospitals, earlier there were only 45,000 maternity beds in 493 maternity hospitals and wards of general hospitals. The total number of beds at that time was 2.75 lakh, i.e., maternity beds constituted less than 17 per cent of total hospital facilities. It should also be noted that most hospitals in India provide no separate beds for women.

The All-India Statewise life expectancy at birth, during the years 1951-95, projected that Kerala, which stands out for provision of maternity services also, has the highest expectancy of life for women, which was 60.7 for 1991-95, and the lowest infant mortality rate. Uttar Pradesh, with the lowest provision for such services has a female life expectancy of 53.7, which is nearly the lowest in India, and the highest infant mortality rate.

There is no doubt that improvement of maternity services has a definite impact on life expectancy of women. States like Tamil Nadu, Andhra Pradesh, Punjab, Assam, Karnataka and West Bengal which have given some attention to these services, have helped to improve their women's expectation of life. The impact, however, cannot be uniform, because of the operation of other factors, like education, employment, general cultural norms, etc., which exert considerable influence on women's utilization of these services.

An important cultural norm which has a direct impact on women's health is the age of marriage. No district in Kerala has below 15 as the average age at marriage and only 3 districts (33 per cent) have an average below 20. In the case of Bihar, Rajasthan and UP, the picture is just the opposite, where 71 per cent, 65 per cent and 48 per cent of the districts respectively have an average below 15 per cent, 35 per cent and 31 per cent of the districts in Andhra Pradesh and West Bengal also come into this category.

Kerala also has the highest female literacy rate which is 53 per cent in rural areas, and 60.6 per cent in urban areas. Tamil Nadu, though well behind Kerala, is still the second highest State in female literacy, which is 19 per cent in rural areas and 45.4 per cent in urban areas. Uttar Pradesh, Bihar, Rajasthan stand out for their low female literacy rate.

We may infer from this that the availability and utilization of medical care for women reflects the general social attitude to women in a region. There is also no doubt that the female literacy rate is an important determinant for utilization as well as supply of medical and health care for this section of the population. This is particularly true of maternity and child care.

Apart from regional variations, the accessibility of health services is also affected by rural-urban and social-economic differentials, including a broad pattern of sex differentials. For example, uncontaminated water is available to 40 per cent of towns, but only 9 per cent of villages. Since about two-thirds of the total number of doctors and nurses, and most hospitals are concentrated in urban areas, the four-fifths of the population living in rural areas get a much smaller share of these services. The National Sample Survey (19th Round, 1964-65) found that 46 per cent of all births in urban India are attended by trained medical personnel, as compared to 9 per cent in rural areas. The household consumption data of the same Round also shows that average per capital private monthly expenditure on medicines and medical services is Rs 1.01 in urban areas, and about half that in rural areas. Majority of doctors in urban areas are private practitioners, charging high fees. Their services can be used only by the upper and middle income groups. Private nursing homes and paying hospitals, with private doctors, are almost totally out of reach of the poorer sections of society....

A recent study on rural health services brings out the peculiar tension created by scarce supply of medical personnel in the villages. On the one hand is the unmet felt need for the services of the Auxiliary Nurse Midwife at the time of child birth. Villagers are keen to have the ANM's services because they consider her to be more skilful than the traditional *dai*. Whether the ANM's have provided the services, the dais' role has become less significant. During our tours we were repeatedly informed of the inadequacy in the number and services rendered by ANMs. Apart from their small number, the area covered by these personnel is too large, with consequent transport and accommodation difficulties. Nighthalts and the problem of security create difficulties for most of these workers in rural areas, and effect their functioning.

Such problems very often obstruct an ANM from really attending to her duties in all places under her charge. Secondly, for an outsider to live and work in rural areas, a degree of social acceptance and security is essential. Protection extended by influential members of the village community ensures this, and prevents her from being handicapped by their hostility. The result very often is that her services are monopolized by the dominant, or relatively well-to-do section of village society. It should also be remembered that the social and educational background of the NMs is likely to be closer to the dominant, or well-to-do groups in the village, rather than the poorest.

This sort of cornering widens the gap between the ANM and the masses of women who need her services. The overall image of the ANM in villages, particularly in North India, is that of a person who is distant from them, meant only for special people or for those who can pay for her services. She is not for the poor. She can be called only when there are complications and then also she has to be paid.

As for sex differentials, they are deep rooted in social attitudes regarding the needs of women for care and assistance during ailments. In many areas we were told that rural society does not always care to report women's ailments, or seek medical aid. Women themselves often prefer to be silent in such matters. The studies in nutritional deficiencies of women indicate that their requirements are often sacrificed to provide a little more nutrition to others in the family. The incidence of diseases caused by malnutrition is higher not only among adult women, but even among female infants. At the same time hospital records reveal that more male children are treated for such diseases.

The two sets of indicators demographic trends, and access to medical care, both reveal the same situation regarding the health status of women.

This increase in comparative neglect of female lives as an expendable asset, observed to persist and increase over several decades, is a matter of serious concern.

Family Welfare

If the masses of Indian women are to be freed from their status as 'expendable assets', some of the obvious and immediate answers lies in releasing them from the bondage of repeated and frequent childbirth, providing them with some choice in the size of their families and in ensuring adequate medical facilities to protect them during and against maternity.

Propagators of the family planning movement in India have been keen to emphasize the improvement in the status of women as one of the direct consequences of acceptance of family planning. The birth control movement in India, from its inception, was associated with the feminist movement, and women's organizations were among the first to start a voluntary campaign for spread of birth control techniques among women. Even now they are active partners of the government's programme to persuade more and more women to accept family planning methods.

Recent researches in this field however make it extremely difficult to establish such an *a prior* relationship. All recent studies seem to agree more on the obverse of the relationship, viz. that improved status of women, with rise in the age of marriage, education, employment, better living conditions and greater general awareness, have a direct impact on the adoption of family planning methods.

There is no doubt that knowledge of family planning methods enables a woman to regulate her biological function and thus gives her a greater control over life and future. This certainly helps to build up her confidence in herself and can enable her to pursue various other ways to develop her personality, e.g., training, career interests and fulfil responsibilities to herself, her family and the wider society. Above all, such control has a direct impact on her health, Ability to prevent frequent and excessive drain on her physical resources undoubtedly helps to preserve her health, and since health is a basic necessity for any kind of development for a person, ability to plan her family ultimately contributes to such improvement of a woman's personality. A third consequence, which is sometimes emphasized is the possible change in husband-wife relationship, leading to improved position of the woman in decision making within the family.

All these results could certainly lead to a general improvement of a woman's status. But each of them are integrally connected with other socio-economic factors and developments, and the relationship between family planning and status improvement depends, in the ultimate analysis, on the presence and behaviour of such variables as social attitudes and opportunities for women's education, employment, pursuit of independent interests and career, size and sex of the family, accessibility of health services, and general economic development.

If the sexual role were the main determinant of male dominance and authority in a society, there would have beèn no communities in the world where the women are dominant, or equal members. The status of women in any society depends on a complex set of social, economic, demographic and political variables, among which the woman's ability to control the size of her family could be a contributory factor. But in our view, emphasizing it as a direct cause of improvement of women's status is somewhat exaggerated, and ignores the evolution of women's status in different societies. The matriarch of many ancient civilizations and primitive communities certainly enjoyed a much higher status than the women with complete control on the size of their families in the developed, modern societies of the West today. Knowledge of family planning techniques may have liberated Western women from excessive pregnancies, but it has not basically changed their status in these societies either economically or politically. Even in the sphere of social attitudes, with all the progress in education, and different types of social freedom and changing roles, their image as sex-symbols has been intensified, not eliminated.

In India, there has been an enormous volume of research on degree of acceptance of family planning, to assist the continuous evaluation of the Family Planning Programme. In one such research by the Ministry of Health and Family Planning, it was concluded that:

> The focus of evaluation of the Family Planning Programme at present is on the purposive assessment of impact of the programme, identification of areas of success and failures and reasons thereof, and feeding back this information for motivation and improvement or programme implementation. Family Planning Programme can be evaluated in terms of its objectives, viz., (a) the immediate objectives, including efforts and performance, objectives set for developing resources and activities for achieving the decision made; (b) the intermediate objective of spreading knowledge, developing favourable attitudes towards encouraging practice of family planning methods; (c) the ultimate objective, which is reduction of fertility so as to bring down the birth rate to 15 per thousand.

Apart from continuous assessment of information received from the States, regarding the success of the programme in quantitative terms, i.e., actual number of couples protected by various methods, provision of services in the way of personnel and equipment, etc., the evaluation includes field surveys on knowledge, attitudes and practices (KAP Studies). The Central Family Planning Institutes, the National Sample Survey, the various demographic and communication action research centres in the country, as well as a large number of individuals and institutions in the university system have been engaged in periodical assessment of the impact of this programme at both local and national levels since its inception. As a result, family planning is now the most heavily documented and evaluated among all major programmes of the Government of India.

One common trend in the results of these studies has been to expose the differentials in knowledge, acceptance and practice of family planning methods between different sections of the population. The results from the national survey conducted by the Operations Research Group, Ministry of Health and Family Planning indicate that the percentage of couples using any family planning method increases with:

(i) Age of wife (from 7 per cent among those below 25 years of age to 17 per cent among those aged 30 years or more);

(ii) Number of living children (from 2 per cent among those without any living child to 25 per cent those with 5 or more living children);

(iii) Education of wife (from 10 per cent among wives without any education to 56 per cent among those who have gone to college);

(iv) Family income (from 10 per cent among those with monthly income of Rs. 100 or less to 30 per cent among those with monthly income of Rs. 1,000 or more);

(v) Size of city or village (from 10 per cent among those living in villages of 5,000 or less to 32 per cent among those living in cities of 1 million or more);

(vi) Community trends that the percentage of current users among the Hindus is higher than among the Muslims.

The survey revealed notable differences in the characteristics of current users, past users and non-users of contraception.

In our discussions with Muslim women in different parts of the country, we did not get the impression that there was any organized resistance to family planning on religious grounds. Some of the very poor women told us that they had heard about the religious propaganda but they could not see their children starve. In every state we asked the lady doctors about the response to family planning from different sections of society. The answers were interesting. Those doctors who had some kind of social commitment and sympathetic attitude invariably said that women from all classes and all regions came to them for advice while the others complained that Muslim women and women from the poorer sections of society were not interested.

Our general impression has been that men, particularly, Muslims, are not very much concerned about family planning, though in Kerala an enthusiastic collector informed us that in the Family Planning Camps a number of Catholic and Muslim men came to him for vasectomy but they did not want anyone to know about it and requested that the operations may be performed at night. He agreed to make the necessary arrangements and the response was good. According to him there was no significant difference in the percentage of acceptors from different communities. In a village in West Bengal while a B.D.C. was complaining that

Muslims were not coming forward for family planning, an old, poor Muslim woman came up and asked where she could take her daughter-in-law for advice, so that she would stop having any more children. She already had 5 children. In Kashmir, the educated and working women are very much interested in family planning and we did not come across any group of women expressing disapproval on religious grounds.

An analysis of variance in five factors, viz., educational level of spouses, family income, number of children, urbanization and exposure to mass media simultaneously has shown that the effect of each of these factors on the use of family planning methods is significant at 1 per cent level. Some studies have suggested that the differential in adoption and use of family planning methods between States may be due to the differences in socio-economic characteristic of couples in actual implementation of strategies or combination of both.

While some of the studies occasionally contradict findings of previous research, one factor which is generally emphasized by most is education, particularly the education of women. The Regional Fertility Survey conducted by the Demographic Research Centre, Lucknow, indicated that mean number of live births varied inversely with the mother's education. The educational level of both husband and wife was found to have a very large influence on their attitudes towards family planning.

The Delhi Fertility Survey conducted by the Demographic Research Centre, Institute of Economic Growth, Delhi based on a total sample of 9,000 households, indicated the inverse relationship between a couple's educational level and average number of live births in a pronounced way only when both husband and wife were educated beyond matriculation level, the variation being 2.73 for this group and 4.47 for literate couples. The Mysore Population Study reported that among the social and economic factors studied, the one which appeared to be the most significant in relation to fertility in Bangalore City was educational status, but education below the high school or university stage was not found to be related significantly to the average number of children born.

Education may affect fertility in two ways: (i) by increasing knowledge and advantages of family planning; and (ii) by generating deliberate efforts for a planned family.

The first is effective at lower educational levels, while the latter operates probably when a sufficiently high level of education is achieved by the couple. The National Sample Survey indicated that the percentage of husbands desiring additional children after 2, declined from 60 when they were illiterate to 41.59 when they were intermediate and above. However, the decline was neither consistent nor pronounced when the educational level was below intermediate and above.

The Dharwar Surveys on the attitudes towards family planning undertaken by the Dharwar Demographic Research Centre indicated that educational level was the most important factor associated with awareness about family planning.

Role of Education: While all the major surveys found a positive relationship between education and knowledge, acceptance and practice of family planning, most of them have revealed the existence of other associational factors which may have influenced this relationship. Education is generally associated with one or more of the following: (a) rise is the age of marriage; (b) diversification of consumption pattern of people, involving both material and non-material aspects which can lead to a decline in the psychic utility generated by the birth of children; (c) urbanization; (d) possible increase in work force participation of women; (e) higher socio-economic status of the couple; (f) higher mobility; (g) higher exposure to mass media and (h) more diversified knowledge of family planning methods. It has been found that couples with primary level education or below have very limited knowledge of family planning and are most often aware only of sterilization and IUCD (Intra Uterine Contraceptive Device).

Methods of Contraceptions: Most of the methods for contraception affect women directly, and acceptance by them would indicate the success or failure of a method.

IUCD: This was introduced in 1965 and initially was very popular. Later the level of acceptance showed a reverse trend. Various studies indicate that the failure of IUCD was largely because enough information on certain side effects of the insertions was not adequately published.

During our tours, the doctors and field workers told us that this method was unpopular and it was a failure. Their observations were as follows: (1)The careless handling of IUCD insertions by the paramedical staff led to complications and there was a whispering campaign everywhere that it was harmful for the health of the women. (2)Proper arrangements were not made for a follow-up treatment in case of bleeding or other side effects.

We found, however, that wherever it was handled by properly trained personnel, e.g., in Haryana and Punjab, it was found to be the most successful method, specially because it was reversible and inexpensive.

Sterilization: This has been performed as part of the family planning programme. Tubectomies accounted for two-thirds of all sterilizations and they exceeded the number of vasectomies, but since then the number of vasectomies has increased more rapidly, and they accounted for more than 80 per cent of all sterilizations. We would like to point out, however, that the validity of these figures has been often questioned.

Since sterilization is a terminal method which is often believed to have consequences on the health of the woman, the possible constraints that may develop in taking recourse to this method are obvious. During our tours we received evidence of this apprehension from a large number of women. They were reluctant to end their chance of child bearing because of an underlying fear regarding the survival of their existing children. They were also apprehensive of the possible consequence of their health. This fear has occasionally been aggravated by the experience of the mass tubectomy camps which very often did not provide adequate medical care or follow-up measures.

Two specific arguments regarding sterilization were brought to our notice by women doctors. A group of these doctors in West Bengal mentioned a number of cases of 'post ligation syndrome' where the women developed psychological disturbances after tubectomy, particularly if any untoward incidence like illness or death of a child happened in the family. In their view, this was due to the tremendous hold of traditional values on the minds of these women, who developed a sense of guilt and regarded these tragedies as being the consequences of their 'unnatural' act. Yet another argument by doctors in the rural areas of Rajasthan was the impossibility of undertaking sterilization for a large number of women, particularly tribal ones, because of their extremely anaemic condition.

Other Methods: About 2.3 million couples are estimated to be using various other types of conventional contraceptives. This is 2.3 per cent of the estimated couples protected in the reproductive age group. For women the most significant is the use of oral contraceptive pills. A number of trials have been conducted to study the medical and social acceptability of oral contraception among Indian women. The pill as a method of oral contraception is useful for the educated urban rather than rural women. It is also comparatively more expensive and constant medical supervision is necessary to check the side effects.

Abortions: The objectives of the Medical Termination of Pregnancy Act 1971 is to reduce the incidence of criminal abortions which pose grave risks to pregnant women by liberalizing the provision of the Indian Penal Code which restricted medical practitioners from terminating pregnancies legally. The Shanti Lal Shah Committee has estimated that for every 73 live births, 25 abortions take place of which 15 are induced. "In a population of 500 million, the number of abortions per year would be 6.5 million, 2.6 million spontaneous and 3.9 million induced." From hospital records it has been observed that 15 to 20 per cent of the direct obstetric causes of maternal deaths are from abortions. Of these, 98 per cent were from septic abortions usually resulting from abortions undertaken by unqualified persons. According to the Registrar General Census (vital statistics); abortions form a high percentage of causes of all deaths due to child birth. According to two studies of the National Institute of Nutrition, Hyderabad, pregnancy wastage from miscarriage and abortions ranges from 16 to 19 per cent to 32 per cent among poor income groups.

The Act allows termination of pregnancy on: (a)Therapeutic grounds where the continuance of pregnancy would involve a risk. (i)to the life of the pregnant mother or, (ii)of grave injury to her physical and mental health. (b)Genuine grounds where there is substantial risk that the child, if born, is likely to suffer from such physical or mental abnormalities as to be seriously handicapped. (c)Humanitarian grounds, where the pregnancy has been caused by rape; or (d)Social grounds: (i)where the pregnancy in a married woman is the result of contraceptive failure, or (ii)that the environment of the pregnant woman during the continuance of pregnancy at the time of childbirth and thereafter, so far as is foreseeable, would involve risk of injury to her health.

Termination can be done only by registered practitioners certified for the purpose in approved places, mainly government hospitals.

While the Act emphasizes its importance as a health measure, the permission granted under section 3(2) to permit such termination for married women in cases of contraceptive failure, has emphasized its importance as an instrument of population control. This has given rise to a strong difference of opinion among medical personnel who are averse to using abortion for such a purpose. Many of them insist on tubectomy as a condition for abortion. In their view, based on experience, abortions often lead to frequent pregnancies, apart from its health hazards.

There is considerable evidence that the measure is being used more for birth control than for other reasons. According to a study undertaken by the Government and Children Hospital, Egmore, Madras, out of 7,957 abortions only 11 were for therapeutic reasons and 617 were cases of induced abortions admitted to the hospital only after complications had set in.

A study undertaken by the International Research Fertility Programme revealed that 88 per cent of abortion cases were among married women, of whom 55 per cent were between the age of 25 to 33, 81 per cent were urban, 19.1 per cent rural; 37 per cent had three or four children. In another study it was found that 72 per cent were married, of whom 60 per cent were in the 20 to 29 age group. The average total pregnancy of these groups was 4.3, where the average number of living children 2.5 and 0.8 had previous abortions. 50 per cent of all the patients had a previous abortion in their record and 17.8 per cent had 2 to 5.

All the studies indicate "that most pregnant women who go in for induced abortions are fully motivated for small family norms if not planned parenthood. These people are very amenable and can be fully motivated for adoption of family planning methods, more often sterilization, if they have two or more living children or other temporary methods of spacing children."

We have given serious consideration to this matter and discussed it with several representatives of the medical profession. While we appreciate the ethical considerations which make some of them reluctant to perform this operation, we feel that it is a woman's right to have control over the size of her family. At the same time it is important that doctors should have the authority to discourage such operations when it possesses a definite risk to the health of a particular patient.

We, however, feel that the condition being imposed in many hospitals, that abortion will only be performed if the patient agreed to sterilization, should not be compulsive, particularly where a woman has only one child. It would be far better to adopt methods of persuasion through expert counselling rather than compulsion. Compulsive conditions of this kind will only drive women to unqualified persons, thus defeating the main purpose of this Act.

We have been informed that there are serious psychological hazards posed by both pregnancies as well as sterilization. It is, therefore, imperative to organize systematic research on this field, to ascertain the impact of these situations and operations on the physical and mental health of women.

The difficulties placed before us by medical personnel regarding the recording procedure and paper work involved in these operations, lead us to suggest that these procedures need to be simplified. It is also necessary to extend facilities for authorized termination of pregnancies, particularly in the rural areas. We have also been informed that though the law does not require it, many hospitals insist on the husband's consent before performing these operations. A special effort needs to be made to convince the medical profession of the social value of this law, from the point of view of both individuals and society.

We have also been informed that most doctors are reluctant to perform these operations in the case of unmarried girls. It is necessary to clarify the point that rape is not the only ground to justify termination in cases of unmarried girls nor is there any legal obligation on the doctor to inform the police of an abortion done in a rape case. We note that the All India Medical Council has introduced this Act in the syllabus for medical jurisprudence, with the object of setting up new norms for the medical profession. This will go a long way in breaking down the resistance of doctors.

Recommended changes in Law: We would also like to recommend the following changes in the Law: (a)According to

Section 4(a) of the Act - consent of a minor girl is not required for operation, while in other surgical operations on children above 12, such consent is necessary. In our view this distinction is uncalled for and may lead to guardians' compelling young girls to undergo this operation even when they do not want it. The consent of the patient should be essential. In the case of a minor girl nearing majority if the doctor and the patient are in agreement, the consent of the guardian may be dispensed with. In all such cases, greater discretion should be permitted to the doctor; (b)Section 8 of the Act provides an overriding protection to the doctor for any damage caused by the operation. Since no such protection is given for other operations, this seems an unnecessary clause and may lead to negligence. It may, therefore, be dropped.

New Policies

During the First and Second Five-Year Plans, Government's approach to the problem of population growth, and the need for family planning, was a long-term objective, depending as much, if not more, on 'improvement in living standards and more widespread education especially among women', as positive measures for 'inculcation of the need' and techniques of family planning. Admitting that rates of population growth could only be altered over a period, it was agreed that programmes to restrain population growth had to complement a massive development effort.

From the Third Plan, however, restraint of population growth received a much greater emphasis and priority, with time-bound targets for reducing the birth rate and heavy investment in the administrative network to mount the programmes on the lines of a military operation, and the adoption of practices like mass sterilization camps, financial incentives and appointment of promoters, to make sterilization acceptable to the people. The legalization of abortions in cases of contraceptive failure was also a step to promote reduction in the birth rate. Some State Governments even adopted measures to deny maternity benefits to Women Government Servants after the third child. We feel strongly about this measure, for the denial of maternity benefits to a working woman is likely to affect both the health of the mother as well as that of the child. In Madhya Pradesh, we met a group of women teachers who complained bitterly that this measure has resulted in a number of them having to work till the day before the child was born. We have already pointed out the results of the absence of this benefit to construction workers.

The result of this change in emphasis was to put excessive reliance on the clinical rather than the welfare approach to family planning. Heavy investment in services, personnel and propaganda, exclusively devoted to family planning, led to a relative neglect of the other health and welfare services. In the case of women, the maternity and child health services, family welfare, adult education, and economic progress, all suffered relative lack of attention and resources, and Family Planning came to be described as the most important governmental programme for women.

The Fifth Plan had changed the emphasis again, mainly in view of a growing realization that the programme is becoming increasingly unpopular among many sections, and is failing to achieve the unrealistic targets. It is also admitted that a purely clinical approach cannot overcome the socio-psychological resistance caused by poverty, ignorance, low survival rate of children among the poor sections, and the economic and social dependence on children.

Though integration of family planning with maternal and child health care was suggested in the Fourth Plan, the policy of integration could not be achieved, since the family planning services had been already placed under a different administrative machinery from the other health services. A new strategy evolved for the Fifth Plan visualizes the integration of family planning into the general health services, particularly its maternal and child care component including nutrition. The principle of integration will be extended to other fields, in particular to efforts at mass motivation through the existing channels for functional training programmes to train multipurpose health workers to deliver the integrated health care services under the Minimum Needs Programme. The impact of this decision to see family planning in its proper perspective is clearly visible in the allocation of resources proposed for the next Plan. According to the Draft Five-Year Plan:

> The primary objective during the Fifth Plan is to provide minimum public health facilities integrated with family planning and nutrition for vulnerable groups - children, pregnant women and lactating mothers. It will be necessary to consolidate past gains in the various fields of health, such as communicable diseases, medical educatión and provision of infrastructure in the rural areas.

During our tours we found that wherever the medical personnel and the village level workers were mature and sympathetic in their approach and worked with a sense of social commitment, their persuasive power evoked a great degree of response. On the other hand there was considerable criticism of the 'motivators', most of whom are very young and inexperienced as well as purely untrained persons. It was a frequent observation that they were responsible for criminal mistakes like persuading extremely young persons both male and female to undergo sterilization, or bringing elderly women who were long past the child bearing age for the same, entirely because of the financial incentives. According to Banerjee:

> Perhaps the greatest mistakes in the formulation of family planning programmes has been a gross overestimation of the effectiveness of the motivators and equally gross underestimation of the resistance to be encountered motivating a community as a whole.... Motivation techniques were viewed as some sort of a magic which would be applied by a person to induce another to accept family planning.

We understand that it has been decided to introduce community incentives and group awards for the programme personnel with a view to increasing the involvement of the community and strengthening the commitment of the staff and institutions in order to improve the quality of the services. Most of the doctors and the women with whom we discussed problems of family planning were of the opinion that while payment to acceptors should continue particularly for daily wage workers, the payment to motivators is not only a waste but has been responsible for much of the unpopularity of this programme. There were also severe criticisms of the lack of adequate follow-up measures. We also came across large gaps both in areas and communities where the family planning services have not reached. One group of women whom we met in Bangalore had never heard of family planning.

During the course of its tours in the States, the Committee met a number of health and family planning officials, social workers, as well as a cross-section of rural and urban women. An analysis of the tour reports reveals that the message of family planning has reached almost everywhere, but access to health and family planning services was most inadequate. Even in slum areas of big cities, there were no family planning clinics in the vicinity, and the women did not know where to go though they were anxious to avail themselves of the information. In the rural areas, there was an acute shortage of maternity facilities, and trained medical personnel.

In Bastar district, and in some tribal areas of Himachal Pradesh, we were informed that the birth rate is 29 per 1000, which is well below the national target for the Vth Plan, and yet we found money being spent on family planning projects in these areas. There were huge hoardings and posters advocating the small family norm, when this money could very well have been utilized for other welfare activities in these extremely backward areas.

In our view, the inadequacy of qualified medical personnel and mature counselling presents the greatest internal drawback to the success of this programme. We are entirely in agreement with the Draft Fifth Five-Year Plan, that integration of family planning with more positive health services like maternal and child health and nutrition, and improvement in the life expectancy of children and mothers, will provide a far greater incentive to the adoption of family planning measures than the hitherto adopted negative approach.

Various Programmes

Programmes for women's welfare and development can be classified under the following broad base

A. ***Programmes in the rural areas:*** Welfare Extension Projects, Family and Child Welfare Projects, Organization of Mahila Mandals, Training Schemes for Workers.

B. ***Programmes in urban areas:*** Welfare Extension Projects, and Working Women's Hostels.

C. ***Other Programmes:*** Grants-in-aid to voluntary organizations, Condensed Courses of Education for Adult Women, Adult Literacy and social education for women. Craft training centres, Socio-economic programmes, Nutrition Programmes, Social Defence Programmes, Border Area Programmes, Homes for Women.

Rural Areas: The concept of rural development as conceived in India covers a wide field and history. Both Mahatma Gandhi and Rabindranath Tagore had seen rural development as an important method of social mobilization which could build the social infrastructure for independence. According to Tagore, it was an effort to make the village a self-reliant and self-respectful unit, with knowledge of its culture and history and to enable the people to make use of modern resources for their full upliftment - physical, social, economic and intellectual. Gandhi viewed rural development as aiming to make every village a 'Republic', in which no person would be unemployed, and everyone would enjoy sufficient nutritious food, houses with adequate hygiene and sanitation, and enough khadi for their clothing. Thus, rural development was not seen only in its micro-dimension, but as a new philosophy for society, which was to bring social consciousness or a revolution among the rural people. Tagore's Shantiniketan and Gandhi's Village Construction Programmes were the forerunners of rural development that was to be taken up by the government after independence. The Community Development Programme undertaken by the Government of India drew heavily from the Gandhian concept.

The application of Gandhian ideas to the field of women's development had been done by the Kasturba Memorial Trust after the death of Kasturba Gandhi, which had been given a concrete form in the objectives and activities of the Kasturba Memorial Trust. This Trust was born with the objective of serving rural women by providing: (i) education for women and children; (ii) medical and health services; and (iii) socio-economic programmes in the form of khadi and village industries to relieve economic distress.

The Trust trained a number of gramsevikas and mid-wives and the training centres were specially conceived to train and mobilize village women, specially widows and deserted wives. The health programmes aimed at prevention of diseases as well as promotion of positive health through maternal and child welfare programmes.

When the Central Social Welfare Board decided to launch the Welfare Extension Projects in 1954, this threefold approach was adopted as the basic framework for provision of services. The activities included Balwadis, maternity services and general medical aid, social education and craft training for women. The original Welfare Extension Projects (WEP) were to serve a unit of 25-40 contiguous villages, with a population of 25-30 thousand through five centres. At the end of the Second Plan, there were 420 such projects with 2004 centres. Eight of these projects, with 40 centres, continue to be operated by the Central Social Welfare Board, while others have either been closed or handed over to Mahila Mandals and voluntary organizations which receive 75 per cent financial assistance.

Since the general objectives and methodology of this programme were similar to those of the larger programmes of community development initiated by the government during the First Plan in 1952, and to eliminate duplication of work, it was decided that Welfare Extension Projects should be started in Community Development Blocks on a coordinated basis. All original Welfare Extension Projects were converted into this pattern as soon as the area was covered by a C.D. Block. These projects covered a block of 100 villages with a population of about 60,000 through 10 centres. The work and the functionaries were supervised by a Project Implementing Committee which consisted of representatives of block officials and local voluntary workers. For the first year the budget was shared by the Central Social Welfare Board, the State Government and Community Development Block in the ratio of 12:65 and at the end of 5 years the total expenditure was shared in the ratio of 24:12:5. Later, there were 264 projects with 2,800 centres.

Since greater importance was increasingly attached to the role of voluntary organizations in the continuance of welfare programmes, 1,629 centres of the Welfare Extension Projects (original and coordinated pattern) were handed over to Mahila Mandals. 442 Mahila Mandals, who have taken over one or more activities of this project were given a grant of Rs. 25.69 lakh.

On the recommendations of the Central Social Welfare Board and an Evaluation Committee of Social Welfare on the Welfare Extension Projects, it was decided to revise services existing in rural areas in different patterns aiming to develop a countrywide programme of integrated welfare services for children. Thus the Family and Child Welfare (F&CW) scheme was initiated, whereas extension projects provided services for women and children, the

Family and Child Welfare Projects aimed at integrated development of the pre-school child, training to young mothers and all services that were necessary for the proper growth and development of the child and rural family.

The family and child welfare projects were funded by the Central and the State Governments in a 75:25 ratio and aided by UNICEF with equipment, stipends and training facilities. They have progressively taken over the functions of the earlier projects of the Central Social Welfare Board and the Ministry of Community Development. The services provided are: (a) Integrated services to rural children; specially preschool; (b) Basic training to women and young girls in home management, health education, nutrition education, child care. General health and maternity services for women were also to be provided with the aid of the Primary Health Centres. Similar collaboration was also envisaged for nutrition. (c) Assistance to women through Mahila Mandals, specially established centres and existing welfare agencies, for getting supplementary work to augment their income. (d) Cultural, educational and recreational activities for women and children.

Initially, there were 221 projects in existence and later, 20 coordinated welfare extension projects were added to this scheme, bringing the total to 240. On 31st March, 1973, 281 projects were functioning.

Maternity and Child Welfare Services: With the integration of the First Plan, Maternity and Child Welfare Services were taken up by the Ministry of Health as part of the overall development programme in health. These services were augmented by WHO and UNICEF. A number of Maternity and Child Welfare Bureaus were established in States, staffed by qualified women medical officers. At the same time, the then Community Projects administration also undertook these services in the Community Development and National Extension Service Blocks. Other Ministries like Railways, Defence and Labour also promoted Maternity and Child Welfare Programmes through the Ministry of Health. The number of Maternity and Child Welfare Centres increased and these services were given an important place in rural development programmes. The Union Government assisted the States in establishment of primary health centres and sub-centres covering a C.D. Block. At present 5,195 centres are functioning in the country. Maternity and Child Welfare Services are also undertaken by the Ministries of Railways, Labour (under Labour Welfare and the various Acts in this section) and public sector undertakings.

Mahila Mandals: Practically from the beginning it was realized that the objectives of these rural development programmes could not be achieved without the active participation and leadership of the local community. Government functionaries, however, efficient and dedicated, can only provide some stimulus and act as catalytic agents to train and release efforts for self-help of the people. This was particularly true of women who had been paralysed by generations of social oppression, and denial of basic rights. Both the Central Social Welfare Board and the department of Community development concluded that the proper agency for the success of this programme would be a committee of local women. The organization of Mahila Mandals thus became one of the objectives of these rural development programmes.

The declared objective of community development is to enable rural women to organize themselves at the village level to assemble on a regular basis to learn from each other and from workers appointed by the Government. The basic idea is to create opportunities for rural women to improve their status as housewives and to take part in public affairs. The department therefore organizes Mahila Mandals, imparts training facilities to their members and provides incentive awards for performance.

Mahila Mandals, were organized in villages and blocks for promoting women's programmes. Nutrition, education, health, mother and child care, home improvement, adult literacy, recreation and cultural activities and training and house and family planning were part of their programmes. There were about 53,000 Mahila. Mandals with a total membership of 14,00,000 averaging 11 Mahila

Mandals per block. Under the Applied Nutrition Programme, additional facilities are being provided for the promotion of economic activities of Mahila Mandals towards, development and management of kitchen and school gardens, organization of fishery units, etc. During the Fourth Plan 7,500 awards in various categories were given to Mahila Mandals.

The Central Social Welfare Board and the State Social Welfare Advisory Boards also realized the importance of Mahila Mandals and now they are being given grants up to 75 per cent for running some programmes of the Board. Subsequently, 442 Mahila Mandals received a grant of about Rs 25.69 lakh. They are also running some Welfare Extension Projects of the Board.

Voluntary-agencies like the Bhartiya Grameen Mahila Sangh have also established a large number of Mahila Mandals. The representatives of the Village Mahila Mandals form the District Mahila Samities and the representatives of the District Mahila Samities constitute the State panel or State branches. According to the Bhartiya Grameen Mahila Sangh, its branches in the 17 States now cover 7,000 villages.

Training Scheme for Workers: The various functionaries required for these rural development schemes are trained at centres located in different parts of the country. The training is organized by some government agencies like the Directorate of Extension of the Ministry of Agriculture and various schools of social work, non-governmental organizations like the Kasturba Memorial Trust, Visva Bharati, Jamia Millia with assistance from the Central Social Welfare Board.

The Department of Community Development in the Ministry of Agriculture has a programme for training associate women workers to enable members of Mahila Mandals to come forward to become organized. The members of Mahila Mandals get to know about the organization of Balwadis, health and nutrition, education, nursery, kitchen gardening, etc. About 20,000 women received training in the Third and Fourth Plans and a sum of Rs 11.17 lakh was spent during the Fourth Plan.

The Directorate of Extension of the Ministry of Agriculture also provides training for village level workers of Community Development Block at 25 centres. The emphasis is on the protection of Agricultural production and nutrition education. In service, training facilities are provided after 2-3 years service and two week refresher courses are given to Mukhya Sevikas. Refresher courses are also given to Instructresses for Gram Sevika and Mukhya Sevika training centres for six weeks. Associate workers such as Gram Lakshmis or Gram Kakis are also given one month's training. Under the nutrition education scheme, training was given to associate women workers.

Farm Women's Training Courses for one week are organized at about 100 training centres for farm women. This farmers' training was started in a few districts and is now being implemented in almost all districts. The emphasis is on agricultural production, reproduction patterns of high yielding variety cereals, stock managements, nutrition, etc. Radio broadcasting is also used for educating the farm women and organizing discussion groups.

The Bhartiya Grameen Mahila Sangh also holds various training camps for rural women. Among these are leadership training camps sanctioned by the Department of Social Welfare in border areas. Similar programmes have also been sponsored by the CSWB. The increased agricultural production programme is a seven-day camp sanctioned by the Ministry of Food and Agriculture for training in improved agricultural methods and covered 650 villages. The Ministry of Health has sanctioned the family planning orientation programme to train village women in methods of family planning.

In Towns

The structure of welfare programmes in urban areas varies from region to region. The municipalities and local administration are responsible for providing basic formal education and health facilities like schools, hospitals, dispensaries, etc. Welfare programmes as such have already been left to voluntary organizations, which in some cases receive grants through the Central Social Welfare Board or the State Governments.

In 1958 the Central Social Welfare Board started Welfare Extension Projects in the urban areas to meet the needs of people living in the slums, particularly in new industrial areas. These projects provided balwadis, creches, arts and craft classes and family planning and maternity advice for women; they also do placement of destitutes. 65 such projects were in existence at the end of the Plan. They were reduced to 33. Later, Welfare Extension Projects received Rs 2.78 lakh benefiting approximately 70,000 families.

Working Women's Hostels: An increasing number of women are leaving their homes and entering employment. The problem of accommodation in metropolitan areas, particularly impelled the Central Social Welfare Board to provide grants for hostels for working women as one of its services. The Board viewed this service as a preventive measure against the possibility of young girls in urban areas being exposed to undesirable and anti-social influences.

The scheme was started during the Second Plan and the Board sanctioned grants to voluntary welfare institutions willing to provide healthy accommodation at reasonable rates for working women of lower income groups. At the end of the Plan, 101 grants amounting to Rs 9.76 lakh had been sanctioned. Later, 29 hostels received a grant of Rs 66,000 from the Board. The Department of Social Welfare initiated a scheme for financial assistance to voluntary institutions for the construction of hostel buildings in capital cities and cities with a population of over ten lakh. The pattern of assistance is under review at present and in the current Plan a sum of Rs 15 crore has been set aside for hostels for working women.

Condensed Courses of Education for Adult Women: The very high percentage of illiteracy amongst women as well as various difficulties in imparting education to them gave rise to the condensed courses of education for adult women which are being implemented by various governmental and non-governmental agencies. The programme was initiated by the Central Social Welfare Board with the dual objective of opening new vistas of employment for needy women and to create a band of trained workers for various projects in the rural areas.

Under the scheme, adult women between the ages of 18 and 30, who have some schooling, are prepared for middle schools, matriculation or equivalent examination within a period of two years. Grants up to Rs 35,000 per course for two years are given for maintenance, stipends, salaries to teachers and educational equipment. Women who complete these courses can go in for vocational training as nurse, mid-wife, gramsevikas, etc. In the Second Plan Rs 58.82 lakh were-sanctioned for 271 courses, though only Rs 28.88 lakh was released. In the Third Plan, a provision of Rs 150 lakh was made for 500 courses. Up to the end of February 1973, 1,386 courses had been started and Rs 3 crore were spent. Of 33,000 women enrolled about 25,000 completed their studies. The programme has been extended to wives of Jawans killed or disabled in action. The Community Development Department also has established adult literacy centres in blocks which cover women.

Socio-Economic Programmes: It was realized at an early stage of the welfare programmes that they would not have the desired impact unless the women were imparted some craft or technical training. This was a part of the three pronged approach of the earliest programmes. While health received some attention and resources from the Ministry of Health, and Family Planning, as well as welfare agencies, the economic schemes did not receive corresponding attention from the concerned governmental agencies. On a very minor scale, some socio-economic schemes were initiated by the Central Social Welfare Board and its grants-in-aid schemes and also organized on a small scale by the Department of Community Development and some voluntary organization. Initially started by the Ministry of Rehabilitation for refugee women, it was taken up by the Central Social Welfare Board, to provide leisure time employment to women in lower income groups and help them supplement their income. This was undertaken in cooperation with the Ministry of Commerce and Industry which provides them necessary assistance in technical training, finance and marketing. The scheme was working in co-operation with State Governments and State Social Welfare Advisory Boards. 95 demonstration-cum-training centres, set up on 26 pilot projects for industries in the Community Development Project areas have benefited women.

At present the socio-economic programme of the CSWB provides financial assistance to voluntary welfare institutions and Co-operative Societies for setting up small production units where needy women or handicapped persons are given initial training and subsequently provided with employment. In the implementation of this programme, the Board as well as voluntary institutions and Cooperative Societies obtain technical assistance from the National-Small Industries Organization and regional offices of the All-India Handicrafts Board and All-India Handloom Board. The categories of the scheme that are being implemented under this programme are: (1) Production units of small-scale industries, such as manufacture of toys and articles, printing books, binding, fruit preservation and canning, bakery, confectionary, ready-made garments, etc. (2) Handicrafts training-cum-procurement and production units; for example, cane and bamboo articles, mat-weaving, traditional embroidery, etc. (3) Handloom training-cum-production units; (4) Units ancillary to large industries; and (5) Industrial co-operative societies set up under the voluntary welfare programmes started by the Board.

Up to the end of March 1972, the Board had approved grants to 130 institutions for setting up production units with an employment potential of about 4,000 under various categories of schemes. An amount of Rs 54.60 lakh had been sanctioned for 140 approved units with an employment potential of 4,235.

The Annual Report of the Central Social Welfare Board mentions that the attention of the State Governments have been drawn to the need for extending some sort of protection or patronage to socio-economic units run by voluntary institutions buying their products. The problem of marketing remains unsolved and unless this is overcome, the objective of a number of socio-economic programmes will remain unfulfilled. A number of Ministries such as Railways, Ministry of Labour, apart from the Ministry of Agriculture and Community Development have small schemes for providing craft training to women. The Mahila Samities of the Ministry of Railways have handicraft centres to help women in learning some trade to enable them to supplement the family income. Some public sector undertakings have Mahila Mandals which also provide such training. While the emphasis on these programmes to improve women's earning power indicates awareness of the dimension of women's problems, it is doubtful whether these programmes are having the desired impact, since most of these women are unable to obtain the raw-material or market the finished goods. It is also remarkable that the governmental agencies responsible for promoting industrial development have completely ignored the reality of the problem that they are trying to solve.

Nutrition Programmes: The Plan emphasized nutrition as a major problem particularly in rural areas, and among the lower income groups. The Department of Social Welfare and the Central Social Welfare Board, the Ministry of Health and Family Planning, the Department of Community Development of the Ministry of Agriculture and the Ministry of Education are all operating various nutrition schemes for women and children.

The Special Nutrition Programme of the Government of India was introduced in 1970-71 to provide supplementary nutrition to children in tribal areas and urban slums, by the Department of Social Welfare. This scheme covers a number of pre-school children in 0-6 age groups and nursing the expectant mothers. Over 19,600 feeding centres have been set up in the tribal areas and about

7,500 in urban areas. The Department of Social Welfare also implements a nutrition programme for children in the age group 3-5, through the Balwadis and day-care centres run by the CSWB, the Indian Council of Child Welfare, the Harijan Sevak Sangh, and the Adimjati Sevak Sangh, covering 2,00,640 children and 5,577 instructions. The Balwadis of the Family and Child Welfare Projects were generally excluded from this Programme because provision for nutrition was already provided in the scheme. The Board, however, feels that it has not been possible to build up adequate machinery for implementation and supervision of this programme at the State and Central levels and it requires greater provision by the Government.

The Directorate of Extension of the Ministry of Agriculture has been running a Composite Nutrition Programme since 1969-70, to provide nutrition education in areas not covered under the Applied Nutrition Programme. It includes nutrition education, through Mahila Mandals, strengthening the supervisory machinery for women's programmes, encouragement of economic activities of Mahila Mandals, training of associate women workers and demonstration feeding. The Applied Nutrition Programme of the Department of Community Development was introduced in collaboration with UNICEF, FAO and WHO. It was intended to educate the rural people in improved nutrition by promoting the production and consumption of protective foods like fruits, vegetables, fish and poultry. From 1966-67, steps were taken to coordinate the operation of the Applied Nutrition Programmes with other schemes like the Mid-Day Meal Programme of the Ministry of Education, and Family and Child Welfare Projects of the Department of Social Welfare. The ANP covered 221 blocks and it covered, 1,101 projects and spent Rs 1.46 crore for this purpose. Under this programme, demonstration, in cooking and feeding is held, particularly designed to give- direction on nutrition through the Mahila Mandals, and to train women workers.

The Ministry of Health has increasingly emphasized nutrition particularly for pregnant women, lactating mothers and pre-school children of the weaker sections, through an integrated programme of supplementary feeding, health care, immunization as well as nutrition education. Now, concentrated attention will be given to these vulnerable sections in rural areas, urban slums, tribal development blocks and school going children of the weaker sections. Within the resources allocated, it should be possible to cover about 11 million additional beneficiaries in the Plan. This programme is under the budgetary control of the Department of Social Welfare.

The Fourth Plan Special Nutrition Programme for pre-school children and expectant and nursing mothers has been redesignated and included in the Integrated Child Development Programme in the current Plan. The services include supplementary nutrition feeding, immunization, health check-up and referral services, health and nutrition education. The entire expenditure for the ICDP during the Fifth Plan will be made by the Centre and implemented through the State Governments and Union Territories. It is proposed to cover about 7,000 nursing and expectant mothers in each project. Women between 15-44 years numbering approximately 23,000 will be provided nutrition and health education. In the tribal areas 2,450 nursing and expectant mothers and 7,000 women in the 15-44 age groups are the target population for each project. The ICDP depends on interdepartmental coordination between the Ministry of Health, State Health Departments, Community Development Department and the Department of Social Welfare. The existing 33,000 feeding centres of the Special Nutrition Programme and Balwadi nutrition programmes are in operation in organized slums, tribal areas and other rural areas. They will initially be included into ICDP centres in the project areas.

Social Defence Programmes: Among the services available in the country for the correction and reformation of persons who come into conflict with the law are the following which apply directly to women: (a) Suppression of Immoral Traffic; (b) After care services; and (c) Welfare Services in Prisons.

These services are provided by the Department of Social Welfare and Rehabilitation Directorate at Central level.

The Suppression of Immoral Traffic in Women and Girls Act of 1956 provides for protective homes and reception centres. There are at present 33 protective homes and 68 reception centres and district shelters in the country. A scheme for short stay homes for rehabilitation of women and girls facing moral danger was approved in 1969-70 and two pilot projects - one in West Bengal and the other in Madhya Pradesh were provided grants of Rs 1.10 lakh in 1972-73. During the Second Plan, programmes were drawn up under Social and Moral Hygiene and After Care Programmes not only for those under the SIT Act, but also those discharged from Correctional and non-Correctional Institutions. The State Governments were assisted to set up special homes such as protective homes.

We visited some of these protective homes. In the Protective Home in Lucknow and in the Nari Niketan in Delhi, efforts are made to rehabilitate the inmates by providing training in sewing and embroidery. There is no formal procedure for marketing of these products, nor are the inmates given any training either to organize production or marketing. We were informed that sewing machines are presented to the inmates when they are discharged to help them to become self-employed. This practice was reported to be prevalent in many States. According to reports by social workers in different parts of the country, most of these young women find it difficult to earn an adequate livelihood from this occupation. Quite a number are compelled to dispose of the machines, and revert to their original profession. We were rather distressed to find that these homes house women rescued from immoral traffic as well as young girls sent under the Children's Act. Even insane women are housed in these homes. We consider this to be a very unhealthy and undesirable situation. We also feel that the training provided for rehabilitation in these homes is not adequate and requires much greater attention and planning as well as resources. We were informed that in some of the homes, efforts are made to return these young women to their families wherever possible, or to arrange marriages for them.

There has been considerable discussion on these programmes for rehabilitation of victims of immoral traffic. During a recent Judicial Seminar on Correctional Services, the speakers, who included representatives of the Association for Social Health, the Director of Social Welfare, Delhi Administration and members of the staff of the Delhi School of Social Work, pointed out the inadequacy of the arrangements for the employment of these young women. Without economic rehabilitation, much of the efforts made for their rescue is wasted. Some social workers have suggested to us that the best way for rehabilitation would be to set up production-cum-marketing centres along with these homes. It is also necessary to diversify the types of training provided to the inmates, since over-dependence on tailoring and embroidery has led to considerable waste. Economic independence is the only way to protect these women from the clutches of persons who have a vested interest in this traffic.

Homes are also provided for the aged and destitute women in various States though the total number of such homes is inadequate in terms of the population to be covered. A scheme for the welfare of destitute women between the ages of 18-44 and 45-65 providing for basic amenities of food, shelter, clothing, besides education and training in craft to enable the younger group to become self-reliant, as also services for dependent children up to 7 years was finalized in 1970-71. For the first group, residential institutions to accommodate 200 persons were to be provided. The scheme was to be implemented by giving grants-in-aid to voluntary organizations up to 75 per cent of the expenditure. The total Fourth Plan provision was Rs 100 lakh. We regret to note that the scheme remains unimplemented.

Grants-in-aid: Grants-in-aid are extended to registered voluntary institutions working for welfare of women, children and handicapped persons. Under the grants-in-aid for women's welfare during the First and the Second Plans, assistance was provided for expansion, development and improvement of activities of voluntary organizations. On the basis of the recommendations of the grants-in-aid Committee, the Board decided to limit the assistance during the Third Plan to consolidate and improve the activities initiated during the First and the Second Plans. Generally all grants except those given for developing special schemes were given on a matching basis.

The amounts allocated to these schemes during the four Plans indicate that while the First and Second Plans brought in a number of voluntary institutions within the network for administration of welfare services, Government's dependence on these bodies has registered a decline during the Third and Fourth Plans.

The NGOs

Voluntary welfare services in India have always been an integral part of the cultural and social tradition. The bulk of the social services were provided by the voluntary sector prior to independence. Social welfare services have always been present in some form or the other for the well-being of the weaker sections of society who, because of various handicaps, social, economic, physical, etc., could not make use of, or were traditionally denied, normal facilities. The weaker sections included women, children, the aged, infirm and handicapped, Scheduled Castes and Scheduled Tribes.

Voluntary organizations may opt for several alternative roles according to their objectives and composition. They may be innovational and experimental activities in fields where government has not entered. They may co-exist with the public sector and the private sector for social development because they may have some advantages over the former or they can provide the government with a supportive base, i.e. they can work like agents of the government at local levels and operate programmes of the government as their own.

Soon after independence, on the basis of a survey made by the Planning Commission, it was estimated that there were about 10,000 voluntary organizations in the field of social welfare. In order to strengthen and encourage these agencies the Central Social Welfare Board was established in 1953, with a nationwide programme for grants-in-aid. It was realized that the voluntary organizations, with the qualities of flexibility, of experimentation, human touch, nearness to the clientele, sensitiveness to the new problems and capacity to discover new ideas could be of great assistance, since it was impossible for any government to take care of all the welfare needs of the people. The voluntary agencies could also mobilize resources from within the community for social welfare.

The relative importance of the role of the State and the role of the voluntary agencies has been engaging the attention of policy makers, planners, social thinkers, administrators and voluntary workers. In 1959, a Study team on Social Welfare and Backward Classes, appointed by the Planning Commission, recommended that whereas all programmes of social welfare arising out of the statutory responsibility of the State should be sponsored by State departments of Social Welfare, other social welfare services to meet local needs, should be implemented through voluntary organizations. A seminar on Social Administration in Developing Countries held in New Delhi in March, 1964, felt that the cooperation of the State and voluntary agencies in meeting social needs would always bring out better results in promoting welfare services on a larger scale.

We met representatives of some national voluntary organizations working for women's welfare and the welfare of socially deprived groups. We also met representatives of voluntary welfare organizations in every State during our tours. Most of the women's voluntary organizations have been confined to the urban areas, with its membership drawn mainly from educated urban middle-class women. Their main activities are conducting literacy classes, adult education centres, Balwadis, promoting women's cooperatives, small savings, handicrafts, etc. Some of these organizations have also taken up family planning programmes. In times of emergency, such organizations have organized canteens, blood banks and other services. These organizations seek to raise the status of women in the social, economic, political and educational fields. They have passed numerous resolutions for the uplift of Indian women, but their constructive activities have suffered from limitations of resources, personnel, and failure to reach rural areas.

Only a few organizations have endeavoured to work amongst rural women, to improve their living conditions, promote leadership and assist them to take part in developmental activities. The government has given grants for some voluntary welfare activities. In some cases, the grant has been for administration and maintenance while in other cases it has been allotted for programmes only.

Apart from the Central Social Welfare Board's grants-in-aid programme, there is no machinery to coordinate and distribute the services provided by these bodies, to ensure greater efficiency and even distribution. Nor are the resources of the majority of these organizations adequate to maintain trained workers for their complex types of work. Initially, the important organizations were able to act as pressure groups in directing the attention of the government to social problems, and to mobilize support for social legislation. Our investigation has shown that these laws still remain unknown to the large mass of Indian women, who have not been able to take advantage of them. Most of these organizations operate independent of each other and as such have not been able to fully benefit the community.

Official Steps

Expenditure for welfare programmes, including programmes meant for women is low in comparison to other sectors, since it has been viewed as a non-productive item in comparison to the economic sectors. In times of stringencies, financial cuts are made first in this sector, since returns from investments are not immediate. A break-up of allocations indicates that a major part of the expenditure is on maintenance and establishment charges, leaving only a small percentage for actual services. The administrative tradition in India has tended to emphasize maintenance of law and order, and economic development, and departments dealing with welfare programmes generally occupy a relatively less important position in the governmental structure. The training imparted to the administrators also emphasizes the same aspects. It has now been realized that administration must also be welfare oriented and recently a working group has been set up to frame a syllabus for social administration for the training of service probationers at the National Academy of Administration and other State level training institutes.

The administration and handling of welfare programmes has become increasingly technical. Administrators have to acquire technical orientation for successful implementation of social welfare programmes. The lack of emphasis on the required technical competence and the limitation of resources have had an adverse impact on the quality and success of welfare programmes.

Certain factors impede realization of a high degree of rationality in organization and flexibility in operation. The federal nature of our policy vests responsibility for implementing social policy and programmes with State and local authorities, but resources and agencies for planning are at the Centre. The weakness of local authorities further complicates the problems. There is dire need for greater coordination between voluntary agencies and organizations built up by Government, between activities of States and the Central Government and of the district or local level organizations and the States.

State Level: At present the majority of the States have a Minister-in-charge of Social Welfare, though this portfolio might include other subjects. State governments give still lower priority to social welfare programmes, and are reluctant to allocate sufficient resources. It has also been found that in the operation of the democratic process, the interests of the weaker sections are sometimes neglected, as they are relatively less vocal and less powerful than the dominant section of the population. Due to existing social prejudice and attitudes towards women, any policy regarding their welfare and development is limited either to education or welfare of special groups like handicapped or destitute women. Therefore, though social welfare is a State subject, the major share of the State's allocations go towards the maintenance of the existing social welfare activities initiated generally by the Centre.

As an illustration, it may be mentioned that during Shri Charan Singh's tenure as Chief Minister in UP, all women's welfare programmes of the Government were summarily discontinued. The State Social Welfare (Advisory) Board was however allowed to continue because of strong representation from the State Finance Department that its abolition would result in stoppage of Central assistance. The closure provoked a protest from the women functionaries whose services were held up as a model to other States, because of their success. The result of the closure has left only skeletal services for women in the States.

Most State governments do not have any machinery for collection of data or planning of welfare services. The State Social Welfare (Advisory) Boards, which might have fulfilled this role, serve mainly as a link organization to supervise, implement and report on the working of aided voluntary organizations in the State as an agency of the Central Social Welfare Board. The relationship between Central and State Governments, the Central Social Welfare Board and the State governments are also not clearly defined and the status of the State Boards differ from State to State.

Local administrations have shown even less interest in women's welfare programmes in general and local bodies authorized to allocate resources have given very low priority to them. Everywhere we were told that the Mahila Mandals were being starved of funds and not being provided even with accommodation. The process of co-opting women into the Panchayats has also not been very successful as their small numbers have prevented them from being more effective in emphasizing the needs of women. As a rule, they have not had an effective voice in policy making or the allocation of resources. The male members of the rural elite, are by and large not favourably disposed towards improving and changing the position of women and consequently women's programmes are prone to be neglected.

Governments' Role

The neglect and indifference to welfare activities by the local and State Governments has led to an increase in the role of central agencies in this field. Within the federal framework the Central government's role should normally be planning, monitoring progress of activities, stimulating particular activities to ensure a national minimum standard, and guiding States through policy directions, giving advice and providing technical and financial help. The reasons for this increase in the role of the Centre can, therefore, be summed up as follows: (a) Limitation of resources of State Governments; (b) Indifference and low priorities for welfare programmes on the part of most State Governments; (c) Absence of proper welfare agencies in most of the States.

The experience of the Central Social Welfare Board suggests that the Coordination Committees as envisaged at the local level of some of the projects of the Board were not very useful since local administrations were not willing to take up women's welfare programmes. The State Boards were not in a position to function autonomously and the State Governments were disinterested in women's welfare programmes.

Under the system of financial relations between the Central and the State Governments, the Centre provides assistance for development programmes during a Plan period either on sharing or on full basis. At the end of the Plan period full responsibility for continuing the programmes devolves on the States. In the case of the women's programmes initiated by Central agencies, State Governments have not always been willing to accept the responsibility for continuation. In such cases, these programmes have had to be discontinued or re-designated as a new programme so that Central assistance could be continued.

Schemes for All

The concept of a local need-based approach to social welfare has gradually been overshadowed as a direct consequence of this centralizing trend. Programmes and policies are initiated at the Centre, and there is increasing distance between the level of policy making and the levels of implementation. National programmes are framed without adequate reference to local variations and needs and this defeats the very purpose of social welfare. It particularly affects the initiative of the local community and the voluntary sector, and leads to increasing bureaucratization. It has also prevented the State Governments from admitting their responsibility in the field of welfare.

Because of this bureaucratization and centralization, the authority and initiative of the field staff is considerably impaired. As an example, the field staff at the State level are not taken into confidence nor are their suggestions considered at the level of policy and planning. For a number of schemes of the Central Social Welfare Board, the State Boards have little authority for initiating and reviewing the programmes.

The delays inherent in routine procedure and functioning of the Government hampers the progress of the programmes. Government organizations and procedures, with rigid rules governing sanctions and expenditure by their very nature, are not suited to the essentially informal and personal approach required for welfare work. Generally the approach of the voluntary workers and organizations is more flexible and personal. Once funds have been allotted for a particular project, they cannot be diverted for any other purpose and these agencies have to function within the rigid framework of the government sanction.

The Shortcomings

An examination of welfare and development activities undertaken in the country so far indicates that there is a multiplicity of programmes, agencies and functionaries. A large number of these programmes have very similar objectives and functions.

These programmes are run by different departments, have separate allocations, and the field staff belongs to different agencies. Areas of implementation in many cases are not rationally demarcated. Since most of these are Central programmes, planning and policy making is carried out by separate Ministries and Departments at the Centre. There is very little or no coordination between these Ministries and Departments, except where a coordinated programme has been envisaged (as in the case of Integrated Child Development Programme). This leads to a waste of funds in the duplication of administrative machinery, leaving a relatively small amount for the actual implementation of the programmes.

There is very little coordination at the State level also. Even though the State Social Welfare Advisory Boards have some government officials as members, this has failed to ensure any substantial coordination of governmental effort in the welfare of women. At the project level, the functional committees and implementation committees are constituted with representatives of the State Governments and State Boards. They have to work in collaboration with the Panchayats or other local organization. The experience of these committees has not been always happy. Besides, their scope of activities is limited, only to the programmes of the Board.

There is little justification for the vast number of agencies for implementing welfare programmes with almost similar objectives. A division in administrative agencies can be justified on one of the three following grounds: (a) territorial distinction, i.e., each agency functioning in clearly demarcated territory; (b) methodological distinction, i.e., if the method of work has to be different; (c) functional distinction, i.e., if the objectives of the agency are such as to warrant a separate organization.

The present allocation of work amongst various agencies has followed no such principle of clear distinctions.

Organisational Setup

As one of the most important agencies for the implementation of social welfare activities, the status of the Social Welfare Boards is currently under consideration. Though in practice the Board has enjoyed some autonomy, legally it has no independent existence. It was given the status of a charitable company in 1969 to meet audit objections in the way of giving grants. This has not solved its problems and its relationship with the Department of Social Welfare in regard to policy, planning and approval of programmes and financial allocations clearly indicates its status as a subordinate agency of the Department.

The justification for creating an agency outside the ministerial framework of the Government lay in the peculiar nature of welfare work, which required a flexible, personalized and committed approach, not easily possible within a government department because of procedural rules and regulations. The intention of the government was thus undoubtedly to create a specialized agency with its membership drawn from the ranks of social workers, with direct experience of voluntary welfare activities. Some other specialized agencies created by the government have been given statutory autonomous status. The unfortunate vagueness of the status of the Central Social Welfare Board, created administrative difficulties and led to its registration as a company in 1969. This arrangement has been admittedly unsatisfactory, and there is an increasing demand for a more autonomous status.

It may also be noted that at the time of the creation of the Central Social Welfare Board, the Government of India had no central department responsible for social welfare. With the establishment of the Department in 1966, and its increasing role in planning and execution of various welfare programmes, the Central Social Welfare Board's position has become still more anomalous. Uncertainty regarding its ultimate status and consequently of the State Boards has had a very adverse effect on their functioning.

At a Conference of State Ministers of Social Welfare held in July, 1992, recommendations were made for the reorganizations of the Central Board. This reorganization was dependent upon the adoption of a general enabling enactment. The State Governments, who had been advised to implement recommendations of this Conference with regard to the State Welfare Boards, were asked to defer action until the reorganization of the Central Social Welfare Board.

At a second Conference of the Social Welfare Ministers and Secretaries held in January 1974, discussion covered four major points. In regard to functions of the Central Social Welfare Board, it was decided that in addition to its executive functions, the Central Social Welfare Board should be responsible for the following: (a) To advise the government on the problems and provision of measures for the welfare of women, children and handicapped; (b) To promote investigation into the study of problems in specific areas, particularly those affecting women and children; (c) To arrange training for social workers at all levels for promoting the involvement of women in national activities; and (d) To provide technical guidance to voluntary organizations for effectively rendering welfare services.

In regard to the composition of the Central Social Welfare Board, the Conference urged that all the Governments of States and Union Territories by rotation, should be represented on the executive committee and the General Council of the Central Social Welfare Board. In conformity with their demand for greater control over the State Boards, the States and Union Territories wanted a greater voice in the nomination of State Board members. With regard to relationship between the Central and State Social Welfare Boards, some States wanted them to be set up by State Governments, while others wished to register them as independent societies.

Difficulties Faced by Field Agencies: Because of the present variations in status and functions of these multiple agencies for welfare and development activity, the field staff experiences many difficulties. The procedure for the release of grants to a voluntary agency often takes about six months and a great deal of hardship is faced by the voluntary agencies whose meagre resources often do not permit continuation of the programme. The uncertainty felt by the staff seriously hampers their work. Many voluntary agencies informed us that they do not have trained workers to manage the accounts in the manner required by the government.

The ad hoc nature of the programmes, their frequent conversion under the various Plans, and the reluctance of State Governments to take over maintenance have also caused a great deal of uncertainty among the field staff. For example, in the case of the Family and Child Welfare Projects, at the end of the Fourth Plan period, 13 States and 3 Union Territories have agreed to accept the responsibility. Six States have not agreed and the continuation of 74 projects are now uncertain. It is proposed to absorb them in the Integrated Child Development Programme. The feeling of the Board in this matter is clear. "With more time, more projects could have been started in consultation with State Governments. The proposed change in the nomenclature and contents of the programme and transfer of all the programmes from the Board to the State Governments, without ensuring continuity by allowing sufficient time for the existing schemes to achieve their objectives, only tend to confuse the rural population."

The staff of the Central Social Welfare Board and the State Boards are not considered on par with government employees and do not enjoy the same facilities and benefits. Their status at the field level is also temporary and dependent on the allocation for the year or the life of the projects. They have a feeling of uncertainty because of the temporary nature of their appointment which is dependent on the continuance of the scheme. They face a number of difficulties, particularly accommodation problems.

We met a large number of these field workers in various States. In our experience, the workers from voluntary organizations and the Board's staff have, on the whole, established better relationship with the village community, since they are better motivated and dedicated to welfare work, as compared to government functionaries who are more concerned with their service conditions, promotion, etc. The Board's cadre are more knowledgeable about the programmes in their areas and can give a better idea about the difficulties with regard to their implementation.

In recognition of this problem, the Department of Social Welfare has, recently examined the service conditions of the staff of the Board, and some of recommendations of the Third Pay Commission have been made applicable to employees of the CSWB. An officer on special duty was appointed by the CSWB in 1973 for drafting service regulations for its employees. The draft is now under examination by the Department of Social Welfare and is expected to be finalized in the near future.

Deficiencies of the Programme: While most programmes for women have emphasized acquisition of knowledge and skills to improve their efficiency as housewives and mothers, and to improve their earning power, they have neglected the dissemination of information, particularly regarding their rights and duties, which could increase their awareness and improve their participation as citizens. The objective of improving their earning power has also not been adequately fulfilled.

Role of Voluntary Agencies: Though it would be difficult to demarcate territories, the relationship of the voluntary and the Government sector should be all along complementary and mutually supportive. The present relationship between these two have not been very satisfactory and a number of complaints have been voiced on both the sides. Ideally the Voluntary Sector should provide services for implementation of welfare programmes, while the financial contribution should come from the Government. Further, the voluntary agencies have a surveillance role to play to see to what extent social legislation and the Government have contributed and can contribute to social welfare.

Voluntary organizations complain of lack of involvement with Government programmes since they are not consulted at the planning stage. Being totally outside the decision-making process, they have been reduced to the level of grant receiving agencies. Due to paucity of funds many voluntary agencies have come to rely heavily on the Government and in this process, the initiative and humanitarian impulse of voluntary welfare work has been considerably reduced. The basic concept of social work is that it should arise out of the local community needs. Voluntary agencies have repeatedly stressed that they should be equal partners with the Governments in the fields of welfare and accountable only for rendering proper accounts for grants. At the policy planning level, voluntary agencies desire that their experience and advice should be taken into account.

The voluntary agencies also express difficulties faced by them because of lack of training of their workers. Training facilities should be provided by the Government, if possible. Without technical and organizational competence, they are unable to utilize resources in the most productive manner. One of the representatives of a voluntary organization needed to review their organizational structure with a view to improving the managerial and professional competence of their workers.

The rising cost of living has reduced funds from private sources. It has also affected the ability of women to devote the same time and resources to voluntary work. Consequently, the area of constructive work of most of these voluntary agencies is limited to their neighbourhood.

The Conference of State Ministers and Secretaries of Social Welfaré held in January 1974, earmarked the following programmes as of interest to voluntary organizations: (1) Socio-economic programmes organized broadly on a cooperative basis; (2) Condensed courses of education for adult women; (3) Functional literacy for women; and (4) Integrated Child Development Service Programme.

It was also agreed that the procedures and rules for making grants should be liberalized, and new ways found for raising and training voluntary workers, to ensure greater coordination amongst them and to improve the dialogue between governmental and non-governmental sectors at all levels, particularly at the district level. This can succeed only with a change in the approach to the voluntary sector.

New Prospects

Health and Family Planning: While welcoming the proposed integration of family planning and maternity and child health services in the Fifth Plan, we wish to offer certain suggestions with regard to its organization at different levels, so that the objective of integration is not defeated by organizational separatism.

1. The rank of the Chief Executive for the integrated maternity and child health services, including family planning, should be upgraded to at least that of an Additional Commissioner, so that this service does not again become subordinate to Family Planning. This procedure should be adopted at all levels of the administration at the Centre and the States.

2. A separate budget head for maternity and child health services should be created, drawing on the provisions now made for family planning and the general health services. It is important to increase the provision for these services to avoid their being neglected, as has been the trend so far.

Since programmes for immunisation and nutrition of infants yield better results when they form a part of general maternity and child health services, we see no difficulty in increasing the allocation for these services.

3. At the level of the primary health centres, the maternity and child health services should be separated for purposes of administrative supervision, provision of medical personnel and budget. While they may share the same buildings and equipment, a separation of the administrative structure required for maternity and child health services will ensure greater priority of treatment. It has often been found that the services of the lady doctor, lady health visitor and the auxilliary nurse-mid-wife, are unavailable to the poorer sections of the rural community. The primary health centres have to cater to the whole population, and women and children do not always get the priority of treatment in the way of medical attention or medicines and other facilities. Separating the MCH Unit will limit the clientele to the women and children, and make the services more accessible to these weaker groups. The allotment of facilities in the way of maternity beds, equipments for immunization of children and family planning for women could be allocated to the MCH Unit. The PHC could be responsible for sterilization operations for men along with other general health services. The proposed Integrated Child Development Programme calls for a coordinating agency at the implementation level, to coordinate all the nutrition and immunization measures which form a basic component of the programme. If the MCH Unit is separated as suggested above, these functions could be allotted to it.

Yet another function that could be undertaken by these Units with suitable provision of staff, is that of maintenance of fertility and morbidity statistics for women and children, the absence of which has made it impossible to undertake any substantial research and evaluation in these fields.

4. We recommend that each MCH centre should collect this data which should be studied and evaluated at the district level by persons of required competence. This will call for a health statistics section at the district level.

   The separation of the MCH Services with family planning as a component at all levels will be a step towards a system of health services which would be reasonably accessible to women and children for preventive, diagnostic and supportive treatment, no matter at which point or stage the patient enters the system.

5. We recommend the abolition of the present practice of providing financial incentives to promoters of family planning.

6. We also recommend that incentives to women who accept family planning should be in the shape of a token or certificate to ensure them higher priority in health care facilities for both the mothers and their children. Such a step will promote greater acceptance of family planning and correct the social attitude towards these practices. Compensation for loss of wages during sterilization operations should however be paid to daily wage earners. Others should be given paid leave for this purpose.

7. The qualifications prescribed for recruitment of personnel for these services in rural areas need to be gradually raised. Until women of requisite higher qualifications are available, the present requirements may continue, but they should be reviewed and progressively increased after every 3 years. Attempts should also be made to obtain the services of older and mature women for these services in the rural areas.

8. We further recommend the promotion of research in the field of female disorders, e.g., puerperal psychosis and the ill-effects of family planning methods on their health.

9. We disapprove the denial of maternity benefits to women in government service after three children, as adopted by some State Governments, and recommend rescinding of such orders.

10. We also recommend that mass campaigns for family planning should also aim to correct prevailing social attitudes regarding fertility and metabolic hereditary disorders, and the sex of the child for which the woman is generally blamed. Correct information in these matters would go a long way to improve the status of women.

11

Planning and Women

Women's development began mainly as a welfare oriented programme in the First Five-Year Plan (1951-56). The Central Social Welfare Board (CSWB), set up in 1953, undertook a number of welfare measures through the voluntary sector. The Second Five Year Plan (1956-61) organized women into Mahila Mandals to act as focal points at the grassroot levels for development of women. The Third, Fourth and other Interim Plans (1961-74) accorded high priority to education of women and introduced measures to improve maternal and child health services, including supplementary feeding for children and nursing mothers, etc.

The Fifth Plan (1974-78), saw a shift in the approach for women's development from 'welfare' to 'development' to cope up with several problems of the family and the role of women. The new approach aimed at an integration of welfare with development services.

The Sixth Five-Year Plan (1980-85), marked a landmark in the history of women's development by including a separate chapter and adopting a multidisciplinary approach with a three pronged thrust on health, education and employment.

In the Seventh Plan (1985-90), the development programmes for women continued with the major objective of raising their economic and social status to bring them into the mainstream of national development. A significant step in this direction was to identify/promote the 'beneficiary-oriented programmes' for women in different developmental sectors which extend direct benefits to women.

The Eighth Five-Year Plan (1992-97), which was launched in 1992, marked 'a shift from development to empowerment in approach to women development schemes. It promised to "ensure that the benefits of development from different sectors do not bypass women" and women must be enabled to function as equal partners and participants in the development process.

In the Ninth Five-Year Plan (1997-2002), two major, steps towards gender justice had been taken for the first time in the history of planning. Their first is the listing of empowerment of women as a major plan objective. The other is to propose inclusion of a Women's Component Plan in the Plan of all Central Ministries/ Departments and State Governments/Union Territory Administrations. The Tenth Five-Year Plan has carried forward this mission. However, its achievements are awaited.

Official Schemes

In addition to the women-specific and women-related policies enunciated in various Plan documents, the government has been creating an enabling environment in which women's concern can be reflected, articulated and redressed by the governments, the voluntary sector and the corporate world. As part of this effort, many policy instruments have been brought forth over the years, leading to Action Plans and programmes in several spheres. Some of the important policy-guiding documents include The National Plan of Action for Women, adopted in 1976, which became a guiding document for development of women till 1988, when a National Perspective Plan for Women was formulated. The National Perspective Plan for Women (1988-2000) drafted by a core-group of experts is more or less a long-term policy document advocating a holistic approach for development of women. Shram Shakti - the Report of the National Commission on Self-employed Women and Women in Informal Sector (1988) examines the entire gamut of issues facing women in unorganized sector and makes a number of recommendations for the betterment of women in the informal sector relating to employment, occupational hazards, legislative protection, training and skill development, entrepreneurship development, marketing and credit, etc. The National Expert Committee on Women Prisoners (1986) examined the condition of women prisoners in the criminal correctional justice system and made a series of recommendations relating to necessary legislative reforms, prison reforms and reforms of other custodial institutions and rehabilitation of prisoners insofar as women prisoners are concerned. The National Policy for Children adopted in 1974 considers children as country's supreme assets. Therefore, the State accepts their nurture as its own responsibility. Further, it also recognizes child development as an important step in building up human resources which are pivotal to the economic and social progress of the country. The National Nutritional Policy articulates nutritional consideration in all important policy instruments of Government and identifies short-term and long term measures necessary to improve the nutritional status of women, children and the country as a whole. The National Plan of Action for the Girl Child (1991-2000) is an integrated multi-sectoral decadal Plan of Action for ensuring survival, protection and development of children with a special gender sensitivity built for girl children and adolescent girls. In addition to these women specific policies, there are many more women-related policies, like National Health Policy (1983), National Policy on Education (1986), National Population Policy (1993), which have been influencing the welfare and development of women and children in the country. The National Policy for the Empowerment of Women has been drafted after nationwide consultations to enhance the status of women in all walks of life on a par with men and to actualize the constitutional guarantee of equality without discrimination on grounds of sex.

The various developmental plans and programmes over four developmental decades (1951-1991) have brought about perceptible improvement in the socio-economic status of women in the country. Important achievements have been made in major thrust areas.

In the field of health, significant gains in respect of women's health status have been achieved. Expectancy of life for females at birth which was 31.6 years in 1951, was estimated to rise 59.7 years in 1989-93. The infant mortality rate for females declined from 131 in 1951 to 75 in 1993. Similarly, the sex differential, which was quite high in the 70s has now been bridged. However, the 0-4 age specific mortality rate, even though it has significantly declined from 55.1 in 1970 to 24.8 in 1993, continue to show higher female mortality. The maternal mortality rate in rural India still continues to be uncomfortably high at 324 per 1,00,000 live births although it showed a declining trend from 468 in 1980 to 324 in 1989 (Source: RG's Office, 1991).

Similarly, in the field of education, a number of steps were taken up for promoting women's education and equality in line with the National Policy of Education, 1986. The main strategy for education was a distinct orientation in favour of women's equality and empowerment. There is considerable improvement in female literacy as it came up to the present rate of 39.19 per cent from 8.9 per cent in 1951. The enrolment rate of girls in primary schools has also improved from 24.8 per cent in 1950-51 to 92.6 per cent in 1994-95. The drop-out rates amongst girls at primary level showed a continuous decline from 62.5 per cent in 1980-81 to 37.8 per cent in 1994-95. However, the higher decadal growth rate of female literacy (66 per cent) as compared to male literacy (43 per cent) provides some consolation.

In the field of employment, the female work participation (total workers) has grown from 19.7 per cent in 1981 to 22.3 per cent in 1991. This could be to some extent, due to the special efforts made by the nodal department of women and child development to capture women's work in the informal sector and, thus, remove their present invisibility. Similarly, number of women in the organized sector has also risen from 12.2 per cent (27.9 lakh) in 1981 to 15.4 per cent (42.3 lakh) in 1995, recording an increase of 51.6 per cent. Of the total 42.3 lakh women in the organized sector, public sector accounts for 61.5 per cent while the private sector accounts for 38.5 per cent.

Further, employment of women in the Central Government has also been rising steadily from year to year. Women's share has grown from 3.64 per cent in 1981 to 7.58 per cent in 1991 reflecting a change in women's participation in the government. At the senior and middle management levels, though limited at present, their participation has increased marginally from 875 in 1985 (based on the data related to 12 selected all India and their allied services) to 1,511 in 1995-96 (8.4 per cent). Women's participation in decision making in the government (taking the IAS, IPS and IFS services into account) has also increased from 379 in 1985 to 631 in 1996 showing an increase of 66 per cent over a period of 11 years.

Actions Taken

Creation of Separate Nodal Agency-Department of Women and Child Development: The first step initiated by the government to strengthen the national mechanism and focus on women's development was the setting up of an exclusive Department of Women and Child Development (DWCD) under the Ministry of Human Resource Development in 1985 and designating the same as the national machinery for the advancement of women in India. The support structures of the national mechanism, as instituted over a period of time include the Central Social Welfare Board (CSWB), a charitable company registered under Section 25 of the Indian Companies Act, 1956 assisting both in promoting voluntary action and implementing programmes fully funded by the Department; the National Institute of Public Cooperation and Child Development (NIPCCD), a society registered under the Societies Registration Act, 1860 extending both research and manpower development services to the Department; the National Commission for Women (NCW), a statutory body set up in 1992 for safeguarding the rights of women; the Rashtriya Mahila Kosh (RMK), set up in March 1993 to extend credit to poor and assetless women through the intermediation of NGOs; the National Children's Fund to support projects of NGOs for Child Development/Welfare and the National Creche Fund to extend assistance to NGOs to open new creches.

In March 1997, Joint Committee of Parliament on Empowerment of Women has been set up with the functions of examining measures for women's equality and considering the reports of NCW, among others.

The Department, in its nodal capacity, formulates policies and programmes, enacts/amends legislations affecting women and coordinates the efforts of both governmental and NGOs working to improve the lot of women in the country. The programmes of the Department, which are women specific, include - employment and income generation, welfare and support services and gender sensitization and awareness generation programmes. These programmes play the role of being both supplementary and complementary to the other women related development programmes in the sectors of health, education, labour and employment, rural and urban development, etc., being implemented by different sectors. Some of the important on-going interventions of the Government of India are detailed below.

Organisations at Work

In order to give the necessary thrust to development of women in the states, Women's Development Corporations (WDCs) were set up in 1986-87. The major objective of the scheme is to play the role of catalytic agents to create sustained income generating activities for women to provide better employment avenues for women so that they can become economically independent and self-reliant.

The functions of WDCs are to identify women entrepreneurs; to prepare a shelf of viable projects and provide technical consultancy services, to facilitate availability of credit through banks and other financial institutions (through the scheme of marginal money assistance); to promote and strengthen women's cooperatives and other organizations; and to arrange training of beneficiaries in concerned trades, project formulations, financial management, etc., through existing institutions, such as women's polytechnic and ITIs.

So far, such WDCs have been set up in Andhra Pradesh, Goa, Gujarat, Haryana, Himachal Pradesh, Jammu & Kashmir, Karnataka, Meghalaya, Orissa, Punjab, Tamil Nadu, Uttar Pradesh, West Bengal and Union Territory of Chandigarh. As per the decision of the National Development Council, in its meeting held in December 1991, the scheme stands transferred to the State sector in April 1992.

Rashtriya Mahila Kosh was set up as a registered society under the Registration of Societies Act, 1860 in March 1993 to meet credit needs of poor women, particularly in the informal sector, who have little or no access to formal credit institutions.

The policies and procedures for lending to women borrowers through the intermediation of NGOs and other women organizations like cooperative societies, WDCs, etc., for which suitable eligibility criteria, such as lending/credit management experience, sound financial management, etc., have been prescribed by the governing board of the RMK.

An amount of Rs 31 crore was released to the Kosh during 1992-93 as the corpus fund. Short-term loans and long-term loans per borrower are extended through the medium of NGOs, and other eligible organizations. Since inception, total sanctions of Rs 3,355-99 lakh have been issued to benefit 1,88,146 women through 154 agencies as on March 14,1997.

Mahila Samriddhi Yojana (MSY). In pursuance of government's policy to empower women by raising their socio-economic status, an innovative MSY was launched on October 2,1993. The scheme aims at promoting self-reliance and a measure of economic independence among rural women by encouraging thrift.

The DWCD implements the scheme through 1.32 lakh rural post offices working under the department of posts.

MSY has received a very enthusiastic response from both rural and tribal women, including those living in the remote areas of the country. Since inception of the scheme, 2.46 crore women have opened accounts with a total deposit of Rs 265.10 crore, till March 1997.

Indira Mahila Yojana (IMY). In order to coordinate programmes and facilitate their convergence to empower women IMY was launched as a strategy on August 20,1995. It proposes to bring out a mechanism by which there could be a systematic coordination and a meaningful integration of various programmes of different sectors to meet women's needs and to ensure that women's interests are taken care of and provided for under each scheme. This mechanism will be operated at the district level as a 'sub-plan' for women to percolate down to the village level appropriately through the Indira Mahila Kendras (IMKs) at village level and Indira Mahila Block Kendras (IMBKs) at Block level to be established as a registered society and supported by mechanisms at both State and Central levels. The ultimate objective of IMY is to empower women by ensuring their direct access to resources through a sustained process of mobilization and convergence of all the on going sectoral programmes. The IMY will be operated as a Centrally sponsored scheme.

The major objectives of IMY include: (1) to ensure convergence of sectoral service at the local, Block and district levels through active involvement of women and sectoral departments; (2) to optimise utilization of scarce resources in speeding up of process of mainstreaming of women in development; (3) to create awareness in women through provision of information on different developmental programmes and issues of specific concern to women; (4) to initiate a process of awareness generation/education to enable them to understand, and analyse their problems and find solutions through their collective interaction; and (5) to help women become self-reliant and independent by their economic empowerment through income generation activities and active participation in decision-making at various stages.

The IMY has three basic constituents, namely, convergence of inter-sectoral services; income generation activities; and sustained process of awareness generation/education. Under the proposed convergence of inter-sectoral services, IMY will provide the umbrella cover and all sectoral programmes aimed at women's welfare, including non-formal education, training, formal primary education, skill development, health, family welfare programmes and other minimum needs programmes like drinking water, sanitation, housing, roads, electrification, etc., would converge at the village level as per the needs, demands and requirements articulated by the IMK. Income generation activities include creation of employment opportunities through group dynamics and participation in a broad range of economic activities suited to the local requirements and use of thrift and credit services to expand the income-generating activities. Under a sustained process of awareness generation/education, IMY seeks to create a general awareness among women through ensuring information specific to equality of social status, legal rights, like those to property and inheritance, constitutional safeguards and on different development, programmes/ issues of concern to women.

In addition to amount of Rs 5,000 given by the Government of India to the corpus fund of the IMK, each member of the IMK shall contribute Rs five as membership fee and will continue to contribute Re one per month to the Kendra. Such nominal contribution by each member will create a corpus of fund and ensure their effective and continuous participation in the group activities.

The corpus so formed will be used as a revolving fund for small credit requirements of the individual members and send money wherever necessary, and for expenditure on holding of awareness generation camps and any other activity resulting in furtherance of the cause of IMY.

The IMY has been taken up in 200 Blocks of the country, on a pilot basis and will be extended in the subsequent years. Selection of these Blocks will be decided by the States keeping in mind the need to ensure maximum convergence of services; care will be taken to ensure that the Blocks are compact and not dispersed over, a number of districts. The IMY will initially be sanctioned for a period of seven years starting from 1995-96. The number of IMBs registered is 113 and the functional Indira Mahila Group (IMG) is 13,717, till March, 1997.

Training for Employment

In line with the Eighth Plan strategy, the nodal DWCD has reset its priorities to accord special emphasis on employment and income-generation activities for women. The ultimate objective in all these efforts is to make women economically empowered and self-reliant. For this purpose, the Department implements some programmes directly through voluntary organizations and interacts with other departments/ministries to ensure flow of benefits to women through their programmes.

The STEP scheme launched in 1987, aims to upgrade the skills of poor and assetless women, mobilize, conscientize, provide training, and subsequently employment on a sustainable basis in the traditional sectors of agriculture, animal husbandry, fisheries, handlooms, handicrafts, sericulture, social forestry, wasteland development, etc., in addition to the training and employment support, the programme advocates gender sensitization, women in development (WID) inputs and provision of support services.

Since inception of the programme 61 projects benefiting 3.32 lakh women, have been launched in various states. Dairying, handlooms, handicrafts and sericulture have been some important areas, since inception of the scheme till March 1997, it has provided employment opportunities for 3.32 lakh women with a total expenditure of Rs 94.13 crore. In 1996-97, 12 projects to benefit 76,875 women were sanctioned with a total expenditure of Rs.17.00 crore.

The second major programme of Training and Employment, which is commonly known as 'NORAD assisted Training Programme for Women', extends financial assistance to public sector undertakings/corporations/autonomous bodies/voluntary organizations to train women in non-traditional trades, like electronics, electricals, watch assembly and manufacturing, computer programming, printing and binding, handlooms, garment making, weaving and spinning, hotel management, fashion technology and beauty culture, tourism, bakeries/ confectionery and office management, etc.

During the Eighth Plan, an expenditure of Rs 38.28 crore has been incurred benefiting 79,797 women. Since inception in 1983, 1,10,002 women benefited with training for employment. In 1996-97, 275 projects to benefit 50,000 women/girls were sanctioned with a total expenditure of Rs 19 crore.

In the recent past, there was a progressive shift and increased attention on the most upcoming modern trades, like computer operation, electrical appliances, bakery and confectioneries, fashion technology, beauty culture, ANM training, canteen and hotel management, tourism, etc. This programme not only plays a preventive role in keeping the young and adolescent girls away from early marriages but also keeps them gainfully engaged with economic independence and self-reliance.

Various Courses

The CCE&VT scheme, in operation since 1968, has been revised from time to time to provide educational qualifications and relevant skills to needy women so that they become eligible for identifiable remunerative work opportunities.

Under these programmes, voluntary organizations are given grants to conduct courses of two to three years duration for women of the age-group of 15 and above for passing primary/middle/matric and secondary level examinations. Under the Vocational Training Programme, grants are given to impart training to needy women of 15 years age-group in different vocations leading to wage/self-employment. Under these programmes, 5823 courses have been sanctioned during the Eighth Five-Year. Plan and a sum of Rs, 39.07 crore was sanctioned to benefit about one lakh women. In 1996-97, 598 courses were sanctioned with the total expenditure of Rs five crore.

Various Programmes

The Central Social Welfare Board had started the socio-economic programme (SEP) in 1958. Under this programme, financial assistance is extended to voluntary organizations to undertake a wide variety of income-generating activities providing opportunities of 'Work and Wage' to needy women, like widows, destitutes, disabled, etc., particularly those coming from economically backward and underdeveloped areas for setting up industrial units, handlooms and handicraft units, dairy units, and other allied economic activities like piggery, sheep and goat rearing, poultry, etc.

During the Eighth Five-Year Plan (1992-97), an amount of Rs 30.33 crore has been released to 2,457 units to benefit about 20,100 women in 1996-97, 13 units have been sanctioned with the total expenditure of Rs six crore.

The national machinery has spread a wide network for women and large number of welfare and support services for women and children belonging to lower economic strata through voluntary organizations. These support services represent an important plank for empowerment of women as they reduce the burden of child care and employment related problems, as detailed below.

The Infrastructure

Hostels for Working Women: In order to promote greater mobility for women in the employment market, the Department launched a scheme of hostels for working women in 1973 to provide 'safe and cheap' accommodation to single working women who come to the cities/towns for the sake of employment. Under this scheme, financial assistance is provided to the extent of 50 per cent of the cost of land and 75 per cent of the cost of construction of the hostel building to voluntary organizations. Assistance is also extended towards purchase of ready-built buildings. Besides, voluntary organizations, public trusts, local bodies, women development corporations, universities, schools/colleges of social work also are eligible for financial assistance programme. Working women, whose consolidated income does not exceed Rs 5,000 per month, are eligible for accommodation. A resident is allowed to stay in the hostel for a maximum period of five years. Till now 805 hostels with attached day-care centres have been sanctioned to be constructed all over the country to benefit about 56,195 working women and their dependent children numbering about 7,558. In 1996-97, 28 hostels were sanctioned to benefit 3,122 women/girls with the expenditure of Rs 8.25 crore.

Creches for Working/Ailing Mother's Children: The Central Scheme of creches for working/ailing mother's children is under implementation since 1975-76. The scheme is implemented through voluntary organizations. The scheme envisages day-care services for children of the age group of 0-5 years. Service includes health care, supplementary nutrition, sleeping facilities, immunization and play and recreation for the children. The creche workers are employed to look after the children. The scheme of running of creches is being implemented by the Central Social Welfare Board through voluntary social welfare organizations and by two other national level voluntary organizations, viz., Indian Council for Child Welfare and Bhartiya Adimjati Sevak Sangh, all over the country. There are 12,470 creches in action all over the country benefiting 3.12 lakh children. Because of paucity of funds, the scheme has not been expanding and is stagnating at this number since 1988-89. In 1996-97, a total amount of Rs.19.75 crore has been sanctioned. In view of the increasing number of working women even in small towns and rural areas, there is a need for mobilizing the community to provide services of creches on a self-sustaining basis without financial burden on governments, etc.

Short Stay Homes for Women and Girls (SSH): The SSH scheme for women and girls, launched in 1969, extends temporary shelter and rehabilitation to those women and girls who are in social and moral danger due to family problems, mental strains, social ostracism, exploitation or other causes. The services extended in these homes include medical care, psychiatric treatment, case-work services, occupational therapy, educational-cum-vocational training, recreational facilities, etc. Under the scheme, grants are given to voluntary organizations to run short stay homes in various parts of the country. As per the approved schematic budget, each SSH receives an annual grant of Re 1,87,300 towards recurring expenses and Rs 25,000 as one time grant to meet the non-recurring expenditure.

National Creche Fund (NCF): The NCF was set up on March 21,1994 with a corpus fund of Rs 19.90 crore made available out of the Social Safety Net Adjustment Credit of World Bank to meet the growing requirement of opening more creche centres. The scheme envisages that 75 per cent of the centres to be assisted by the Creche Fund would be general creches and 25 per cent centres would be Anganwadi-cum-creche centres. The general creches assisted by the Fund would be on the pattern of the Creche Scheme of the Department of Women and Child Development and would provide children below five years, services which would include day-care facilities, supplementary nutrition, immunization, medical and health care and recreation. Children of parents whose monthly income does not exceed Rs 1,800 are eligible for enrolment. The voluntary organizations/ Mahila Mandals selected for opening the creches are required to open creches in schools or in places close to schools, in rural areas and urban slum areas dominated by SCs/STs. The creches have a maximum of 25 children and normally work for eight hours a day. The voluntary organizations/ Mahila Mandals are encouraged to involve the community in the implementation of the scheme so that the creches become self-supporting.

Gender Equality

Great deal of importance is attached to efforts which, trigger changes in societal attitudes towards women. An integrated media campaign projecting a positive image of both women and the girl child through media and film is the most important component of the governments communication strategy. A large number of TV spots, quickies, documentary films, radio programmes with positive messages about the girl child and women, have been produced by the department to undertake publicity and coverage.

Gender Sensitization: The Women's Development Division (WDD) of the NIPCCD, New Delhi organizes training programmes with a focus on gender issues under the DANIDA Bridging Arrangement as well as its regular activities. These training programmes were organized at national, regional and state levels. Some of the important programmes include para legal training; training of elected women representative of Panchayats; leadership of organization, training of voluntary agencies reaching women; awareness and gender sensitization programmes; incorporation of gender issues in development programmes, etc. The participants of these programmes include government officials, representatives of voluntary agencies, academic and technical institutions.

Under legal literacy, para legal training programmes were organized by the WDD in collaboration with these agencies working for women's emancipation. The major objective of these training programmes were to sensitize the participants about the constitutional, political and legal provisions relating to rights of women; to inform participants about legal structure and procedures; to create awareness about existing support schemes of government and non-governmental agencies and to conscientize them about the scope of rights, their potential to act as pressure groups, to access the entitlements of women. These programmes were organized in West Bengal, Delhi, Himachal Pradesh, Bihar and Haryana.

In the field of training for Panchayat members, training programmes were organized for women elected representatives of Panchayats in Orissa, Karnataka and Madhya Pradesh. About 300 elected women members were trained. The main objectives of these training programmes were to sensitize the leadership qualities among elected women members, to enable them to understand the structure, function and responsibilities of Panchayats and make them aware about various development programmes implemented at the grass roots level.

Besides, the WDD also organized training programmes on leadership and organization of grass roots level women, incorporating gender concerns in Prime Minister's Rozgar Yojana, courses for superintendents of remand homes/jails on custodial justice to women and children sensitization programmes for law enforcement machinery, media campaign on pilot project on gender issues in credit and support services, orientation training programmes for police personnel on atrocities against women, issues and interventions, consultation on women in human settlement development, awareness generation on constitutional and legal rights for women, consultation on violence against women, etc.

Awareness, Generation Projects for Rural and Poor: The programmes of Generation Awareness Projects was introduced in 1987-88. It aims at identifying the needs of rural and poor women and generating awareness among them of their status in the family and society and to activate them to work for achieving their rights and to deal with social issues, like community health and hygiene, technology application and environment, etc. The camps organized under the programme provide a platform for rural poor women to come together, exchange their views and ideas and in the process develop an understanding of their problems and come out with ways to tackle them.

Safety Measures

The programme of Education Work for Prevention of Atrocities Against Women, started in 1982, extends financial assistance to research and academic institutions like universities, colleges/ women's study centres and institutions of higher learning etc., and voluntary organizations for various items of education work, propaganda, publicity and research work such as production of publicity materials, research studies on particular aspects of violence/ atrocities against women; awards for best films, short stories, poems and other creative efforts, etc. Dissemination of information/publicity materials in regional languages is also envisaged under this programme. The focus is on those women who are subjected to deprivation, brutality, extortion and exploitation.

Supportive Programmes

The ICDS - gift to millions of children and mothers living in the most backward rural, tribal areas and urban slums all over the country - aims at improving nutritional and health status of preschool children, expectant and nursing mothers and adolescent girls through a package of services, viz., supplementary nutrition, immunization, health checkup, referral services, treatment of minor illnesses, pre-school education and nutrition and health education. Started in 1975-76, with 33 projects, the scheme has expanded gradually and reached, by June 30, 1997 to 5,614 ICDS projects by covering 3,663 Community Development Blocks and 260 major urban slums. Of the 5,614 projects, 3,397 are under Central sector projects and the rest of the 510 projects (including 316 TINP projects) are in the state sector. These projects benefit around 198.44 lakh (19.84 million) children and 35.37 lakh (3.54 million) mothers/women.

Of the total 5,614 ICDS projects, around 1000 projects located in Andhra Pradesh, Bihar, Madhya Pradesh and Orissa are receiving assistance from World Bank to enrich the services with innovative activities.

It is proposed to universalize ICDS at the earliest to cover all Child Development Blocks/urban slums. Of these, 500 Blocks/slums are being taken during the current year, while the balance of over 1400 Child Development Blocks/slums are proposed to be covered during 1996-97 or in future years depending on the resource position and capacity of the States to operationalize the new Blocks.

For the first time in India, a special intervention has been devised for adolescent girls using the ICDS infrastructure. The scheme of adolescent girls focuses on school drop-out girls in the age group of 11-18 years and attempts to meet the special needs of nutrition, education, literacy, recreational and skill development of adolescent girls. It attempts to make the adolescent girl a better future mother and tap her potential as a social animator. The scheme for adolescent girls has been sanctioned in 507 Child Development Blocks and, when fully operationalised, would benefit about 4.50 lakh girls.

Revolutionary Steps

National Commission for Women: In January, 1991, the government constituted a statutory body called National Commission for Women (NCW) with a specific mandate to study and monitor all matters relating to the constitutional and legal safeguards provided for women; review the existing legislation to suggest amendments wherever necessary; and to look into complaints involving deprivation of the rights of women. Similar Commissions have also been set up in nine States. The NCW has taken up a number of activities which include (a) Setting up of 11 expert committees to tender advice on various women's issues; (b) conducting Pariwarik Lok Adalats, to which nearly 35,000 cases were referred; (c) Complaints and Pre-litigation Cell; (d) Legal awareness; (e) Welfare of women prisoners under trials; and (f) Action on issues of women and children.

Legal Literacy Manuals: Ten legal literacy manuals were brought out in 1992 to educate women about the laws concerning their basic rights. These manuals have been written in a simple and illustrated format so that even semi-literates and neoliterates are able to comprehend them. They cover a wide range of subjects, namely, laws relating to working women, child labour, contract labour, adoption and maintenance, Hindu, Muslim and Christian Marriage Laws, including right to property, dowry, rape, kidnapping and police procedure. The manuals have been distributed to State governments and NGOs for wider dissemination and are being translated into many of the Indian languages.

The National Plan of Action of Children (1992) and The National Plan of Action for the Girl Child (1991-2000 AD): The two Plans of Action are both integrated and multi-sectoral in their approach to ensure survival, protection and development, of children with an ultimate objective of building up a better future for children. While the Girl Child - being an integral part of the total target group of children - is expected to derive full benefits from the general Plan of Action, her gender-specific needs will be taken care of by the Plan of Action for the Girl Child with a focus on the adolescent girls.

National Resource Centre for Women: Government is also finalizing a proposal to set-up the National Resource Centre for Women and three State Resource Centres for Women which will act as an apex body for promoting and incorporating gender perspectives in policies and programmes of the government. A pilot project to test the concepts and methodologies underlying the National Resource Centre has been successfully implemented.

For the first time in the history of demographic records, an attempt was made to capture women's work in the informal sector in 1991 census. The provisional data of 1991 census on 'Workers and their Distribution', has shown that there was a substantial increase in the female work participation during 1991 census compared to that of 1981.

Reservation for Benefits for Women Under Poverty Alleviation Programme: Under various poverty alleviation programmes of rural development sector, 40 per cent of benefits have been reserved for women belonging to the below poverty line groups (families whose annual income is about Rs 6,000 to Rs 11,000).

Reservation for Women in Grassroots Democracy: The (73rd and 74th) Constitutional Amendment Bills passed in 1992 by the Parliament marks a holistic event in the lives of Indian women as amendments ensure one-third of total seats (33.3 per cent for women in all elected offices in local bodies whether in rural or urban areas). As a result of this, women have been brought to the centre-stage in the nation's efforts to strengthen democratic institutions at the grassroots level. About 0.8 million have emerged as leaders/decision makers at grassroots levels and entered into public life through the existing 0.23 million all over the country. Of these, about 76,200 are at the village, Block and district levels.

Training in Leadership Development: A massive country-wide training programme was launched in 1993 to extend leadership training for eight lakh women Panchayat members/chairpersons, emerging as a result of the elections to Panchayats and urban local bodies since 1993 when the 73rd and 74th Constitutional Amendment Acts came into force.

Voluntary Action: India has a rich tradition of selfless voluntary action. While the governmental interventions in this sector are operationalized largely through NGOs, the initiatives that the latter have themselves developed are rich and diverse. These efforts have often demonstrated success of alternative models of empowerment and development. Whether it is in the field of credit of poor women or women's health or women's awareness generation or women's literacy, or participatory rural appraisal involving women or organizing women's self-employment groups in traditional and non-traditional sectors of the economy. The Central Social Welfare Board, which is an apex agency of voluntary organizations at national level promotes voluntary action and community participation through its country-wide network of more than 12,000 Voluntary organizations at the grassroots level. Besides these, there are many more voluntary organizations working at block/ district/ state levels in the field of women and child development.

Further Prospects

Holistic Development: The major approach for the future will be to bring in holistic approach for women's development. This underscores harmonization of various efforts in different fronts - social, economic, legal, political and cultural. This calls for consolidation of various programmes and efforts in different sectors of the Government and their integration in a logical fashion to converge various services and facilities required by women. A Sub-Plan approach to package all relevant resources and benefits for women's development will be laid down to ensure their systematic focus on women.

The over-arching strategy component for women's development in the Ninth Plan will comprise mobilization and convergence orchestrated by women's groups and supported by Panchayati Raj institutions. The organization of women will by itself empower them and provide them a forum for articulating their needs and contributing their perspectives to development. This will also give them experience in participatory decision making, thereby building up a cadre of grass root leaders, capable of effective participation in institutions of local government.

This capacity building has to start in the womb, without any deprivation, for the mother of the child, particularly the girl child. Her survival, protection and development as identified in the National Plan of Action for the Girl Child (1992) has to echo through all sectoral programmes. Access-to education, health, information and resources are, therefore, the vital areas of concern, that need to be effectively addressed in future to attain many of the goals for the next millennium.

The thrust in the future has to be on identifying traditional sectors of employment that are shrinking due to technology changes or market shifts, and retrain the women to take up jobs in the new and expanding areas of employment.

The provision of support services is another critical input that can greatly improve women's enhanced economic participation. Promoting women's labour market mobility through an expanding network of working women's hostels, the provision of toilet facilities for women in places of work and widespread provision of creches for working parents are essential if women are to derive maximum benefits from the economic liberalization process.

Future Programmes for Empowerment

Keeping in view the aforementioned experiences, the following specific programmes could be considered for adoption in the future: (i) Expansion of education and training among women; (ii) EDP training; (iii) Provision of child-care support facilities for men and women workers so that either parent can avail of this facility at the work-place and not make it a cost on women's employment; (iv) Provision of hostel and residential facilities to enable women take up employment away from home; (v) Special employment and placement services which should seek to promote employment of women in non-conventional sectors through dissemination of information, counselling, etc.; (vi) Legal protection and legal aid services, (vii) Promotion of women workers organizations through voluntary effort; (viii Protection against flexibility. Considering the new trend towards economic liberalization such protection cannot be ensured through statutory means and should, therefore, be attempted, through negotiations and collective effort. The State, the employers as well as the workers must have separate layers of protection against loss of employment, (ix) Introduction of flexitime, multi-entry, conducive personnel policy on leave, transfer and promotion and training opportunities, to help women retain their jobs or move to new and higher areas of work, (x) Conducive credit policy to access credit to women through appropriate organizational and institutional mechanisms including self-help groups, and (xi) Improvement of the bargaining strength of women workers by encouraging their participation in trade-unions.

The DWCD has recently launched the IMY which is intended primarily to mobilize the women around an integrated delivery system. IMY is a major step towards participation of women in the planning and development processes of their areas. It is also a mechanism that can establish a system of coordination and integration of the sectoral activities. In order to put the need perceptions and the sequential priorities of these women into the Sub-Plans, women would be organized into groups and empowered to participate in the planning process. A sub-plan, consisting of the women's components, would emerge through an interactive process of discussions at the district, block and Panchayat/local levels.

Different developmental schemes and programmes already have quantified components of SCP and TSP. In a like manner, these schemes and programmes could also have a "Mahila Plan" component. It will therefore, be helpful if all Central Plan schemes/ programmes, Centrally sponsored schemes/programme, State plan schemes/programmes and non-plan schemes/programmes identify a Mahila Plan component, with both physical targets and financial outlays. For plan schemes/programmes, such a component should exist for both the Annual and Five-Year Plans.

The basic approach to women's development and empowerment should continue to be based on the theme of convergence, i.e. convergence of the development programmes of different departments of the government to target women through a single delivery system as well as convergence of the efforts of both the government functionaries and community or NGOs in achieving a common objective.

This Women's Day there was reason to rejoice. The Ninth Plan draft document has said that 'empowerment of women' is one of its prime objectives. While this is significant, what is also important is the sub-Plan that was evolved in the run-up to the preparation of the Plan, the fact that a think tank of women was set up to evolve a document that spelt out the specific demands of women in the country. Way back in 1974, the report of the Commission on the Status of Women had called for a sub-Plan, one that would address gender inequities but it was not taken seriously. So while some attempts were made in subsequent Plans to give women a place in the developmental process, it tended to be sectoral and haphazard.

The think tank, comprising academicians, activists and researchers held consultations with the Planning Commission, the Department of Women and Child Development, various ministries and women all over the country. The focus was on building consensus with a view to understanding what women wanted and what is perhaps even more important on what was working and what was not.

The concerns voiced were varied, but the key ones were the right to information about changes, opportunities, options, schemes, services and technologies, the gender sensitization of government functionaries particularly the police and the local administration in the areas of health, agriculture and animal husbandry, and the right to work and employment guarantee schemes.

Liberalization, it was pointed out, is here to stay but women were losing out and will continue to lose out because they have neither the skills nor the legal safeguards to be included.

Other important demands were gender analysis and gender audit of all plans, policies and programmes, the elimination of violence against women and girls through the strengthening of institutional capacity and legal provisions and the decentralization of democracy so that decisions can be taken at levels that are ipso facto more accessible to women.

Happily, if one is to go by the Ninth Plan draft, there is a veritable sea change in Plan perspectives. Until now women's development, to quote the document, was primarily 'welfare oriented'. The focus was always on health, nutrition, education and in the early nineties, on training for employment. Demands that they be recognized as participants in development made little headway. The approach was patronizing and chauvinistic.

The draft is therefore significant promising, as it does, "to create an enabling environment where women can freely exercise their rights within and outside homes as equal partners along with men". It goes on to add that "this will be realized through the early finalization of the 'National Policy for the Empowerment of Women, which lays down definite goals for targets and policy prescriptions along with a well-defined Gender Development index to monitor the impact of its implementation in raising the status of women from time to time. Also significant is the fact that the Ninth Plan directs both the Centre and the States to adopt the 'women's component plan' through which no less than 30 'per cent of funds and benefits are earmarked to the women related sector.

To quote Madhu Dandavate, Deputy Chairperson of the Planning Commission "Women have moved from 'footnote' to an 'objective' in the Ninth Plan" but a lot more will have to be done to ensure that policies are evolved along the lines of the Plan initiatives. Perhaps, as Anita Anand, a member of the think tank suggests, an autonomous body on the lines of the National Organisation of Women in the USA should be set up. Bandhs and dharnas will no longer suffice and a much more sophisticated approach is required in which people with expertise in policy analysis and advocacy will lobby for change. In fact, it must work in tandem with the Planning Commission to ensure the economic and political empowerment of women and gender sensitizing of issues.

The tendency all along has been to direct jobs, resources, political positions, credit et. al., to men especially in the macro sector. The assumption was that the benefits would percolate down to the women and children but, in actual fact, it has only further marginalized them. Panchayati Raj will of course go a long way in remedying these aberrations. Since the passing of the 72nd and 73rd amendments four years ago, almost a million women have come into local politics and in Haryana and Kerala there are all women Panchayats. But, the issues raised by them at the grass roots level will have little success if women's representation in the upper echelons of democracy remains low. Studies conducted in the US on disparities between the blacks and whites have shown how important it is to have a 33 per cent reservation. Anything below this has proved to be ineffective. This is why it is absolutely imperative that the 81st Amendment Bill providing for 33 per cent reservation for women is reintroduced and passed in the next session of Parliament.

12

Benefit of Reservation

Women throughout the world have a low socioeconomic and political status. Even though democracy made great gains in 1989-1991, women members average only 11 per cent of world's legislatures. The presence of woman in formal democratic process is woefully inadequate at all levels, centre, state and local/grassroot level. They are on margin in political decision-making processes. This fact has evoked concern in recent years about the political status of women. It has been increasingly realised that unless empowered politically. the socioeconomic status of women cannot be improved. Thus, the movement for the political empowerment by women has steadily gained momentum today.

World View

A brief outline in international arena regarding the voices raised for political empowerment of women, becomes essential. Preparations were made by the United Nations Organization (UNO) for a convention, way back in 1952, about women political rights. Again in 1967, there was a Declaration on Elimination of Discrimination against women by the UN General Assembly. 1975 witnessed an international conference in Mexico, where a world plan of action was drafted. It emphasised that political participation comprised of women having voting power, their acting as pressure groups, their being elected as representatives and as governmental employees. Again in 1980, there was a conference in Copenhagen, which was named as 'Participation in the Political and other Decision-making Processes and participation in Efforts to Promote International Coperation and Strengthen Peace.' The year 1985 witnessed a conference at Nairobi, where forward looking strategies for the advancement of women and the international blue print for action until year 2000 was planned.

In this context, the 1995 Beijing conference was a landmark, where the focus was on political empowerment of women, and consequently, on the issue of women's reservation. This received an international recognition. The Inter -parliamentary union meeting held in New Delhi on 1997 February 14-18, attended by about 240 representatives from 78 countries, focussed on the theme: 'Towards Partnership between Men and Women in Politics.' The final consensus was that establishment of quota for women's political participation was legitimate and practical. It was also felt that women need to be established in the political system as well in the membership and hierarchies of political parties, and with respect to candidates chosen by them to contest election.

Experiences have proved that despite the constitutional arrangements, women all over the world have not been given actual power. It was realised that democratic norms cannot be realised if marginalised sections, which include women, are not in the mainstream of political process. There will be no change in the political milieu of the country, particularly since most women both as voters and voteseekers are within the patriarchal structure. Not only a change within the existing political structure is required, but also within women's own perception of sensitive issues that directly concern their lives. Why we need the strategy for affirmative action or positive discrimination in favour of women is because the age-old traditions have kept women out of the periphery of political power. This calls for a debate, devising methods through law for their access to political power. This again brings us to the debate on quota system/ reservation for women as a strategy for their political empowerment.

With this backdrop, an attempt has been made to understand the extent and magnitude of women's political participation in free India.

Scene in India

True to the spirit of freedom struggle, and in recognition of the important role played by women in freedom struggle, and also the promises made by the leaders of the nation, the Constitution of India pledges itself to full equality among men and women. The Preamble to the Constitution of India resolved to secure to all its citizens: Justice, social, economic and political; liberty of thought, expression, belief, faith and worship; Equality of status and opportunity; and to promote among them all fraternity assuming the dignity of all individuals and the unity of the nation.

To action these national objectives, the Constitution guarantees certain fundamental rights and freedom such as freedom of speech, protection of life and personal liberty. While these may be termed as positive rights, the negative rights are the prohibition of discrimination on the basis of race, caste, religion, sex or denial of equal protection on such grounds. Indian women are the beneficiaries of these rights in the same manner as men. Article 14 ensures equality before law and Article 15 prohibits any "discrimination" interalia of sex. All these provisions ensure equal opportunity of political participation by women along with men, and that they needed to be represented within the system and the status quo. This false sense of complacency that women have been granted political right along with men on an equal footing by the Constitution, remained for quite some time. Thus, in the 1950s and the '60s there was no such open expression. However, with the '70s studies undertaken by the Committee on the Status of Women in India (CSWI), revealed shocking data (as per 1971 census). This was a watershed year which raised concern among lawyers, thinkers, planners, regarding the servitude position of women in India. Since then, the demand for improvement and the political empowerment of women started at the global level.

The Logic

Before coming to the issue of the strategies, debates and resultants of the problem of women reservation, it becomes necessary to debate on the need for reservation. A very pertinent question arises as to why reservation is the only alternative for the victims of age-old oppression and exploitation? The remedy, if rationally thought upon, can only be either 'equal opportunity' or 'reservation'. For some time, equal opportunity will not work because of the top-dog/under-dog attitude that dies hard. Can there be equallity immediately in an unequal society? Reservation is a means of protecting the weaker sections of society, who have for centuries been socially, historically and politically exploited, giving them a chance to come on a par with the stronger sections and be prepared to take advantage of equal opportunity. Women are in this category a historically victimised group. Women are nowhere in the planning process after five decades of democratic politics. Economic independence cannot alone suffice. Power at political level would only change the status quo, Parliament is a sad spectacle. Reservation, thus, aims at giving not only panchayati women, but all women participation in public Life.

The Committee on the Status of Women in India (CSWI) though agreeing to the problems especially of rural women's life, only recommended the establishment of statutory women's panchayats. In case of state assemblies and Parliament, the committee failed to address the problem of under representation caused by institutionalised inequalities, which 25 years of democracy had failed to dislodge. But with an increase in grassroots organisation, the new groups of poor women demonstrated for greater dynamism and challenge. The issue of reservation was periodically raised by political activists as well as serving women legislators in various government-sponsored conferences.

The Rajiv Gandhi government in 1985, took the issue of women as a priority issue. Subsequently, women's division within social welfare became a Department for Women and Child Development within the Ministry of Human Resource Development. But this did not make much impact, as in 1988, the first draft of the National Perspective Plan (NPP) for women to the year 2000, which recommended 30 per cent reservation for women in all elective bodies - from Panchayats to Parliament, put in a proviso that in the initial years, this quota may be filled by nomination co-option. The final version of NPP, however, only recommended 30 per cent reservation in Panchayats and municipalities to be filled by election. During Rajiv Gandhi's regime, efforts were made to amend the Constitution so as to provide for 33 per cent reservation to women in local grassroots level Punchayat bodies. But the amendment (73rd) was made in 1992 under the next government providing for 1/3 reservation to women in the women panchayats with Schedule Castes and Tribes inbuilt quotas for women. The bill was released is April 1993.

The conferring of constitutional status on local self-government as an integral part of the Indian governance structure, and mandating 1/3rd reservation for women in all these bodies, with an in-built quota for Schedule Castes and Tribes women were quietly ratified in April 1993.

Between 1993 and 1996, women's organisations united for a joint demand for reservation in state assemblies and Parliament. The demand was accepted and featured in the manifestoes of the major parties:

Janata Dal (JD)	The reservation on 30 per cent elective post in local bodies for women has to be extended to union and state legislatures.
Congress	The Congress has already reserved seats for women in the gram panchayat and municipa-lities. It also proposes to provide reservation for women in state assemblies and Parliament.

CPI	Having made a beginning with panchayats, the next step should be to reserve 1/3rd seats for women in state assembly and Parliament.
CP1 (M)	1/3rd of the seats in legislature and Parliament be reserved for women.
BJP	In state assembly and Parliament and all elected position, 33 per cent reservation will ensure that at the dawn of the 21st century, Indian women will have true participation.
Samata Party	The party will initiate legislation for the reservation of constituencies for women candidates in rotation for one third of the seats in both the Lok Sabha and state assemblies.

But against these theoretical assurances, the major political parties are taking vogue positions on the issue of caste-based and religion-based women's reservation regarding four sub-categories within the women quota-backward castes, Muslims, Christians and Sikhs. In September 1996, when the reservation bill was brought before the house, the first obstacle was about the fixed quota women from the other backward castes (OBCs). The main votaries were Sharad Yadav, Ram Vilas Paswan), Mulayam Singh Yadav and other OBC MPs. The main argument advanced by them was that with a blanket reservation, the upper caste women would grab all the party tickets and get supremacy in Parliament.

The pressure was mounting by the women activists. It gained momentum after the ratification in 1993. In 1996 general elections, only 34 (that is, 6.3 out of 537 declared) seats went to Women.

Mainstream national level parties which had a longer history of involving women such as congress, the janata Dal and the Communist Party did not do much better. Only 103 women out of 388, who contested the election to the 11th Lok Sabha were supported by the parties. Congress had 16 women in Parliament. BJP had 14 women and JD had only nine seats. Such induction reflects tokenism rather than power sharing. It could also be termed as the patriarchal frame of society, which has marginalised women in mainstream parliamentary politics.

Political Mockery

Amidst, such a scenario of opposition, the double face of parties and MPs, the Constitution amendment (81st) Bill 1996 was introduced by the United Front Government. All hopes were dashed to the ground at the end of the discussion on an aggressive plea for proportional representation of seats for women belonging to OBC. The bill was then referred to a joint select committee of 32 parliamentarians under Gita Mukherji for amendments with a brief to see if the demand of having reservation for the OBCs from within the 33 per cent could be met. The committee in its final recommendation wanted the bill to be passed at the earliest and rejected the demand for an OBC quota. Both the houses witnessed clamorous scenes with members cutting across party lines.

Once again the government failed to put the bill before Parliament due to strong objections to the bill in its present form. It was deliberately attempted to keep the bill in cold storage by stating that the consensus needed to be evolved.

Although, Prime Minister Atal Behari Vajpayee assured representatives of the women's organisation that he would not only introduce the bill in the Budget session but also put it to vote and the Union Cabinet also approved the introduction of the bill, It was once again put under the lid on the issue that the quota should be slashed to 15 per cent for OBC women. The women's bill was stalled in the Lok Sabha and was finally deferred on July 17.

What does this show? Women's reservation bill is surrounded by shame and hyprocisy and more by male chauvinism. The shelving of the Women's reservation bill calls for a serious debate on the text of the Bill.

Bill : A Piece of Paper

The proposed bill is debated upon from many angles. It requires analysis and discussion. The bill envisaged reservation by rotation of the constituencies through lottery system so any constituency could be selected for the reserved category. The debate and doubt is on the issue of rotational principle.

The Discussion

Senior advocate of Supreme Court Abhishek M Singhvi, has opined that though the rationale is unclear, it appears evidently to be actuated by a desire not to permanently shut men off. He reiterates that the constitutional mandate for rotation of constituencies reserved for women is impracticable and harmful. Madhu Kishwar, Women's activitist also contends that the bill has been drafted irresponsibly. She opines that the rotational principle means that neither male nor female aspirants will know which constituency they can stand from. The result, at least 1/3rd of male legislators will be routinely uprooted and denied seats from their chosen areas of work and Influence, and an equal number of women will be told at the last minute where they can fight an election from. This will further erode the incentive to serve a constituency because everyone will remain forever uncertain about whether or not they can actually get elected from their areas of influence.

To this problem, Madhu kishwar comes out with a suggestive measure. Instead of 33 per cent rotating lottery system of reservation, we provide for 50 per cent reservation by having double member constituencies. This would give women a share of seats in proportion to their population. That is to say, each constituency should be represented by two members, one of which has to be a woman. The other constituency would remain open and general, which means there would be nothing to prevent even two women be elected from it on the basis of winning the highest common vote and the other on the basis of acquiring the highest vote among women candidate. This system will encourage team work among men and women in parties. It will also create a healthy competition between them to serve the constituency. Doubling the figure of MPs will also lighten the load of work and remove the possibility of 'biwi-beti brigade'.

If the rotational principle is not to be eliminated, it may be provided that in case reservation for women in legislatures is to continue beyond the presently mandated duration of 15 years, the next round of reservation after 15 years may commence with new and rotated constituencies.

The delay and debate on the issue of absence of reservation for OBC women, impartially seen has no actual link to the issue of women's reservation in general. It has already marred the process of the actual proposed bill. Reservation for backward classes generally never existed in Indian legislatures. Reservation for Schedule Castes and Scheduled Tribes on the contrary, was a subject of debate in the constituent assembly and found specific inclusion in a specific set of constitutional provisions. Ever since 1992, women reservation in Panchayati Raj institution operated without any linkage with the lack of reservation for OBC women in these institution. Even as CP Bhambhri rieterates that the logic that women should participate in the decision making process gets diluted if participation is on the basis of their religion or caste because they are reduced to the level of sectorial leaders and not women leaders. Veena Nayyar too on the issue contends that the talk of quota within quota is a blatant attempt to divide the women. That they forget about OBC & when it came to the 73rd Amendment because it concerned only governance at the village level and there was no need for considering a system of proportional representation whereby the legitimate political aspirations of each group can be satisfied without breaking down the whole system with competing quotas.

Therefore, quota or no quota only the most deserving should get the benefits. Why not pass the bill as it is first and later decide about the quota within a quota. Women have to begin somewhere. As Kannabiran and Kannabiran contend that women are fighting for the principle of reps mentatim. Women's representation in politics will somehow improve the status of all women including the Dalits, OBCS, etc.

Another argument put forth disfavouring the bill in its present form, is the concern for creating a zenana dabba argument. The objection seeks to encapsulate the apprehension that men will limit women to only 33 per cent which might become a maxima or an upper limit for women's presence in legislatures. But then assuming without conceding that in the first phase women's reservation will result in an upper ceiling of only 33 per cent. It is for stronger presence than the present 6-7 per cent. With the time pace, this would reflect a sufficiently strong voice to result in allotment of ever increasing number of seats.

The one more objection on proxy control and the 'biwi brigade' deserves to be considered. The proposed reservation will be cornered by elite women, by wives, daughters etc. It would be a conflict of personal interest between them and the women at that level.

Basically, the OBC politicians used a clever tactic to stall women's reservation. Caste and communal card was used to confuse the whole issue. The OBC leaders too, were not sincere about either the backward caste women or the Muslim women's share. Supporting the quota for OBC, several women leaders too have come out with their expressions like Salija Kumari, Meera Kumar (CWC member) and Uma Bharti (BJP) Uma Bharti's comment "I'm for 'Mandal and Kamandar' is indeed surprising. Because what is essential today is the general involvement of women at all levels of power structure to ensure a true society, without any quota within quota for political leverage. Mamta Banerjee rightly affirms: "What percentage of OBC and Muslim women candidates Laloo Yadav and Mulayam Singh Yadav had put up in the last election ?" As Brinda Karant opines, there is no reservation for OBC in any state assembly or in Parliament and nor has any such demand ever been raised by OBC. Therefore, to raise the demand, OBC women now is nothing but a pretext to shelve the bill, as it protects the interests of OBC men. The last Parliament had about 200 OBC male MPs. Why are OBC women not there if OBC women's representation is their real concern? Their talk of quotas within quota is a blatant, attempt to divide the women. Madhu Kishwar maintains that mothers and mistresses of powerful men will be used by them as agents or nominees of proxy control. When party tickets are given to the wife of a Kamal Nath as a means of keeping him in power through her, or when wives of local politicians are given panchayat and Zila parishad seats simply because a certain number of women have to be compulsorily fielded in the elections, it makes a mockery of women's participation of politics. Some of the women candidates may be representatives of the parivar syndrome, but it is not a permanent phenomenon 'Biwi brigade' would be easily overshadowed once women realise their power in a democracy; more and more women would come forward to participate in elections, and would be elected on their own merit. Evaluation reports have suggested that women leaders in panchayats have given a greater thrust to the developmental activities in their respective areas. Moreover, the parivar syndrome is not restricted to women alone, this malaise affects men too. Could Laloo Prasad Yadav be stopped from bringing his wife? In any case would Prakash Singh Badal or Farooq Abdullah or Karunanidhi be stopped from fielding their sons? Just because they are men, no one points finger at them. So why question women? This very culture of male-female segregation prevalent in our society adds to the disabilities suffered by women in the political world.

Amongst the various objections to the proposed bill the suggestion for constituencies may be clubbed into one and represented by one male and female member (as also suggested by Madhu Kishwar, discussed earlier in this chapter) - is actuated by an apprehension that simple reservation for women would result in ghettoisation of women and pitting women against women. But this does not have much Innovation. This kind of suggestion does not operate in any legal system or legislatures in the world. Moreover multi-member constituency would not fit in with our existing constitutional alteration of several provisions and chapters of our

Constitution based on representational democracy. It would also raise several other issues regarding the total strength of our Parliament (whether it would remain 550 or become 1, 100), the potential enhanced expenditure involved in maintaining double the member of MPs, the Issue as to which of the two members would speak for the constituency.

Though probe and thought on all these issues still requires more open debate and discussion, one can impartially admit that through reservation the state intervenes to admit the imbalance in an effort to at least rectify it. Abraham Lincoln's (Lincolra's) concept of democracy is an ideal, unachieved in the world. Democracy falls short when women of whatever colour or ethnic group cannot vote or cast an effective vote cannot expect success in electing representatives of their choice or being elected to the legislative bodies, and have little hope for enactment of laws they believe are critically needed.

The arguments pro and against the issue of reservation of women in Parliament, have been quite conflicting and mixed from various comers even after the debate and discussion of the basic text. The politicians, women activists and thinkers are divided on the issue of women's reservation.

Argument against the issue has come up from Shatkari Mahila Aghadi that experience of reservation in panchayat in Maharashtra has not been favourable. The relatives of established male leaders are fielded, with no impact on inefficiency and corruption. Yogendra Makwana calls the bill as an inflated one. What is needed is more women candidates in elections, rather that providing statutory reservation for them in Parliament. Nearly 50 per cent of the voters in our country are women. Should they not exercise their voting strength to get more tickets instead of begging for statutory reservation? He reiterates that in a country where a women ruled for 17 years as Prime Minister in EUP and Congress Vijaya Raje Sindhia and Sonia Gandhi have respectively reached the top position, Najma Haptullah is elected deputy chairperson of Rajya Sabha for the third term and earlier. Margret Alwa was also elected to this position thrice - it seems paradoxical to talk of women reservation in Parliament. Vishwa Hindu Parishad Lobby among EUP MPs does not want women reservation. Ram Vedanti – a VHP block Lok Sabha MP from Pratapgarh along with Uma Bharti and Ganga Charan Rajput agitates on women's quota in business: "Women should not be given any reservation." The Congress Party was no better off than BJP on the women's bill. It forced even its women president Sonia Gandhi to buckle under party MPs' pressure. Rajesh Pilot and P Shiv Shankar led the revolt within the Congress. They demanded 27 per cent OBC quota within the overall 33 per cent women reservation. They questioned why shouldn't BC women get a share when the very concept of women reservation is based on the backwardness criteria. Madhu Kishwar counters the demand for reservation of seats in Parliament and the state assemblies for women with the contention that it would stultify the political process and prevent the emergence of outstanding women who practice better politics of renewal and change.

On the other hand, Promila Dandavate, an avid crusader of women's rights, is in the forefront of the struggle for reservation and a chunk in the power structure for the women of the country. She opines that the quality of parliamentary debate will definitely improve with at least 180 women MPs. Former Union Minister, Margaret Alva too is playing a leading role in mobilising women MPs and other organisations, and is quite disgusted by the way the bill has been treated. Veena Nayyar also favours the bill suggesting there can be no empowerment without power. With the amendment what women are seeking is not reservation but de-reservation that is, male representation be scaled down to 67 per cent from 95 per cent is only when women will acquire an 'effective voice' and become a legislative force will agenda's for women in terms of education, health, shelter, access and control to set targets for their empowerment can be implemented. Margaret Alva has showed her concern for the 5 per cent of meagre representation of women of the total contestants. Of these who get elected constitute a still smaller percentage. Therefore the big task before us today is to ensure justice to reduce the disparities in the opportunities and facilities available to women and make them equal partners in development.

However it would be dangerous to conflate the two discrete spheres of political activity, namely that of Panchayati Raj institution and that of legislatures and Parliament. At the level of Panchayati Raj institution, what matters is the nature and strength of familial and social patriarchy no matter what caste the women may belong to. On the other hand, the women who make it to the legislature and Parliament have usually attained a class status that enables their movement out of the household, and thus, it is the patriarchal power arrangement of the party that matters more. All parties have thus found it convenient to deploy women only strategically, resulting in the emergence of 'biwi brigade'. But today reservation has become an. imperative not an option. The policy of 'tokenism' by having a few women in the legislature and executive wings of government offers serious obstacles to their acting as spokespersons for women's rights and opportunities. If this process continues, women would loose their faith in political process to change their condition. Reservation would provide an impetus to both the women and political parties to give a fairer deal to nearly half the population in the various units of government. The system would generate greater freedom to articulate their views, increase women legislators sense of responsibility and concern for the problems affecting women. Instill socioeconomic change and broadening the political elite structure.

Moreover, women reservation cannot lead to their becoming isolated pockets in the nation because women are not marginal to society as a minority group. It might be a transitional measure to break through the existing structure of Inequalities. This will not be retrogression 'from the doctrine of equality of' sexes and the principle of democratic representation' as felt by representatives of political parties and most women legislators, but it may serve a long-term objective of equality and democracy in a better manner. Women need to represent their own interests. Statistics and social indicators show that women's interest have not been served.

The argument that women should come into Parliament only on their merit, against the 'parivar syndrome' is true, but then their representation is negligible in a merit based system. Reservation should result in less inequality and increased confidence of women. Women if encouraged to participate through reservation will emerge even in nonreserved constituencies. Once women emerge, we can revert to a merit based system. Also, the argument that women's reservation is a play of the upper castes to bring their women into Parliament is not true. Schedule Castes and Scheduled Tribe and OBC men have come into Parliament either through constitutionally mandated reservations or by being given tickets by their parties, they have significant representation in Parliament within their party organisation. It is upto the 'same people' to ensure that party tickets are given for women from minorities and disadvantaged communities.

The possibility that 33 per cent reservation will ghettoise women, has its own reasoning. In the face of the fact that women today are already marginalised, this provision alone could arrest this trend. It will provide them an opportunity to escape from ghettoslation imposed upon them by patriarchal norms and practices.

Reservation reflects the will of the people. It is the part of the common minimum programme of all parties, which make up the United Front (UF) government. The then prime Minister had himself introduced the 81st Amendment Bill in Parliament. The leader of the opposition has fully endorsed the bill in his public address to the nation. The National Policy on Women of the Ministry of Human Resource Development (HRD) has stressed the need for more women to be part of the political decision-making process. The national alliance of women's groups have strongly articulated the need for reservation for women in Parliament and the assemblies. Even after looking at over 100 submissions including the attorney general, the law ministry and the National Commission for Women, the select committee made up of representatives of all parties from both houses has strongly recommended that the bill as amended, be passed without delay and that necessary legislation to give effect to the provisions of the bill may be brought before Parliament at the earliest. So how can it be reiterated that reservation for women is the demand of only a few urban elite women and does not reflect the will of the people? It was indeed surprising, when a positive response in favour of bill, came from a male MP, Anand

Mohan, on the fateful day of July 14, 1998. He seemed to be the only honest male politician in the house to have questioned amidst revolt, "Speaker sir, what about the women's reservation bill?"

The bill would bring roughly 181 women in Parliament. The integration of women in the political process at all levels of political life is essential for the democratisation of politics. Although it is known that some sections of people in the country including the women should take more active interest in public life, this cannot be ensured by a system of reverse preference to ensure a quota for women in legislature. This is the surest way of ensuring that women do not achieve equal status in life. The idea is to bring about a qualitative change with women's participation in these fora rather than bring the level of functioning down further with women simply joining as puppets in this enterprise.

In future electoral contests, parties that show themselves to be sensitive - voluntarily rather than under compulsion to the need for greater female representation could well reap a proportional harvest. This would salvage the issue of gender justice from the detritus of caste prejudice that today surrounds it. Another strategy would be for a diligent study of the patterns of social representation that have emerged from the women's quota in local bodies. The large number of women who have recently assumed office as mayors of important cities is an index of the substantive impact of this measure. Objective observers are convinced that in their social origin, the women who have gained seats in local bodies are as representatives of the underlying caste sub-stratum as are the men. If the appropriate lessons are avidly disseminated before the extrapolation of the principle of reservations to legislative institution many of the political insecurities that have recently emerged well be placated.

13

Social Change

Modern methods of production, marketing and planning call for a higher level of knowledge and those skills that are required by a traditional economy. The increasing complexity and interrelationship among production, investment and the process of competitive selection, increases the importance of education and dissemination of information.

Though educational opportunities did expand in the post-Independence period, it was relatively slower among women, particularly at the primary and secondary levels. The rate of expansion was much faster at the level of higher education, and was the virtual monopoly of the middle-class. In the case of women, both secondary and higher education was practically confined to the urban middle-class. On the other hand, the number of illiterates, who remained outside the reach of the educational system also increased the women outnumbering the men. This pattern of educational development, coupled with the changes in the economy, has, inevitably affected the economic opportunities of women.

The work participation rate by educational level shows that while employment opportunities for educated women have increased, there has been a negative trend in the participation rate of illiterate and semi-literate women, whose share in employment has declined.

During 1981-91 the participation rate for illiterate women had declined substantially from 71.1 per cent to 55.3 per cent in urban areas, but showed marginal variations in rural areas. As pointed out in already, the employment of women has declined significantly both in unorganized nonagricultural occupations and in organized industry. Our review indicates that there is a large-scale displacement of illiterate and semiliterate women workers from organized industry and non-agricultural occupations in the unorganised sector. This is also evident from the fact that the drop has been more marked in the urban areas. A superficial conclusion that could be drawn from this data, is that the decline in the numbers of illiterate or semi-literate women workers, indicates a rising level of education.

The pattern of women's educational development in the years since independence, however, indicates that it has failed to penetrate, in any significant manner, the large mass of illiterate adult women, whose numbers have increased over the years. Since they also come from the poorest section of the population, where employment is a dire necessity, this change in the composition of the women workforce has to be regarded as, an indicator of the displacement of this section of women from the workforce, a consequence of the changing levels of technology, and methods of business organization. The increase in the participation rate of the technical diploma holders from 0.6 per cent to 2.3 per cent, indicates the growing demand for modern technical skills in new industries like electronics, pharmaceuticals, electricals, etc., and in new services for technical personnel. The distribution of degree holders and technical female personnel by labour-force status and level of education indicates that the majority of them were employees and only 2.1 per cent being self-employed.

Among the educated women, the worker rates for women who have received a technical degree and diploma (mainly in teaching and medicine) were substantially higher than those who had received non-technical degree or diplomas or had studied up to the Higher Secondary level. The differential according to fields of specialization of technical degree and diploma holders are smaller among males than among females. The distribution of women degree holders and technical personnel by sector of employment show that 58 per cent are employed in the public sector, 36.6 per cent in the private sector and 5.4 per cent are selfemployed.

The extent to which persons of different educational levels undertake productive roles in the economy is an indicator of the nature of utilization of the investment in their education. Women with degree or diploma in medicine and teaching generally pursue a career. The differential participation rate between such women and their male counterparts in not more than 20 per cent.

The rising participation rate of educated women is also witnessed by the Employment Exchange statistics. Since 1963 the number of female job seekers with matriculation as well as higher education on the live Register has increased more rapidly than for males. Between 1964-68 the number of female job seekers registered with Employment Exchange increased by about 81 per cent while that of male job seekers increased by only 14 per cent. For matriculates and higher educated job seekers the corresponding increases were 72 per cent and 116 per cent for males and females respectively (Visaria, 1971). In 1973 the percentage increase of women work seekers over the previous year was 25.7 per cent for those with qualification below middle school, 39 per cent for matriculates and undergraduates and 95.4 per cent for graduates and postgraduates. This phenomenon assumes importance in view of the relatively rapid spread of women's education in urban India and the paucity of employment opportunities. Taking different subject fields together, the average duration of unemployment is higher for women than for men.

According to the Census of 2001, the average waiting period for a male graduate before getting employment was 9.9 months as against 11.6 months for a woman graduate. The only exception to this is the field of medicine and nursing where the average waiting period for men with postgraduate qualification and with doctorate is higher than for women. This sometimes acts as a strong deterrent for many a woman without specialization from seeking employment.

The total stock of degree holders and technical personnel by subject field, level of education and sex, and the distribution of degree holders and technical personnel who were found unemployed, was obtained by CSIR on individual enumeration slip in 2001. The study revealed that out of 7 lakh women degree holders only two and a half lakh were employed which is only 5 per cent of the total working women in the country. Of these employed women, 52 per cent earned less than Rs. 1000 and 20 per cent earned between Rs. 1000 and Rs. 2000. Of total number of unemployed women graduates only 160,000 women were seeking jobs and the largest number of this component were holding degree -in Arts and Humanities and the next were those holding degrees in Science. Of the women who were not seeking employment, 65 per cent had degrees in Arts and humanities, 60 per cent in Science, 20 per cent in technical or engineering and 10 per cent in vocational courses.

The Tight Corner

The paradox of women's employment is that while illiteracy drives many out of employment, education does not necessarily lead to their employment.

> That participation ratios are not higher has at least as much to do with considerations of status and prestige as with the absence of jobs for those who seek but cannot find them. It is of course conceivable that a more progressive and expanding society could elevate the position of women and change attitudes towards female work. But an economy whose capacity to absorb men of working age is strained, does not encourage the elimination of traditional forms of discriminations against economic activity by women. G. Myrdal (Asian Drama).

Idleness can both be voluntary and involuntary. Since our labour market does not provide full, productive and freely chosen employment and jobs are at a premium, many women prefer to avoid the competitive pressures. Utilization of labour in any society depends to a certain extent on social institutions, taboos and inhibitions related to status and work which affect women more than men. These attitudes are reflected in social institutions, and the relationship between institutions and attitudes is mutually reinforcing.

The development of education has been mainly confined to middle-class families, among whom the attitude to women's employment outside the home had been most restrictive. This attitude however has been changing rapidly under economic pressure and the changing social scene. The real difficulty lies in the failure of the economy to absorb all its labour power and to appreciate the need for an institutionalized pattern of labour utilization that takes note of women's roles as housewives and mothers. So far, in spite of occasional lip service to the idealised image of women in these roles, little attempt has been made to assess its productive value. Still less attention has been given to providing the necessary infrastructure to remove women's disabilities in the labour market. Education alone cannot remove these disabilities.

Professional Education

The need to relate education and particularly vocational training to actual employment opportunities has been repeatedly emphasized by various expert bodies like the ILO, the National Commission on Labour, the All-India Council for Technical Education, the Institute of Applied Manpower Research and the University Grants Commission, Committee on Coordination of University Education with Manpower Requirements.

In view of the current social prejudices against employment of women and their large-scale displacement from employment as a result of structural and technological changes taking place in the economy, vocational training for women requires special attention and priority. This has been emphasized by the International Labour Conference in 1965 and the UN Commission on the Status of Women in each of its reports. In India, the National Committee on Women's Education, had pleaded strongly for better and more extensive facilities for vocational training for women particularly since the general educational system paid little regard to the needs of industry and commerce.

The inadequacy of vocational training opportunities for women, widens the productivity gap between men and women at all levels and makes them unwanted by the economy. Training facilities when they are provided, display the existing social bias regarding the suitability of particular occupations for women which leads to over concentration in a limited group of subjects.

Our examination of opportunities for vocational and technical education for women is based on the following: (a) on the job training; (b) pre-employment training—technical and professional; (c) training programmes undertaken by different Government Departments and Voluntary Organizations for developing skills and human resources. We have not included professional training at the university level because, as will be discussed in the next chapter, there is no real evidence of discrimination or any substantial wastage of training at this level.

The major factor limiting women's contribution to the modern industrial sector is lack of adequate opportunities for on the job training. We have already pointed out that women have been greater victims of rationalization and modernization in industry. Some of the new industries like electronics, simple engineering, telecommunications, etc., provided in-service-training to women with comparatively higher educational qualifications. In spite of opportunities provided by these few industries, however, the disparity in opportunities available to men and women is glaring. Under the Apprentices Act, 1961, 161 trades with 87,000 places have been located for apprentices in 101 industries. 52,500 apprentices have actually been engaged against these places of which only 104 are women. The bias for confining women trainees to limited group of trades is clearly visible.

Representatives of trade unions informed us that the training provided to workers for handling new machinery in different industries, seldom extends to women except in the few specific industries like machine tools, telecommunications and electronics in which women's greater aptitude for particular operation has already been recognized.

In the non-engineering trades where women constitute 64.6 per cent of the total number of trainees, the most popular, trades are cutting and tailoring, embroidery and needle work, knitting, and stenography. Of these, the first two are completely monopolized by women even in co-educational institutions. The situation is very different in the engineering trades where they form a mere 2.7 per cent of the total trainees. The most popular courses are for draftsman, instrument, mechanics, radio and T.V. mechanics, electronics, surveyors, carpenters and painters.

On the recommendation of the National Committee on Women's Education, the Ministry of Education took up a scheme to establish women polytechnics for post-matriculation training in various skills in industrial, commercial and public service occupations in accordance with developing needs of the national economy and to promote awareness of new opportunities and needs for women workers in such fields as social welfare, nursing, chemical and pharmaceutical industries, etc., in which women could be gainfully employed'. The total admission capacity of all these polytechnics is over 3000 for courses which require 2 to 3 years for completion. According to the Ministry of Education in commercial practice, stenography, catering and food technology, the admissions exceed the sanctioned capacity, while in other trades they fall short of the available number of seats. The out-turn for all the courses is considerably lower than the admissions. The total out-turn during 2000 amounted to only 1820 against an admission figure of 4500. This points to both wastage of available facilities as well as a failure in the realization of the objectives of this scheme. In the absence of inadequate assistance in placement, quite a few women on completion of these courses remain unemployed. The second reason for this is that the courses are not designed with any particular consideration for the employment potential of the locality. For example, during the Committee's tour of Andhra Pradesh we were informed by officials of the Industries Department that though there was an increasing demand for women in the telecommunication and electronic industries, none of the women's polytechnics in the State were providing training in these subjects. On our asking why nothing has been done, the officials replied that the control of polytechnics rested with the Department of Education and not industries. In Himachal Pradesh we received a number of requests from women's groups for training in food technology so that the products of their orchards are not wasted but no training facilities of this type exist in that State. Courses introduced are not always in relation to the demands of the region, e.g., dress and costume designing, a significant avenue for employment of women in bigger cities, hardly constitutes an important or a significant source of employment in the interior of the country. A heavy concentration on the same course, e.g., tailoring, also leads to minimization of job opportunities.

In 1968-69 the All India Council for Technical Education had reviewed the functioning of women's polytechnics and came to the conclusion:

1. A direct relationship should be established between course of training provided and employment opportunities available. For this purpose, for each polytechnic, there should be an advisory Committee including representative of employing organizations. Before any new course is started, close consultation should be held with the prospective employers to determine available job opportunities.

2. Each polytechnic should establish a production centre in the relevant field to provide practical training and improve standards and content of the courses. Such production centres might be started with the assistance of small-scale industries departments of the State concerned.

3. Polytechnics should offer short term job-oriented courses in selected fields where employment opportunities exist.

4. Start an employment advisory service for its students.

5. Service units should be established in these institutions to cater to the needs of the local public in such matters as providing practical, services blueprints, model estimates, etc.

Earlier 75 per cent of the non-recurring expenditure and 75 per cent of the recurring expenditure was borne by the Central Government. Since the commencement of the 4th Plan the Central Government stopped direct financial assistance for implementing specific development programme and now it is for the State Government to implement these recommendations.

Unfortunately while the Ministry of Education supplied information regarding the list of sanctioned courses and admission capacity in each of the 24 polytechnics, we were unable to obtain actual information regarding the teaching facilities available in the different institutions. Unofficially information received from different sources suggests that in many of the institutions some of the courses exist only on paper, particularly since the stoppage of central grants. Many of the State Governments find it difficult to provide adequate support to these institutions for their general maintenance. This could account for the very poor number of admissions against the courses for the country as whole. The second reason is the failure to implement the recommendations of the All India Council for Technical Education regarding the opening of production centres and provision of employment advisory service. Technical training for women is a relatively new field in India. In the absence of greater assistance in the placement of successful trainees, parents will be reluctant to send them to these institutions.

It is to be noted that some private institutions providing similar types of training to young women in the large cities, including a placement services, which connect training to the actual employment potential of the area, have proved to be highly successful. Mention may be made here of two institutions in Delhi. The Secretarial Training School, started by the Young Women's Christian Association some years ago has proved to be so successful as to justify its expansion to other types of vocational courses during the last few years. A similar unit started by St. Thomas Girls Higher

Secondary School has also expanded rapidly, and is attracting students with even university degrees. Their success lies in their placement assistance and in the liaison that they maintain with employing agencies.

In the present socio-economic set up, self-employment of women requires much more than training in a particular productive trade. Without knowledge of the market mechanism, and capital resources, training alone cannot help women to face the competition. The production centres recommended by the All India Council for Technical Education as a part of polytechnic training have remained conspicuous by their absence. In our view, without supportive assistance in the way of training in organization of production and marketing and in procuring capital and raw materials, it will not be possible for the majority of these young trainees to utilize their training in self-employment.

The officials of the Industries Department in Andhra Pradesh informed us that in spite of the existence of a Government scheme to provide financial assistance for generating self-employment, the Department has been unable to assist many women to obtain the required help from banks. Even when such projects are sanctioned by Government, banks hesitate to provide the loans as they feel that the life of the projects may terminate when these young women get married.

Organisations at Work

Unlike the more formal programmes of pre-employment training, in the sphere of informal training programmes, a great deal of emphasis has been given to training women by various agencies in charge of development and welfare. All agencies specifically concerned with women's welfare and development, both government and voluntary, have always attached the highest priority to improving women's earning capacity.

Schemes for Betterment

Programmes have been developed to solve the economic needs of women hard pressed by the processes of social change and break-down of familiar obligations to support needy women widows, deserted and aged women as well as women from lower income groups.

(i) The Central Social Welfare Board is the most important agency providing assistance for these programmes operated by autonomous and voluntary organizations. It provides financial assistance for setting up production units in small-scale industries, handicrafts and ancillary units for larger industrial undertakings. In 1999-2000, 54 handicraft units were functioning with an employment potential of 2000. Apart from this, 31 handloom training-cum-production centres are being assisted by the Board. Some training centres have also been set up in association with the All-India Handicrafts Board. There are 30 institutions running production units for handlooms under this programme in various States with an employment potential of 1900. According to information available, a total of 240 units are in existence under this programme providing employment to 7500 workers.

(ii) Training of development cadres: Under the insistence of various developmental agencies, particularly the Central Social Welfare Board, training courses have been developed for village level workers (Gramsevikas, Gramlakshis, Mukhya Sevikas, Balsevikas, etc., by agencies like the Kasturba Memorial Trust, Visva Bharati, Jamia Milia and various schools of social work. They are mostly pre-service or in-service training for these cadres, fully financed by Government.

(iii) The programmes by the Kasturba Memorial Trust, Visva Bharati and Jamia Milia, have displayed considerable innovative acumen in developing new types of cadres for working in rural areas.

(iv) The Indian Council for Child Welfare also runs 45 centres in different parts of the country for pre-service and in-service training for Bal-sevikas. The training is financed by the Government.

(v) The Ministry of Health has training programmes for Health Visitors and auxiliary nurse midwife for developing health services in both rural and urban areas.

The Ministry of Food and Agriculture has also organized 43 community canning and food preservation centres. There are four institutes of catering technology and applied nutrition in the country. Though not exclusively for women, they train some women. Under the co-ordinated programme for community development, training is given in selected productive activities like kitchen-gardening, poultry keeping, dairy science, etc.

The Ministry of Home Affairs has a scheme for training of women and children of Central Government employees belonging to the low income groups. There are 80 centres under this scheme. Training is provided in cutting, tailoring and embroidery. Students are recommended as private candidates for the diploma courses of the Industrial Training Institutes. Some home employment is provided to these women through Government contracts.

Similar programmes have been initiated in few of the States by the Department of Welfare, Labour, Industry and Education for training mainly in sewing, embroidery, handicrafts and tailoring.

We visited a number of these training centres. In our view, much of these well-meant efforts end in futility, because they are not linked to production and marketing. The bias for traditional or home crafts limits their scope since the indigenous markets for these products are now on the decline, and marketing, both internal and for export, is mainly in the hands of intermediaries. Strangely even the Government Emporiums are also dealing through middlemen and do not buy directly through the production centres, even though the latter are financed by Government. Even without these handicaps, the scope of the programmes are so limited that they can only make a marginal impact on the employment needs of women. Another difficulty lies in the multiplicity of agencies engaged in this work, leading often to duplication and over-concentration in a few areas, leaving the large areas of the country completely untouched.

It is unfortunate that though the training programmes developed by welfare and other developing agencies have shown greater understanding of the employment needs of women, their efforts suffer from lack of adequate resources and coordination. In our view, better degree of planning, coordination and redistribution of responsibilities in these fields would prevent considerable wastage of resources and instil a greater sense of urgency and productivity in these schemes for improving women's earning power.

14

Role of Education

Education is the most important instrument for human resource development. Education of women, therefore occupies top Priority amongst various measures taken to improve the status of women in India. In recent years, the focus of planning has shifted from equipping women for their traditional roles of house-wives and mothers to recognizing their worth as producers, making a major contribution to family and national income. Efforts have been made over the past three decades of planned development to enrol more girls in schools and encourage them to stay in schools, to contribute their education as long as possible, and to provide non-formal educational opportunities for women. The fulfilment of the Constitutional directives in respect of providing free and compulsory education up to the age of 14 years has been included as one of the components of the 'Minimum Needs Programme' and given over-riding priority.

Education in India is constrained by the socio-economic conditions of the people, their attitudes, values and culture. During the pre-British era, education was linked to the socio-religious, institutions, reinforcing the patriarchal social structure. During the British period, education became a tool of colonial power, enabling a small minority to have access to education, and all the benefits it entailed. The social reformers of the nineteenth century raised the demand for women's transformation but to make them more capable of fulfilling their traditional roles. Since Independence, the policy makers have argued for universal education and for making education as a tool for bringing about social equality.

In spite of concerted efforts to improve the enrolment of girls and provide adult education for women, their educational status is still far from satisfactory. Female enrolment in educational institutions is low as compared with males and drop-out rates are higher. There are also regional and inter-group disparities.

The factors which do not permit the closing of the existing gap between the education of men and women are many. While undertaking a review of the educational system at the time of formulation of the National Policy on Education 1986, if was noted that the system is caught in a state of ambivalence, aiming at creating an equal society, while at the same time not disturbing the class, caste and gender relationships. Issues in women's education are, therefore, not issues only of educational sector, but they extend to issues of environment, employment production processes. Indeed, the entire gamut of social and, economic policy has a bearing on women's education. The need for educating girls is not considered worthwhile. In urban areas, by and large, there is a greater acceptance of its need than in rural areas. Some other factors responsible for low enrolment are:

(i) The requirement for older girls to stay at home to take care of siblings when mothers are away at work;

(ii) Need for girls to work in order to help in augmenting the family income;

(iii) Early marriage of girls;

(iv) Social customs that hinder female mobility after puberty;

(v) Lack of relevance of school curriculum; and

(vi) Lack of facilities in the form of school buildings, hostels and women teachers, etc.

Basic Elements

Women's education has assumed special significance in the context of the country's planned development.' This is because women constitute nearly half the nation's population representing a valuable human resource and play an important role in the development of the community and the national economy. Education enables women to acquire basic skills and abilities, and fosters a value system which is conducive to raising their status in society. Recognizing this fact, great emphasis has been laid on women's education in the five-year plans. The First Five-Year Plan advocated the need for adopting special measures for solving the problems of women's education. It held that women "must have the same opportunities as men for taking all kinds of work and this presupposes that they get equal facilities so that their entry into the professions and public services is in no way prejudiced". It further added that "at the secondary and even at the university stage it should have a vocational or occupational basis, as far as possible, so that those who complete such stages may be in a position, if necessary, to immediately take up some vocation or other". Accordingly the educational facilities for girls continued to expand in the subsequent plans. The major schemes undertaken encompassed elementary education, secondary education, university education, postgraduate education and research, technical education, scholarships, social/adult education and physical education. The Second Plan continued the emphasis on overall, expansion of educational facilities. The Report of the National C committee on Women's Education (1959) made a strong impact on the Third Five-Year Plan. It launched important schemes like condensed school courses for adult women, Bal Sevika training and child care programmes. Subsequent plans supported these measures and also continued incentives such as free text-books and scholarships for girls. This trend continued in the Fourth and Fifth Five-Year Plans.

Although there was a large-scale expansion of facilities for education up to the Fourth Plan, vast disparities existed in the relative utilization of available facilities by boys and girls at various stages of education. Hence, the major thrust in the Fifth Plan was to offer equality of opportunities as part of the overall plan of ensuring social justice and improving the quality of education imparted. To promote enrolment and retention in schools in backward areas and among underprivileged sections of the population, in addition to the incentives like free distribution of textbooks, mid-day meals, etc., girls were to be given uniform and attendance scholarships. In spite of these schemes, it was noticed that insufficient numbers of women teachers resulted in low enrolment of girls. To remove this bottleneck, scholarships were given to local girls to complete their education and training leading to a teaching career. Besides, condensed and correspondence courses were organized for the less educated women. Emphasis as also laid on the need for orientation of the curriculum to meet the special needs of girls.

A landmark in the Sixth Plan was the inclusion of women's education as one of the major programmes under Women and Development which was an outcome of the publication of the report of the Committee on the Status of Women in India. The programmes for universalization of elementary education were specially directed towards higher enrolment and retention of girls in schools. It was envisaged to promote Balwadi-cum-creches attached to the schools to enable girls responsible for sibling care at home to attend schools. Women teachers, where necessary, were to be appointed in rural areas to encourage girls education. Science teaching in girl schools and colleges had to be strengthened to achieve greater participation of women in science and technology. Streamlining the admission policies to promote greater enrolment of women in engineering, electronics, agriculture, veterinary fishery and forestry courses was stressed. For boosting the education of women belonging to backward classes, the number of girls' hostels were to be increased. Instead of adding more separate women's polytechnics, which were developed as multipurpose institutions for imparting training in arts, crafts, etc. coeducational institutions were encouraged as far as possible. The adult education programme too received a fillip.

The Seventh Plan envisages restructuring of the educational programmes and modification of school curricula to eliminate gender bias. Enrolment of girls in elementary, secondary and higher education courses, formal as well as non-formal, has been accorded high priority. At the elementary stage, education has been made free for girls. Sustained efforts are to be made through various schemes and measures to reach 100 per cent coverage in elementary education. Financial assistance schemes to voluntary agencies to run early childhood education (pre-school centres) as adjuncts of primary/middle schools are to be expanded, particularly to help evolve innovative models suited to specific learner groups or areas. Efforts are to be made to enrol and retain girls in schools, especially in rural areas, and also to enrol children belonging to Scheduled Castes, Scheduled Tribes and other weaker sections. Teacher training programmes are to receive continued priority with a view to increase the availability of trained women teachers, and thereby to enhance girls' enrolment and retention in schools. Incentives by way of distribution of uniforms, free textbooks and attendance scholarships to needy girls are to be continued. Non-formal elementary education is to be expanded to benefit girls in the age group of 6-14 years. Talented girls are to be encouraged to pursue higher education. It is also proposed to expand the 'Open Learning System', including correspondence courses for them. In order to promote technical and vocational education for girls, more women's polytechnics are to be set up and programmes for vocationalization of education are to be expanded.

To expedite education among the girls of the Scheduled Castes and Scheduled Tribes, additional facilities will continue to be provided under the "Development of Backward Classes" sector.

Girls above the matriculation stage will get higher scholarships/ stipends than male students. Financial assistance is envisaged for construction of hostel buildings for girls at the district level and for purchase of equipment, furniture utensils, books and periodicals in these hostels.

Under the National Sports Policy, participation of women and girls in sports and games is to be encouraged. Stress is to be laid on the identification of sports talent among women, and provision made for sports scholarships, coaching and nourishment support for promising girls with a view to improve the standards of their performance in competitive games. Besides, the schemes for encouraging traditional folk, tribal and hill arts and cultural activities are to be expanded and strengthened.

Assessment of Conditions

Notwithstanding the planned objectives and endeavours, actual progress in upgrading the educational status of women has been slow. The literacy level among women has risen from 7.9 per cent in 1951 to 24.3 per cent in 1981 (excluding Assam). Among males, the corresponding rise was from 24.9 to 46.3 per cent. Thus the gap in percentage literacy points between male and female literacy increased from 17 in 1951 to 22 in 1981. In absolute terms too, the number of illiterate women has increased during the period, from 158.7 million to 241.7 million. (excluding Assam). Women comprised 57 per cent of the illiterate population in 1981, and girls formed 70 per cent of non-enrolled children in the school age group.

There are disturbing regional variations in the levels of literacy in the country. The literacy rate for women varies from 65.7 per cent in Kerala, as per 1981 census, to 11.4 per cent for Rajasthan. The gap between male and female literacy, rates in percentage points is only 9.5 in Kerala, but 24.9 in Rajasthan. States like Madhya Pradesh, Uttar Pradesh and Bihar are also lagging behind in girls education. Certain ecological constraints like difficult terrain, variety of dialects as in Arunachal Pradesh, migratory habits due to unfavourable weather as in parts of Jammu & Kashmir, etc. have also been instrumental in perpetuating low levels of literacy in such areas for the population as a whole and particularly for women.

Primary Education

High Priority has been accorded to elementary education in the National Development Plans to fulfil the requirements under Article 45 of the Constitution for universal, free and compulsory elementary education for children upto the age of 14 years.

By the end of the Sixth Plan, it was apparent that in order to achieve universal elementary education, an additional enrolment of 255.3 lakh is required of which the girls constitute 140.7 lakh, i.e., a little more than 55 per cent. Besides, there is a sharp fall in the number enrolled at the middle level, viz., from nearly 332 lakh to 91 lakh indicating a large dropout rate, wastage and stagnation. The enrolment ratio falls from 76.7 to 36.3. The retention of girls in schools from classes I to VIII, therefore is a task requiring urgent attention.

Among Scheduled Tribes particularly, the enrolment of girls is far below that of boys. At the primary stage, the enrolment of Scheduled Tribes boys is almost double the enrolment of girls, and the difference increases at higher stage. Girls belonging to Scheduled Castes communities are also lagging behind boys. The ratio of Scheduled Castes boys to girls in the elementary classes is 2:1. In the VI to VIII classes, 61.9 per cent of girls in the general Population are enrolled, whereas among Scheduled Castes this proportion is only '20.9' per cent; The reasons for Scheduled Castes and Scheduled tribes girls lagging behind boys. The ratio of Scheduled Castes boys to girls in the elementary classes is 2:1. In the VI to VIII classes, 61.9 per cent of girls in the general population are enrolled, whereas among Scheduled Castes this proportion is only 29.9 per cent. The reasons for Scheduled and Scheduled tribes girls lagging behind the boys are mainly rooted in socio-economic conditions and environmental constraints such as inaccessibility of schools in tribal areas. Irrelevance of formal education curriculum to the immediate environment is also responsible for low initial enrolment and subsequent drop-out rates. Among the urban and rural poor, the compulsion on girls to assist in household chores including care of younger siblings, and on children of both sexes to work for their own survival and contribute economically to the household income, forces them to remain outside the education system.

According to the Fourth Educational Survey (1978), in the plains 95 per cent of the rural population have access to a primary school within one kilometer of their habitation (having a population of 360 persons or more). Middle schools are available to 78.8 per cent of rural people within three kilometres from their habitation. But commuting to distant schools does pose a problem for girls. There are very few separate schools for girls. The parents, particularly in rural areas, are reluctant to send their daughters to co-educational schools. Moreover, in most schools, the teachers are male. Despite considerable emphasis in the plans, the proportion of women teachers continues to be low Provision for accommodation for women workers including teachers is far from satisfactory.

A large number of primary and middle schools, in rural areas especially, lack facilities such as a proper building, adequate number of teaching rooms, drinking water and toilets for girls. More than 85 per cent primary and 70 per cent middle schools in rural areas do not have these facilities, according to the Fourth All India Educational Survey (1978). Hostel facilities for girls continue to be meagre.

School Education

There is a progressive rise in the rate of enrolment in secondary education of girls during the various Plan periods as seen below:

The enrolment ratio of girls in the age group 15-18 years for secondary classes is 14.3 per cent as against 29.3 per cent for boys. Secondary education continues to be more or less confined to urban areas, and is affordable and accessible largely to the higher castes and the upper and middle economic strata. Although a large number of secondary schools have come up in rural areas, their enrolment particularly, in respect of girls is low. The main constraints in improving secondary and higher level education among girls have been a lack of availability of trained lady teachers, dearth of separate institutions for girls and lack of hostel facilities.

The 10+2+3 system of education has been introduced with the aim of establishing a uniform pattern of education all over the country in terms of its structure, curriculum and mobility across the States. This system has laid a common foundation for higher education without differentiation between boys and girls. Both girls and boys under the new system Will learn the rudiments of science and mathematics, social sciences and humanities up to matriculation and thus gain a holistic base education which will equip them to play an active and meaningful role in the employment market.

College Education

In the higher educational courses, girls constitute 24 to 50 per cent of the students enrolled depending upon the type of courses. The most popular course with girls has been teachers training where they already constitute nearly fifty per cent of those enrolled. The number of girls in science courses had risen to 41 per 100 boys in 1984-85. In engineering and technology courses, however, the enrolment of girls is only 6 for 100 boys. This Proportion has to be enhanced through suitable incentives in the form of scholarships and other facilities for girls studying for these courses.

Girls enrolled for higher education, particularly those in science and technical courses, are mainly from the higher economic strata. There is a need to introduce positive measure to improve the enrolment to girls in higher education courses in rural areas and, among backward groups like SCs and STs.

Private Education

The concept of adult education has found support in several Plan Programmes. However, until the Sixth Plan, no special emphasis was given to women's education. In the Sixth Five-Year Plan, adult education was included as a part of the Minimum Needs Programme and the goal of reaching 100 per cent literacy by 1990 was set under the New Twenty-Point Programme. Adult education centres exclusively for women were set up, which provided education in subjects like health, nutrition and family planning. An effort was made to build up an awareness about these subjects among women through discussions, talks and distribution of relevant literature.

Under the Adult Education Programme, apart from increasing adult literacy, the contents of education was to be modified to incorporate new value systems regarding the role of women in the family, and community. The Seventh Plan also envisages, among other schemes, the preparation of district level plans with local community participation, both for activating, and implementing the literacy programme, and the creation of special mechanisms to monitor the progress of implementation at the State level. The Integrated Rural Development Programme (IRDP), National Rural Employment Programme (NREP), Training of Rural Youth for Self-employment (TRYSEM), and other such programmes, are also to have a component of functional literacy for women beneficiaries. The programme of Functional Literacy for Adult Women (component of the ICDS programme) was unfortunately abandoned, though the concept of utilizing Anganwari workers, who belonged to the villages and were in contact with young mothers, could have been an effective mechanism for imparting non-formal education. The scheme has since been revised to focus on issues of immediate relevance to women but has yet to be introduced.

The scheme of 'condensed courses of education and vocational training' for adult women was started in 1958 under the aegis of the Central Social Welfare Board, and was suitably expanded over the years to vocational training in areas with high employment potential. Measures are to be taken to enhance the competence of the teaching staff / training institutions involved in this programme.

The various programmes, however, have not yet been able to make any significant impact on literacy levels of the Indian population, particularly on women. According to a World Bank Report in 2000 A.D., there will be 500 million illiterates in India, constituting 54 per cent of the world's population of illiterates. As per the Seventh Plan, the total number of adult illiterates is about 900 lakhs of whom 580 lakh are women. Although it is encouraging to note that the proportion of women in the adult education centres has gone above 50 per cent (52.34 per cent in 1984-85), women still constitute about 5.7 per cent of the illiterate population. Among these, literacy levels of SC mad ST women are still worse. Even those treated as literates, have very low levels of literacy, scant opportunities for continuing education and use of literacy skills. Therefore they often relapse into illiteracy.

Effect of Education Policy

The National Policy on Education (NPE)-1986 is a landmark in the approach to women's education. It has attempted for the first time to address itself to the basic issues of women's equality. In the section titled "Education for Women's Equality", the policy states:

> Education will be used as an agent of basic change in the status of women. In order to neutralize the accumulated distortions of the past, there will be a well-conceived edge in favour of women. The National Education System will play a positive, interventionist role in the empowerment of women. It will foster the development of new values

through redesigned curricula, textbooks, training and orientation of teachers, decision makers and administrators.

It gives overriding priority to the removal of women's inhibiting their access to and retention in elementary education. Emphasis has been laid on women's participation in vocational, technical and professional education at different levels as also to promote women's participation in non-traditional occupations and existing and emergent technologies.

The Programme of Action for Implementation of NPE (POA) spells out the meaning of women's empowerment:

> Women become empowered through collective reflection and decision making. The parameters of empowerment are:
>
> (a) Building a positive self-image and self-confidence.
>
> (b) Developing ability to think critically.
>
> (c) Building up group cohesion and fostering decision making and action.
>
> (d) Ensuring equal participation in the process of bringing About social change.
>
> (e) Encouraging group action in order to bring about change in the society.
>
> (f) Providing the wherewithal for economic independence.

The programme entails the following:

> (i) A phased time bound programme of elementary education for girls, particularly up to primary stage by 1990 and up to the elementary stage by 1995.

(ii) A phased time bound programme of adult education for women in the age group 15-35 by 1995.

(iii) Increased women's access to vocational, technical, professional education and existing and emergent technologies; and

(iv) Review and reorganization of educational activities to ensure that they make a substantial contribution towards women's equality, and creation of appropriate cells/units therefore.

A number of measures have been suggested to achieve the state's objectives of the National Policy on Education. The Action Plan enunciates that every educational institution should take up by 1995 active programmes for the development of women. All teachers and non-formal education/adult education instructors should be trained as agents of women's development. Special programmes should be developed by research institutions to promote general awareness and positive self-image amongst women through programmes like discussions, street plays, wall papers, puppet shows, etc. Preference in recruitment of teachers up to school level should be for women.

National Literacy Mission (NLM) which aims at eradication of illiteracy in 15-35 age group by 1995 concretizes what is envisaged in NPE as regards literacy and adult education. The Mission document emphasizes the importance of imbibing the values of national integration, conservation of environment, women's equality, observance of small family norm, etc., and goes on to say that "the focus of NLM would be on rural areas, particularly women and persons belonging to the Scheduled Castes and Scheduled Tribes."

For universalization of elementary and adult education, the present programme of non-formal centres for girls needs to be extended to all educationally backward pockets of the country. Increased assistance should be given to voluntary organizations to run non-formal education centres for girls. In rural areas, special support services should be provided to relieve the girls from sibling care and other household work like fetching water, fuel, etc. Skill development linked to employment opportunities in the villages is required to be given priority so that there is an incentive on the part of the parents to educate girls. It is necessary to develop adult education programmes for women linked with upgradation of their skills and income generating activities. Skill development for girls should be a continuous process of learning and should be supported by programmes administered by others such as Polytechnics, Industrial Training Institutes (ITIs), Women's Centres in Agricultural and Home Science Colleges, etc. Centres should be set up in a phased manner vocational training, provide opportunities for retention skills and application of this learning for improving their living conditions. Their are 104 ITIs functioning exclusively for women and 97 wings in general ITIs reserved for women would need to be revamped during 1988-90 in terms of diversification of trades and courses, keeping in view the job potential and facilities for vocational counselling, imparting information about credit, banking, entrepreneurial development and women's access to technical education, etc.

Women's studies programmes would also have four dimensions, viz., teaching, research, training and extension. Women's issues would be incorporated in courses under various disciplines. Research would be encouraged on identified areas/subjects. Seminars/workshops would be organized on the need for women's studies, and for dissemination of information and interaction. Educational institutions would be encouraged to take up programmes like adult education, awareness building, legal literacy, information and training support for socio-economic programmes of women's development, instructional programmes through media, etc., which directly benefit the community and bring about the empowerment of women.

All the foregoing endeavours will be planned, coordinated, and evaluated continuously both at the national and state levels. The Women's Cell in the National Council for Educational

Research and Training would be revived and strengthened. National, Institute of Educational Planning and Administration and Directorate of, Adult Education would have cells to plan and administer women's training programmes. The Women's cell in the University Grants Commission would, be strengthened to monitor the implementation of various programmes at the higher education level. It is proposed that women cells should be set up in all the States.

Wide Angle

The programmes for women's education will have to be implemented as a priority so that women attain a comparable level of education by 2020 A D. The strategy to be adopted for raising literacy levels and education among women has to keep, in view the vast cultural, geographical and ecological variations as also the problems relating to poverty and ignorance. The cultural and geographical variations call for decentralization of educational planning. Within the national perspective planning, implementation and monitoring of educational programmes has to be done at district and block levels, keeping in view the socioeconomic and geographic parameters of the area. The vocational and occupational components have to be designed in accordance with the availability of resources and job opportunities in the regions. Voluntary organizations and women's groups active in the area should be involved in the task.

In view of the social and cultural handicaps that have operated against women's education and taking account of the multiple roles that women are required to play, the need for adopting set of objectives specific to women's education is imperative. The objectives to be achieved by 2000 A.D. in regard to women's education are:

(i) Elimination of illiteracy, universalization of elementary education and minimization of the dropout and stagnation rate in the age group 6-14 years, to negligible proportions.

(ii) Ensuring opportunities to all women for access to appropriate level, nature and quality of education and also the wherewithal for success comparable with men.

(iii) Substantial vocationalization and diversification of secondary education so as to provide a wide scope for employment and economic independence of women.

(iv) Making education an effective means for women's equality by (a) Addressing ourselves to the constraints that prevent from participating in the educational process; (b) Eliminating the existing sexist bias in the system; (c) Making necessary intervention in the content and scope of education to inculcate positive and egalitarian and (d) Ensuring that teachers perceive this as one essential role.

(v) Providing non-formal and part-time courses to women to them to acquire knowledge and skills for their social, cultural and economic advancement.

(vi) Impetus to enrol in various professional degree courses so as to increase their number in medicine, teaching, engineering fields substantially.

(vii) Creating a new system of accountability, particularly of the basic educational services, to the local community, inter alia, by active involvement of women.

In brief, it is reiterated that the goals and strategies spelt out in the National Policy on Education, POA and the National Literacy Mission will ensure a much larger access for women to education.

High priority has to be accorded to creating awareness, through the various communication media, of the need for women's education and their active participation in economic and political development of the nation.

The curricula for school as well as university education have to be reviewed and revised so as to remove sex bias, inculcate among the masses a recognition of equality between men and women, and make women aware of their own potentials as well as provide them necessary opportunities to develop their capabilities in every field. Greater accessibility of educational facilities to girls is to be achieved by reducing the distance of schools from village habitations, and expanding non-formal elementary education, adult education, and the open school system. Appointment of lady teachers in schools would help draw more girls to schools and instil confidence among their parents. Towards this end, provision of quarters for lady teachers would be essential. Efforts should be directed at training local women as teachers. Provision of creche facilities and Balwadis near the elementary and secondary schools for girls would enable the girls to attend schools and ensure care of younger siblings. Incentives like midday meals, better rates of scholarships, freeships, etc., would go a long way in preventing dropout.

Above all, better health facilities, smaller families, and relief from drudgery through improved technology for household chores, are essential prerequisites for better enrolment of girls at school and higher educational institutions. Inputs from other sectors are, therefore, important. Greater coordination of health, employment, welfare and education interventions will have an effect on the status of women and girls.

According to Educational Statistics for 1984-85 published by the Ministry of Human Resource Development, the enrolment of girls at primary level, which covers the age group 6-11 years, is 331.9 lakh. Surveys and field research have pointed out that there is 25 per cent inflation in the enrolment figures, and 22 per cent enrolment is outside the age group. Thus the effective enrolment gets reduced by about 47 per cent. Accordingly, the coverage for

1984-85 for the 6-11 years age group may be estimated as 176 lakh. The population projected for the age group is 422.7 lakh. This means that only 40.7 per cent of the girls in the age group 6-11 are enrolled in schools. On a similar basis, the enrolment of 11-14 years age group gets reduced to 48.1 lakh (from 90.7 lakh) which is only 19.2 per cent of the population of 249.9 lakh estimated for the age group. The population projections for the girls in the age group 6-11 years and 11-14 years for 1989-90 are 462 lakh and 2,67 lakh respectively. In order to have full coverage, the additional enrolment required would be 286 lakh for 6-11 age group and 219 lakh for 11-14 years age group, the total being nearly 5 crore. The task appears to be stupendous. Along with enrolment, there is the problem of very high dropout rates. Stemming from highly inflated enrolment rates and subsequent dropouts in the 6-11 years age group, enrolment of 11-14 years age group girls, even at primary level, may not be possible even by 1995.

In view of the social and cultural handicaps that have operated against women's education, the need for adopting a set of objectives specific to women's education is imperative. These would need to encompass the elimination of illiteracy and measures for retention of girls in schools, substantial vocationalization and diversification to enhance economic opportunities for women, improvement in the quality of education in terms of the values it promotes and inculcates, and finally the provision of access to professional courses for women. Such measures would be necessary as also efforts to remove the inherent prejudices working against women's education.

The Prospects

1. Awareness needs to be generated among the masses regarding the necessity of educating girls so as to prepare them to effectively contribute to the socio-economic development of the country, to strengthen their role in society and to realize their own capacities. The media and various forms of communication have to be geared to this end.

2. A fruitful rapport has to be established between the community at large and the teachers and other education personnel. As per the Programme of Action under National Policy on Education-1986, every educational institution should actively participate in bringing about such awareness.

3. Involvement of local leaders, voluntary agencies and women's groups is also necessary. Mahila Mandals need to be revitalized and reoriented to provide an effective forum for the purpose. One measure to achieve this could be to assign the responsibility to Mahila Mandals for ensuring that all children in a community attend school. An incentive scheme should be introduced to motivate panchayats to ensure 100 per cent enrolment of girls in their villages.

4. Early childhood care and education introduces children into the school system gradually and smoothly. When children get used to attending schools, it ensures in some measure retention of children, including girls, at elementary stages also. Hence there is needed to have a comprehensive and effective programme of early childhood care and education linked to an integrated package of learning for women. The most comprehensive example of this is the Integrated Child Development Services Programme which needs to be universalized.

5. For improving enrolment and minimizing drop-outs and wastage in case of girl students, it would be helpful if learning is made more attractive by providing adequate teaching materials in schools.

6. The number of teachers should also be increased so that the interaction between the teacher and the taught, which is so essential for good education also increases. This would help in the retention of girls in schools and would

be more effective if teachers from the area are employed. In single teacher schools, the teacher must be a woman. In Orissa all jobs of primary teachers have been reserved for women.

7. School curricula should be imaginatively developed to stimulate creativity 'largely through play rather than overburdening children' with formal or rote learning. Regional language should normally be the medium of instruction.

8. School timings should be flexible and fixed to suit local conditions and the needs of the working girls and must be available within the walking distance of the child. A substantial increase is required in the number of schools for girls.

9. In addition to incentives like free textbooks, free supply of uniforms, award of attendance scholarships and mid-day meals, facilities such as proper school building, safe drinking water, and toilet, etc., need to be provided to encourage school enrolment and retention of girls especially girls from educationally deprived social groups and from hilly, tribal, desert and remote areas and urban slums.

10. Local talent must be developed in order to meet the need for recruiting women teachers at the primary and elementary levels especially in rural and tribal areas. In this endeavour national agencies like CAPART and CSWB, voluntary agencies, Mahila Mandals and local self-government agencies can make a significant contribution. They can also play a useful watchdog function to ensure that educational and other programmes are run efficiently and effectively.

11. There should be a reservation of 50 per cent posts for women teachers in elementary schools. Women teachers

working in the rural areas should be provided suitable accommodation.

12. Multi-entry system for girls who cannot attend schools continuously should be adopted.

13. Wherever necessary, schools meant exclusively for girls may be set up. The recommended distance of 3 kilometres for locating a middle school is a handicap for many girls. To ensure participation of girls in middle schools, it is necessary to provide hostel facilities.

14. The Savitribai Phule Foster Parent Scheme of Maharashtra could be adopted in other States/Union Territories to help poorer families to at least complete primary school. Under the scheme, well to do persons and organizations are persuaded to adopt one or more out of school girls and contribute in cash or kind or both @ Rs. 25 per month for her education. The money can be spent on uniforms, stationery or anything else, needed by the girls or also partly used to alleviate the economic distress of the parents. The Zila Parishad, Block Education Officer and head-masters play a pivotal role in implementing the scheme, which is purely voluntary and if district level officers are appointed for coordination of programmes for women, they could also actively take it up.

15. Condensed courses of education at elementary and middle school levels for girls must be started in all the rural areas and for weaker sections of the urban community.

16. Many girls in the 11-14 years age group would first have to be brought into the primary stage through non-formal education. By devising alternative education approaches non-formal schooling and through like intelligent use of technology, the pace of middle school education can be accelerated. If retention up to 73 per cent is achieved up to

class V, universal elementary education may be possible in some parts of the country by 2000 A.D. Other backward areas would have to be given much more attention in, professional as well as financial terms to enable them even to universalize primary education for girls by 1995. The National Literacy Mission will need to address these issues on a priority basis.

17. Special efforts are necessary for bringing tribal children particularly, girls into the school system. Tribal dialects, extreme poverty, problems of commuting, rigidity of formal education and its irrelevance to the tribal culture and the tribal's distrust of the ways of the mainstream society, must be borne in mind in formulating strategies.

18. The educational forecasts, may look more achievable if the system is opened up for flexible non-formal education which 'the below average states' should be persuaded to adopt in a large measure. The existing educational infrastructure particularly, in tribal and rural areas should be made effective and responsible.

19. Non-formal education is an alternative to the formal system which has the potentiality of becoming the major programme of education for girls who cannot attend school during normal school hours due to various reasons. The Central Government is already implementing a centrally sponsored scheme under which grants to the extent of 90 per cent are provided towards maintenance of non-formal education centres exclusively for girls in nine educationally backward states. This programme should be strengthened further and extended to other states where education of girls is lagging behind. It should at least cover all the pockets of low enrolments of girls and areas of high dropout rate. Besides literacy, it must also provide relevant information on skill development and inculcation of positive self-image among girls.

20. Secondary education for girls should entail:

    (i) A ten-year course in general education learning and diversified higher secondary education which may be either terminal or lead to further professional preparation; and (ii) Diversified courses after Grade VIII in technical subjects, viz., agricultural technology, health services, food production activities such as dairy and poultry and non-traditional areas need to be untroubled. A legal literacy component is also recommended at this stage.

21. Diversified courses leading to occupational preparation should be of parallel duration to the general secondary courses. In addition, there should be a variety of short and long term, whole time, part-time and apprentice courses. The trend of thinking is now to place emphasis on the last. Keeping in view the rapid modernization and advancement in technology for agriculture, there is an urgent need for skilled artisanship, for promoting productive activities on the one hand, and a variety of learning programmes for adjustment of the rural society to socio-economic change on the other. Efforts should be made to ensure that girls have every opportunity to enter into apprenticeship in areas that are non-conventional, and incentives be provided for the same. Further, at least 30 per cent seats should be reserved for girls in apprenticeship training courses on a non-transferable basis.

22. General and vocational training courses should be combined so that prospects of a career immediately on completion of schooling may attract girls from weaker sections. While designing the vocational courses, available occupational opportunities as well as the need to overcome market stereotypes should be kept in view.

23. Since secondary education has remained almost beyond the reach of weaker sections, liberal incentives and other

facilities to release the girls from household chores appear to be essential. It would also help to locate the institutions in the areas of their habitation.

24. Multiple entry system should be introduced in the secondary classes. Part-time education facilities should also be made available.

25. Condensed courses should be organized in cooperation with local vocational training institutions to cover all rural areas and areas inhabited by weaker sections in urban areas. Such courses may be organized for small groups of girls, and combined with job training. Efforts should be made to cover atleast 215 lakh women in the age group 15-30 years under the condensed courses programme wherever possible the condensed courses of the CSWB should be expanded and strengthened. New programmes that are to be initiated must avoid duplication in the areas where the CSWB's programmes exist.

26. Correspondence courses and self-study programmes can be especially useful for girls desirous of continuing education but are unable to do so because of circumstances. Apart from imparting elementary education and knowledge about farming techniques, the curriculum for non-student girls should include courses of training in occupational skills. Similar programmes should also be designed for girls in the urban areas.

27. The open school system should be expanded extending the facility to all the girls in rural and backward areas.

28. Science education for girls has been neglected so far. Secondary schools for girls must be helped to build good science programmes over the Eighth Five-Year Plan. Special scholarships for girls opting for science courses need to be instituted at the secondary and higher education levels.

29. Special scholarship may also be offered to rural women, who opt for teachers' training, especially those who complete the condensed courses at the secondary stage.

30. There is a need to open more colleges and polytechnics for girls, especially in rural areas.

31. Incentives like scholarships, freeships, etc., should be provided to enable girls from rural areas to pursue higher education for girls belonging to weaker sections. In addition to freeships and scholarships hostels should also be provided to meet their requirements for food and lodging.

32. Girls should be encouraged to enter professional courses. Reservation of seats for girls in such courses may be considered to level out the existing bias in access to certain professional streams.

33. Vocational counselling and guidance service be organized exclusively in a more meaningful way to help girls in colleges and universities opt for suitable courses relevant to their talents and interests, and free of traditional bias.

34. . Vocational and technical education for women, both formal and non-formal, should be a major feature of the programmes of rural universities. The women's wings of the universities could undertake large-scale extension programmes in order to activate girls and women in the surrounding areas to take advantage of educational and occupational facilities of various types, particularly those leading to meaningful employment, essential for reducing women's marginalization.

35. In order to increase the representation of rural girls in higher education courses, 30 per cent seats, may be reserved for girls to begin with.

36. All agencies, involved with preparation of curricula prescription of textbooks and organization of educational processes will have to evince awareness towards women's issues. University/College Departments of Women's Studies, appropriate voluntary agencies, women's groups, etc., should be involved in giving a new perspective to the various issues of content and processes of education. Women's universities and women's centres in colleges need to take an active role in women's development and in influencing the attitudes of Future generations.

37. Facilities for part-time self-study and correspondence courses should be provided on a large-scale to enable girls who are not in a position to join higher educational institutions on a regular basis, to continue their studies.

38. In addition to courses leading to degree/diploma, short courses in specific subjects through summer school sessions, and ad hoc programmes like seminars, workshops, etc., should be organized for working women with a view to upgrading their knowledge and skills, not necessarily leading to degrees.

39. Integrated learning programmes for women are recommended which will not only lay emphasis on literacy but on empowering women through awareness building on social issues, bringing about attitudinal change, promoting skill training for employment, providing information on healthcare, nutrition and hygiene as well as on legal rights. Such programmes are beginning and must continue to be designed and structured so as to be relevant for the vast majority of rural women. The revised scheme linked to ICDS known as the 'Women's Integrated Learning for Life', should be introduced as an integral part of the non-formal education system.

40. Entrepreneurship development programmes should be organized separately for education of women in the age group 18-30 years, with a minimum of matriculation level of education. The objective of such training should be to:

    (i) Make them aware of the various opportunities for self-employment; (ii) Motivate them to take up self-employment; (iii) Impart needed skills and training; (iv) Promote motivation for achievement among them; and (v) Create access to resources such as capital, credit, etc.

41. A large number of girls cannot participate in whole day education programmes. Provision of non-formal and part-time programmes, with flexible school hours and sensitivity to the agricultural cycle are, of particular importance. In addition to the primary and upper primary stages, distance learning opportunities need to be provided at secondary and higher secondary levels.

42. Adult education will have to be composed of three interrelated stands aimed at:

    (i) Continuous flow of new information especially to rural and tribal areas, particularly to inculcate positive attitudes towards women;

    (ii) Continuous training of the people in the use of modern tools and methods of production; and

    (iii) Acquisition of permanent reading and computation skills.

    Following from the above, three types of programmes may be offered to the learner:

    (a) Information and literacy.

(b) Information and training in new technology and literacy.

(c) Information and training in new technology with or without literacy. Continuous information flows relating to human affairs, gender relations and the use of science and technology for betterment of life would be the common factor in all the three programmes.

43. The growing availability of communication media should be directed towards keeping up information flows and portraying positive images of women in non-conventional roles. Audio-visual materials, combined with non-formal training arrangements, could impart to various population groups the kind of instruction they need in the use of new technologies. Involvement of mass media in motivating women to attend literacy classes is most essential.

44. Rapid strides in the development of technologies and tools for the reduction in women's drudgery and easy access to work places, water and fuel supply, child care, health services and population control can contribute significantly to the success of learning programmes for women. Women's literacy programmes would succeed better if they centre around women's concerns and also provide opportunities of recreation and sharing of experiences.

45. District plans should be prepared keeping in view literacy requirements of the learners and identifying agencies which can take up such programmes in districts.

46. All women working in industries or employed elsewhere should be made literate by the employers by allotting time from the working hours for their education. Place of teaching, teachers and teaching material should be arranged by them. Necessary legislation to this effect may be enacted.

47. At least 50 per cent seats in pre-service courses in all teachers training institutions should be reserved for women. Spatial planning to ensure that women from rural areas are selected as teachers is essential.

48. Provision of composite teacher training courses for women who have had insufficient education to improve their educational qualifications along with their training, should be made.

49. The existing Integrated Rural Development Programme, National Rural Employment Programme, Development of Women and Children in Rural Areas, Training of Youth in Self-Employment Programme, Integrated Child Development Programme, etc., should have a component of literacy for their women beneficiaries. Training should be provided to the functionaries of various development departments by Directorate of Education in the States.

50. The State Resources Centres should produce suitable learning material for women on a priority basis. Literature for neoliterates should be suitably devised by experts, keeping in view the needs of different groups of learners.

51. Decentralization is the key to the successful application of the strategies outlined above in this decentralized approach, the village cluster or the block level is seen as most appropriate for the delivery of programmes. It is, therefore, necessary that the block is allocated a flexible budget so as to make funds available to village clusters/ villages for innovative educational activities and for equalization of educational opportunity.

52. An overall coordination of health, welfare and educational inputs would be most desirable. This would entail (a) Convergent policies in these sectors; (b) Coordination of delivery mechanisms; and (c) Pooling of allocations.

53. The strategies spelt out in the National Policy of Education, 1986, the Programme of Action for its implementation and the National Literacy Mission and the successful achievement of the goals, imposed in these documents, would be important for improvement in the status of women.

Denial of Education

As centuries rolled on, Aryan culture was firmly entrenched in this land. Indian women were trapped more and more in the web of myth and lost their sense of self and will. The goddesses were robbed of their glory even though they were still seated on a high pedestal. Men's obsession was to pull them down to earth by having the women sing their praises and do their will. Only when the women pleased them and satisfied their ego-needs, did they call them the goddesses of the household (Girhya Lakshmi). The moment women defied male idiosyncrasies, they were called devils. Men took upon themselves the responsibilities of protecting and feeding the women who were consequently destitute and completely dependent. The women were not allowed to move outside the household without male company since it was taken for granted that they were incapable of defending themselves. Women became frail and weak creatures and believed that if any man other than their husbands touched them or cast a lustful glance towards them they were defiled and dishonoured. Hence, their only path to an honourable existence was to give the men unflinching loyalty, submit to their care and deny their own self and will.

Perhaps in no other culture does such a duality exist where women have been mythically placed upon a high pinnacle while at the same time pulled down to dust in reality. In no other civilisation the women's status in the social milieu has been raised so high and simultaneously, so brutally lowered as in the Indian culture. In other cultures women are usually labelled as either saint or sinner, while in India she is both. Years of being enmeshed in the many strands of this web have deeply affected the position of the Indian women.

Women of the early Aryan civilisation were highly respected. This society, however, as patriarchal, therefore, the birth of a girl was generally an unwelcome event. As early as in 2000 BC charms and rituals ensured the birth of a son in preference to that of a daughter. These charms are reported in the ancient Atharva Veda. Even though a son was desired and preferred, the birth of a daughter was a source of great pleasure to the family. Alteker points out that some scholars of this period were of the opinion that a gifted and well-mannered daughter might be a source of pleasure to the family. No restrictions were placed on girls in performing religious rites. The marriage of a daughter was not a difficult problem since she was free to choose her husband.

The marriage of girls used to take place at the age of 16 or 17 years. The women were not restricted and were allowed freedom of movement within the society, even in the company of their lovers. The wife occupied the honoured place in the family as the mistress of her household. Marriages were mostly monogamous. Widow remarriage was usually permitted within the family. Parents desired their daughters to marry the husbands of their choice. During the early Vedic period, the prayer of an anxious father used to be "May Saviter lead and bring to thee the husband whom thy heart desires". Pinkham notes: It is important for us to note that a wife was on a level of equality at the hearth which was the altar of sacrifice.

Around 1500 BC, the education of the daughters confined to the family. Religious and secular training was given only to girls from rich and cultured families. Men performed functions in the religious sacrificial rites, which had previously been the wife's domain. Girls were married at about the age of sixteen years, and divorce and widow remarriage were, still permitted.

Gradually circumstances changed. As ancestor worship gained popularity, sons alone were permitted to perform religious rites. Women became "valued only as the vehicles for bearing sons, and when they were unfit or unwilling to perform this function, they were considered useless". The value of the sons increased further, and they began to be regarded as investments for the future. Without a son, no man or woman could hope to go to heaven. The position of the daughter was greatly undermined. Still the women were not debarred from the study of the Vedas and there existed very few taboos regarding the rearing of girls.

During the Epic period in India, the birth of daughter became an exceedingly negative event because of the prevalence of marriage customs, which subordinated the position of women. Still, a daughter was regarded as a prized possession, and family took a keen interest in her rearing. In Mahabbarata, Draupadi is described as the common property of the five brothers. She was put at stake in a gambling bout. Sita, the ideal woman character of Ramayana, was put to fire ordeal to prove her chastity. She was denounced by Lord Rama to prove himself as an deal king. Draupadi did not accept her subordinate position and fought in an open assembly when Duryodhana the winner of the bout, sought to derobe her. Sita, on the other hand, took her humiliations with fortitude and goodwill toward her husband. However, by this time the right of the husband over his wife or a man over a woman has generally accepted by the society irrespective of whether women acknowledge it willingly or not.

This willing acceptance, even today, is considered as the ideal of womanhood. Sita is worshipped in most of the devout homes for her absolute obedience to her husband. Everywhere in India her example is exalted to be followed by all women. Sita had great strength of character and virtue. She pursued what she considered to be right. Her love for the husband was limitless. Her character was of utmost purity and chastity. If we for the sake of argument forget for the time being the divinity of Rama and Sita there arises a doubt in our minds that such a character might have been drawn to satisfy the male ego by the male poets. It might be possible that Sita's character was enfolded in the myth of male supremacy and female subordination so that the women's sole aspiration in life became the loyalty and the service to her husband who was put at the level of God to her. This emphasis on chastity and service to the husband may lead to the conclusion that the women of this period were put on pedestal as goddesses only if they lived the ideal and the virtuous life according to the most rigid standards set by a male dominated society.

The witch type of the nature of women is demonstrated in the Ramayana through the story about Kaikeyi and Manthra. Kaikeyi tried through deceit to obtain the throne for her son. Manthra prompted her to do so. Hence both are branded as great culprits at the opposite end of the spectrum from Sita.

An aspect worth noticing in the character portrayal of Mahabharata heroines is the strong willed women. They are depicted as "resolute, full of fire, passionate in comparison with the often slackened, spineless men". Perhaps the Indians of this period were not in full control of their women and were frustrated enough to seek means of controlling them. One such means was to put an exceedingly high value on loyalty and chastity. Meyer points out that in Indian literature no ideal of a man is found; however, idealistic character portrayals of women are outstanding, especially in the Epic period". We may not entirely agree with this view as the portrayal of characters of Shri Rama, Shri Krishna and other heroes of Epic period cannot be ignored and yet there seems to be truth in this observation that women of this period were certainly of strong will.

During the post-Vedic period the age of marriage of girls was nine or ten years. Since the marriage was performed at such a young age, the choice then was not that of the girl but of the parents or other elders. A woman was debarred from revoking her marriage but the husband was free to throw his wife out of his household if she was not submissive. Widow marriage became unacceptable and was banned by 500 AD. The dictum that "the wife ought to revere her husband as a god even if he was vicious and void of any merit was accepted as applying to all women". The Law of Manu became the accepted way of life. It stated that the father should protect his daughter while she was young, her husband when she was married, and her son when her husband was no longer there. This law contributed to woman's inferior status in society and denied her all decision making rights.

Kautilya was in favour of marrying girls at a tender age. He advocated the marriage of girls when menses appear. He advocated the punishment of parents who did not marry their daughters at proper time. According to Jha: "Probably Kautilya advocates early marriage with a view to maintaining the chastity of girls, preventing 'women' from joining nunneries, check love marriages, utilising the fertile period of girls for bringing forth offspring, and increasing the population at a time when frightful wars of conquest reduced Hindu population by one-half". Kautilya propagates the subjection of women in married life. The wife must remain under the control of her husband. As the girls were to be married at an early age their education was totally neglected. Kautilya considered that a wife must be fully devoted to her husband and blindly follow him. The woman's freedom of speech was totally curbed and since her individuality was denied she was kept ignorant.

At this time, Buddhism developed in India as a revolt against Brahmanism, a too formal ritualistic religion prevalent about six centuries before the birth of Christ, Buddhism soon spread throughout India and dominated the nation until about 800 AD. Buddhists still maintained women in an inferior position through an emphasis on celibacy for men who made women appear unclean or as objects simply for men's pleasure. Women were admitted to the Buddhist order as a gradual change occurred. According to Altekar, "this change was the beginning of a movement, which led to new attitudes about female education among ladies in commercial and aristocratic familes". Several ladies from Buddhist families led lives of celibacy with the aim of understanding and following the eternal truths of religion and philosophy. Some women like Sanghamitra went to foreign countries to propagate Buddhism. Also, many women of the Jaina faith devoted their time to learning and became famous scholars. However, these were early exceptions. For the majority of women, no educational gains were made between 300 AD and 800 AD because of either Buddhism or Jainism. The celibate Jaina monks considered women as the temptresses that perpetuated the misery that was life. This attitude certainly did not deter in general the Jainas from marriage or begetting of children. Women were given place of honour in the household. However, the monkish tales about celibacy did contribute to ambivalence among the Jaina men in their behaviour pattern with their women. Jaina men enjoyed their women in spite of the religious discourses about their evils.

The road back to educational equality was slow and difficult. By 500 AD the religious influence had obligated all education for women. The model women were exposed to re-modelled. Women were exposed to such literature, which highlighted dependence and punishment for breaking the norms of conduct imposed on them by indifferent priests. A blind faith developed among the women through a process of awe and forced reverence. The Puranic literature cites examples where the husband was carried on his wife's shoulders to the house of a prostitute. The wife's willingness to put her husband's needs above hers' proved that she was a sati.

This literature which seems to have been developed by male Hindu priests completely subjugated the will of women. It emphasised husband worship along with the notion that a woman's salvation was possible only by doing that which her husband desired. An abundance of stories about Pativarta Nari or the husband worshipping woman influenced women to perform every kind of unnatural act for the sake of their husbands. Women started taking pleasure in their morbid existence. Eventually they became even greater fanatics than men in opposing their freedom. Perhaps they were so removed from the idea of an independent existence that even the thought of such responsibility frightened them. It may be said that it is human nature that one wants to stay with the familiar even if it is destructive because the unknown is scary.

Muslims considered marriage as a contract. In certain respects the Muslim law gave woman a higher position in the society than the medieval Hindu law. However, the purdah or veil as well as the women's ignorance of the law diminished this small difference. The Muslim men believed that their women would remain safe only if they were not exposed to temptation. Thus the women were denied the right to make choices.

The Muslims like Hindus believed that the women's only path to salvation lay in the service to their menfolk. Divorce was shunned and many myths were woven about the dutiful wife who was prepared to sacrifice her all for her husband. Muslim had put all types of restrictions on the movement of their women outside their households and by and large they were restricted from having any contact with men who did not belong to their immediate family. Chastity was valued and the husband considered it his conjugal duty to keep his wife away from temptation.

According to the Holy Quran women were respected because they bore children. Progeny was very important to the Muslims as defenders in warfare against unbelievers. Hence among Muslims there also developed ambivalent feelings towards their women. Women were respected for being mothers but at the same time they were restricted from having any freedom of action. They were completely subjugated by the dominant males. Due to a number of environmental factors affecting the Indian Muslims the feelings of respect were overcome by the need or restriction. Most of the legal rights of the women were virtually subjected to the male will.

The early Muslim period was one of great instabilities. Local feuds and conversions were dominating the social life. The fanaticism and religious intolerance closed the doors to rationality. The women were the worst sufferers of the irrationality of the ignorant priests and religious fanatics. Their spirit of inquiry was crushed, as they were not allowed any interaction with learned or open minded persons. The women were left with no option but to submit to their submissive role and suffer indignities and cruelties in silence. Dubey describes the personality and the character of the women that emerged during this period: They had no status in society; none in their own estimation. They were more like puppets, which move when someone pulls the strings than individual human beings with minds of their own.

At this time the patriarchal type of family in its perfectly developed state was generally in existence. The senior male in the family was the undisputed head. Hindu women could not claim any patronage since the law of succession did not give them independent right of inheritance. The inheritor of the property was made responsible for looking after the widow oı the deceased. However, in spite of their low social status, women were still the ideal of conjugal devotion, and the family was the most intimate and enduring social relationship. Dubey considered that "the Hindu family was an ideal family, the Hindu parents, mothers were not equalled by any people on the earth in tenderness towards their progeny and attachment to the family ties".

This attachment to their families was not an exercise of free will for the women. They only knew to be dutiful wives and loving mothers. No other options were open to them. In most cases, motherhood was the only solace for them in their subordinate existence. As mothers, they elicited respect, and through their sons, they ruthlessly made attempts to dominate their daughter-in-laws and other poor and dependent relatives. The condition of the women in the Indian society continued to remain low. The disruption of the Mughul Empire in the eighteenth-century and the consequent confusion throughout the country added to the women's miseries. At the beginning of British rule, the marriage age was lowered to three or four years. Since hygienic conditions were poor and disease and famine were common, a large number of girls became widows in their early childhood. These child widows were ill treated and considered a curse to their families.

The use of the veil became popular, particularly among the Muslims. The higher-class women were kept away from the males by means of purdah even a glimpse of a woman's fully clothed and veiled body by a stranger was not tolerated. While travelling, dark clothes also covered the vehicle, and when the women entered it and left it, the male servants or the carriers had to be removed from their presence.

The observance of purdah was not only to safeguard the honour and chastity of women, it also kept them for special pleasure of the men. Certainly, the veil produced a special type of feminine beauty, which was pale and passionate with mystic eyes, and the mind of a child. Such women seemed to appeal to the morbid taste of the pleasure lovers. When a woman is unlimited and has free social interaction with the opposite sex, her sexual impulses are toned down. Perhaps those who put their women in purdah do so to obtain more sexual pleasure out of them.

During the period of Muslim rule, quite a number of upper caste Indian widows burned themselves on the funeral pyres of their husbands. This was known as the sati system. The Sanskrit word sati means "true wife" or "good woman." Thus a woman was considered true to her husband when she burned her body with him after his death. Akbar, the Mughal emperor, made efforts to stop this practice about 1600 AD. He, however, was unsuccessful. When the British became the rulers, they found this practice so firmly entrenched that they also had no luck in disrupting it. The magnitude of the tradition is further understood by noting that in the year 1803, 275 women were burned at their husbands' funeral pyres within 30 mile radius of Calcutta. Within six months of the year 1804 in the same area, the number was 115.

The British passed an Act in 1829 to stop the burning of widows. However, the practice continued in rural parts of India as late as 1905 when a few people participated in a sati ceremony in Bihar and were condemned to prison. The Hindu priesthood strongly resisted the British India law. They argued that Vedas, their holy text, sanctioned the practice, therefore, alien rulers could not suppress this practice. When the religious texts were examined, it was found that the Hindu priests had falsified them to support this rite. The prevalence of the sati system and the opposition of its abolition by the orthodox priests show the extent to which a society can degenerate in the name of religious law. It also shows the strong influence of myth which the men and women came to believe. The honour of a family became so strongly linked with the widow burning that the kinsmen of a widow could cruelly push her into the fire. Unfortunately, the abolition of sati system did not end the miseries of the Hindu widows. Their burning was stopped, but they were still treated worst than the pet animals of the household. They were not allowed to remarry and had to pass their lives depending on the charity of their kinsmen and serving them like domestic servants. The plight of the young widows was extremely bad. They were not only tortured but also many times sexually exploited by the unscrupulous males in the family or the neighbourhood.

Unfortunately sati system is still not completely wiped out. In September 1987, a young widow of 18 years Roop Kanwar was burnt at the funeral pyre of her deceased husband, a bare seven months after her wedding. The burning took place before a large gathering of people. The illiterate village folk endorsed the sati pratha and the rural women developed worshipful attitude toward the burnt widow. She became a deity. The myth woven centuries ago around the virtuous wives and self-destroying satis as goddesses seemed to persist in the minds of the people. It is worth noticing that all those women and men who supported and organised the burning of Roop Kanwar were not totally illiterate. They were some that were educated. Yet the type of education which they had received did not result in opening the vistas of their minds. This has in fact opened the question of quality of education, which these persons had received. In the case of these persons education which they had received had completely failed in developing in them a positive attitude towards modernity and a will to fight against orthodoxy perpetuated by a corrupt and ill formed priestly class.

The institution of prostitution continued to flourish as a respectable way of life and the dancing girls were patronised by the nobles and landowners of their villages or towns. Chakraborty writes that in 1853, the Chief Magistrate of Calcutta reported that his town with its 416,000 people supported 12,419 such women. Of these upwards of 10,000 were Hindus including several daughters of the Kulin Brahmins.

Existing along with the customary form of prostitution, which was quite common in large part of the country there was another form of prostitution that of Devdasi cult or temple prostitution. In early times, the practice of offering virgins to the deity was common. Some examples can also be found in the temple precincts of Sumerian culture in Mesopotamia. In India, the Dravidians who may have borrowed it from Egypt or Mesopotamia probably introduced this custom. In the Rig Veda there is a clear reference to the dancing girl. Usha, the goddess of dowri, is compared to a dancing girl wearing embroidered garments and baring her bosom. In the Atharva Veda there is also a reference to the existence of women called Gandharva grihtas (possessed or owned by Gandharvas). They do not marry and exist for the pleasure of gods and men.

The cult of Devadasi originated in the early civilisation and became prevalent in South India between the sixth and the thirteenth centuries AD. During the reigns of Pallavas and Cholas all big temples recruited girls for temple prostitution. The temple dancers were married to the temple deity at a young age. They were taught music, dancing and the classical literature. After seven years of practice, the rite of worship of anklets (gajjai puja) took place. This was the first wearing of the anklets for the dancer. It has been traditional for families to offer their daughters as Devadasis or servants of the gods. In spite of the Devadasi Protection

Act of 1934, some families still continue with this tradition in Maharashtra and Karnataka. In most other parts of India, this practice has been abolished.

The courtesan in India has filled a need for the men, which the wives were unable to meet. It seemed normal to a wealthy male that wives are kept for progeny and prostitutes for pleasure both sexually and aesthetically. The high-class courtesans throughout most of India's history were the most learned women in the country. Santosh Chatterjee in one of his articles has observed that "Be she of heaven or this earth, the courtesan in India had dual purposes in her life. She was in one way an object of lust for men, in another way she was the repository of all the delightful acts of music, dancing and personal decoration'.

The cult of Devadasis supported the envelopment of women in the web of myth regarding self-sacrifice and negation of will for men's pleasure. Women lost their individuality partly due to the contrivance of men and partly due to their need for the advantages they gained by being submissive.

Many factors contributed to women's dependent state. Numerous pregnancies during their most active years left her unfit and unable for engaging themselves in any type of employment except in the case of very poor or destitute women. Men accepted the responsibility of looking after the material needs of the women but in return for this they demanded from them unflinching loyalty and devotion. They denied them any opportunity to develop them physically or mentally or to develop their own will power. Thus women became weak and inferior to men as human beings. This degeneration of the women in India was at its peak by the end of the eighteenth century. By the beginning of the nineteenth century the entrapment of the women in the mythical web was so complete that in almost all the spoken languages of India women were, described as evil, an appendage of men, and always open to temptation.

And so such sayings were quoted:

> "To educate a women is like placing a knife in the hands of a monkey".
>
> "Where there are women, there is trouble".
>
> "Woman is a poisonous creeper, avoid her company; her love destroys faith, caste, wealth and money".
>
> "He who is guilty of sin easily begets daughters".

15

Force of Intelligence

Are women different from men because of their physiological development? This question is raised time and again. The men establish their superiority by pointing out the biology of the female sex. Whenever the question of the equality of sexes is put someone is sure to say: "But it's just a matter of biology. You know women are different from men-they are more intuitive, nurturing, emotional, but also weaker and subject to fits of weeping once a month." Women are born to be mothers. Men are stronger, both physically and psychologically and so are fit for work and to play role of dominant partners in the men-women relationships. It is because of such notions that the education of women is considered not of as much significance as the education of men. But is it the right conclusion? We will now try to focus our attention on this question.

There is much divergence in the opinions regarding the basic biological differences between sexes. One viewpoint is that sex differences are biologically determined while the other viewpoint emphasises that the only difference between the sexes is reproduction. Only men can impregnate women and only women can give birth and lactate. It is true that one is born either male or female (not talking into consideration a small percentage of those born with no explicit sex or as eunuch). But there are six determinants of gender: (1) Chromosomes, XX for females and XY for males, (2) Gonads, testes in males and ovaries in females, (3) Hormone level, more androgens in males and more oestrogens and progesterone in females, (4) Internal accessory organs, which are the uterus and the organ of menstruation in female and the prostrate gland and seminal vesicles involved in the secretion of seminal fluid in male, (5) External genital appearance. (6) Assigned sex and rearing, usually based solely on external genital appearance (Hampson and Hampson, 1961).

There is research evidence that indicates that after birth the brain regulates secretion of sex hormones. Puberty seems to be initiated by an interaction between the sex hormone and certain cells of the brain. In normal child, both male (androgen) and female (oestrogen) sex hormones are almost undetectable in the urine until the child is eight to ten years of age. At this point the male hormones sharply increase in both sexes, while the female hormones increase only in females. In girls the production of sex hormone becomes cyclic at about the eleventh year and is accompanied by the beginning of menstruation, the appearance of secondary sexual characteristics, and a growth spurt. Thus in terms of hormones there are no appreciable differences between males and females up to puberty. After puberty both adrogenic and oestrogenic hormones are present in both sexes but in different proportions. Males have high level of androgens and low level of oestrongens, while females have high level of oestrogens and moderate level of androgens.

A very relevant question that may be raised here is: Do hormones determine our personality and behaviour completely or in their determination social factors are also involved? The biological determinists consider that hormones give us energy and direct that energy into natural channel such as sex and fighting. Thus our moods and behaviour are related to our own body state and socialisation factor is irrelevant. But this view is open to controversy. Research has shown that even our private emotions and their interpretation are shaped by reaction of those around us.

While visceral sensations such as heart palpitation, flushing and tremor tell us that we are emotionally aroused, we have to learn whether that arousal means that we are excited, angry or happy. All body chemical hormones produce a physiological state that must be translated into personality and behaviour through a specific social control. Thus sex role probably enters into the very way we perceive and interpret our own bodily sensation even those due to hormone. This is not to say that hormone levels are irrelevant to personality and behaviour. It merely suggests that even with such purely biological differences as hormones, we need to keep a sharp eye for ways in which social factors help to translate these biological factors into every day behaviour. We may say that the differences in personality and behaviour of male and female are not only because of hormones but also the process of socialisation of girls and boys creates such differential behaviour, which is known as typically male or female behaviour. We may give a few more research findings to establish our above-mentioned belief.

The hormone androgen is found in greater quantity in males than in females. This is then considered as a factor governing more assertive behaviour among males. But Moss (1967) found that mothers tend to comfort crying female babies more than they do crying male's. It may be that the male infant experiences visceral sensation, such as stomach contractions of hunger pains. He cries but mother's attention is not drawn. He then learns that crying is not enough. He has to assert himself physically to attract the mother's attention. When this situation persists for months or years the male child may then associate this visceral sensation with greater activity or aggression and he may show it in his emotion of anger. On the other hand the female infant when experiences the similar visceral sensation due to stomach contraction she may also cry but in her case the mother comforts her. Gradually the female may come to associate these visceral sensations with comforting which may lead her to the emotion of happiness. The mothers perhaps do not attend to the male infant's cries as quickly as that of female infants because they may feel that males ought to be tough and should not cry. The finding of Moss may be taken with a sense of skepticism, in the case of Indian male child. In this country because of too high aspirations for a male child more attention is given to him by the mother. But this might be leading the male child becoming too much attached to the mother and an entirely dependent individual to the parental wishes.

It cannot be said that hormone levels are irrelevant to personality and behaviour. It merely suggests that even in dealing with such purely biological differences as hormones, we need to keep a sharp eye for ways in which social factors help to translate these biological factors into day to day behaviour.

The controversy surrounding aggression is not about whether males act more aggressively than females but about the causes for these sex differences, for regardless of how aggression is defined and measured, males of all ages show a consistent tendency to be more aggressive than their female peers. The greater male aggression is expressed not only in a variety of behavioural modes but also in a variety of situation and culture. But how do female hormones affect aggression? Unfortunately we know little about the answer to this question. Most researchers have assumed that male hormones increase aggression while female ones decrease it. Bronson and Desjardins found that administering female hormones to newborn may decrease the aggressiveness of males but increase the aggressiveness of females. Thus in females the oestrogens may mimic the effect of androgens in males, when given to males, however, oestrogens may interfere with the action of the androgens.

Further more, male androgens administered shortly before or after birth seem to increase aggressive behaviour in females but not in males, while female hormones administered at that time also seem to increase aggressive behaviour in female while decreasing it in males. Thus XX hormones, whether androgens or oestrogens seem to increase aggressive behaviour in females more than in males. This conclusion then suggests that it is the absolute level of all hormones androgens and oestrogens together that underlies aggression in women, rather than a level of androgens relative to that of oestrogens. The basic argument is that both the sexes are actually equally aggressive in their underlying motivation but carry out desires to hurt others in different ways. This argument takes two basic forms. The first maintains that the two sexes are reinforced for different forms of aggression: Girls are allowed to show hostility only in subtle ways, while boys are encouraged to show it more directly by physical attack. The second form of argument maintains that aggression in general, is less acceptable and hence more discouraged for girls, leading to greater female anxiety and conflict over aggression.

It is now widely known that there are no sex differences in over all scores on intelligence tests. Some psychologists have, however, suggested that the sex hormones influence general intellectual capacity. The most popular view has been that male hormones enhance intellectual functioning and development in both sexes and, perhaps is based on the assumption that several social and physical behaviour levels of male hormones are related to aggressive or energetic intellect. There are also some psychologists who argue that female hormones may underlie intellectual ability.

The fact that males and females obtain similar overall scores on intelligence tests which does not mean that there are no sex differences in intellectual abilities. The pattern of intellectual abilities that make up the overall IQ score differs for the two sexes. In fact IQ tests are carefully constructed to weight the various portions on which men and women, typically score higher in such a way that their average overall scores will be equivalent. Females generally excel in verbal ability while males in visual-spatial and mathematical ability. The females superiority in verbal is found in both "lower level" measure (fluency) and "higher level" tasks (comprehension of different material and creative writing). The males' visual-spatial advantage is about equal in non-analytical tasks (matching similar shapes and completing routine numerical operation, perceiving and manipulating parts and performing complex numerical operations).

The idea of difference in male and female brains continue to have popular appeal and has been hotly debated and researched for many decades in spite of numerous contradictions in both theory and data. About the differences between the male and female brains the researchers are only able to find that the issue is extremely complicated and does not offer any conclusive evidence that biological sex differences exist in intellectual performance.

Utilisation of Wisdom

Can the sex difference in intellectual abilities be erased through altered social experience or specific training? If they can, these differences might be attributed to differences in the training that males and females receive in the usual course of growing up in our culture.

Our entire educational system is based on the premise that training is crucial, that without it children would not be able to reason clearly or to complete complex verbal and non-verbal tasks. Yet every teacher knows that there is limit to what the best instruction can accomplish with each child. There seem to be a basic intellectual capacity that sets the limit for the rate and perhaps for the total amount of learning. With no instruction only a few children will develop complex skills, yet with the best instruction no all children will become highly skilled. The issue is whether instruction helps a child use basic cognitive abilities he/she already possesses, or whether instruction can affect the development of these basic intellectual abilities themselves.

Research on the training effect has focussed on the Embedded Figures Test (EFT) and the Rod Frame Test (RFT) developed by Witkin, in 1950. These tests assess spatial decontextualisation, or the ability to extract key elements of a stimulus from a confusing background. They measure "fields dependence versus fields independence" that is one's ability to assess external or internal stimulation independently of the environment. It has been reported that women are more fields dependent than men are." In other words, women have lower spatial ability scores than men have. It was also reported that the field independence does not increase with training. But these findings and Interpretations have been challenged. Mazy Brown Parlee (1973-74) conducted a thorough review of all published studies and concluded that sex differences were not nearly so conclusive as usually reported. Parlee maintained that field independence scores tend to improve with practice or training.

Cross-cultural research results lead to the conclusion that the greater field dependence in women is an indication both of basic female dependence on others for emotional support and social stimulation and of a general lack of psychological differentiation" or development of a clearly defined and separate self-identity. Kogan and Kogan (1970) conclude that not only child rearing practices are associated with spatial ability scores in the predicted fashion, but sex roles are also implicated, i.e. men tend to score higher in spatial ability in those cultures with marked differences between the social roles assigned to the two sexes. The assumption is that greater sex role differentiation is associated with greater encouragement of dependence in females, and this dependence in turn interferes with spatial ability as measured by field independence and other measures.

The cross-cultural argument is organised around the theme of dependence and assumes that the trait of dependence interferes with the restructuring of external physical and social stimulation and hence inhibits abstract reasoning. When cultures begin to adopt a modern lifestyle, allow children more autonomy, or define the proper role of the sexes less strictly, they are increasing the independence of their population. This more independent population then scores higher on field independence and other spatial ability measures. But increased childhood autonomy, decreased sex-role differentiation, and increased technological innovation are all associated with higher levels of formal education for the population in general and for women in particular. Thus increase in visual-spatial ability scores may be reflecting increased formal education rather than a personality trait of independence.

Intellectual Differences

To conclude the argument regarding physiological differences influencing the intellectual differences between males and females we once again raise the question: Do biological sex differences underlie any possible differences? It seems unlikely. Owing to traditional sex roles females are discouraged from being assertive and independent and therefore, their intellectual development and performance are inhibited. It is very well known that the parents treat male and female newborns differently. They encourage gross motor behaviour in males while viewing females as littler, cuter, cuddlier, and generally more fragile. The cross cultural research echoes this social theme by demonstrating that most cultures encourage males to be independent and assertive while encouraging females to be dependent, nurturing and responsible.

In 1912 in his book, The Psychology of Education Walton wrote that the profound physiological differences which distinguish the sexes are the correlates of equally important mental differences. While man lives by reason, women's outlook is molded and determined by feeling. In his opinion the advocates and promoters of equal education to the sexes sadly ignore the mental and intellectual differences between the two sexes. He is against coeducation. He emphasised that, as the psychological differences between man and woman are so intimate, so deep that the other cannot give the real training in character and in outlook in life of the one sex. A man cannot be a really sympathetic guide to a girl, nor a woman to a, boy, simply because the man has never been neither a girl nor woman a boy. But Walton clarifies that it must never be supposed that woman is an imperfectly developed man. That woman differs from man in intellect does not mean that she is in any way intellectually inferior to him. He proposes a different type of education for woman as her functions differ from that of man. He proposes a system of education which lays stress on preparation for an efficient woman.

Howard in 1928 drew attention to the prevailing educational system in which the boys and girls studied very much the same things even when their schools were separate. He advocated a separate system of education for boys and girls. In his opinion girls are liable to fatigue more readily after puberty when the amount of haemoglobin in the blood becomes lessened. With their thinner blood with lowered content after puberty, they are nearer to the threshold of anaemia. These girls in general are not so strong physically as boys are. They are also highly-strung and liable to nervous strain, which possibly is associated with the fact that physiologically they are liable to heavier drains upon the circulating calcium of the blood. These considerations of the physiology of the girl, Howard advocates, must weigh when laying down a particular system of education for girls.

Many other psychologists have also pointed out the physiological differences between men and women and recommended a different type of education for women. Geddes and Thompson in their book Sex (1927) argue that though certain differences between men and women are undoubtedly modification and natural, that is to say, the individual results of disparities or peculiarities in their education, training and occupations, many of the differences are constitutional, inborn and not acquired. They say that "the tenacity of life, the longer life, the characteristic endurance, the greater resistance to disease, the smaller percentage to genius, insanity, idiocy, suicide, and so on, are all correlated with the distinctively female constitution which may be theoretically regarded as relatively more constructive in its protoplasmic metabolism".

Stanley Hall (1920) has stressed the psychological differentiation between man and woman. Woman, he points out, are more emotional, altruistic, intuitive, less judicial, and are less able to make disinterested and impersonal judgment. He is of the opinion that woman thinks more in terms of the concrete, is slower in logical thought and has less patience involved in science and invention.

The psychologists, physiologists and social reformers till quite recently were pointing out the different physiological make-up of women as a ground for giving them a different type of education than that was to be given to men. They were emphasising that the existing female education was incompatible with the nature and need of woman. It had entirely ignored her function and mission in life, namely motherhood. The educational curriculum for her was a complete imitation of that of the man, as if like him she was going to be in future an office bearer. With only a few exceptions most of the women were going to be married and the motherhood was a undoubted fact. Hence they needed an education which would prepare them for motherhood. These persons were quite critical of the modern feminists whom they considered were criminally ignoring this vital fact in their zest of following the standards of male pursuits. According to them the girls should be given education in domestic economy, nursing of children, hygiene of pregnancy, general household management, and in all such subjects which would be intimately personal to them.

Dr. Saleeby in the Report of the Proceedings of the English Speaking Conference on Infant Mortality has remarked: "Education of a girl must be to prepare her for womanhood and not to show that at a pinch she would be a boy".

Truby King in the same report has mentioned that: proper education should be given but above all there must be a development of love of human life, and interest in children, and a development of proper womanly qualities".

The ideas expressed above are considered redundant now. The technological and scientific advancement has refuted all the arguments put as above in view of the women's physiology. It is now being said that because of technology, tomorrow's most challenging and rewarding careers will require the powers of mind, not muscles. The most modern psychological and brain research have made it very clear, despite all of yesterday's cliches, that women have all the intellect and ambition needed to go after these jobs. Science is also relieving the women from the tyranny of the biological clock, allowing women the freedom to delay bearing children until late thirties or sixties.

The changes in work and reproductive choices are women's family lives, encouraging "Parallel" marriages in which husband and wife both share the work inside and outside the home.

The study of biological and other sex differences is being carried out on many fronts by the anthropologists and psychologists, who catalog human behaviour, neuroscientists, who probe the brain, and endocrinologists, who trace the action of hormones in the body. It is still a very young science. But this science has given us new dimension regarding the biological and psychological differences between man and woman.

Male and female brains are different although not in ways that would support most of the stereotypes of the past. The distinction is certainly not one of intelligence, for the average female brain is as smart as the average male brain by whatever test we use to measure it. The difference lies in question of values, interests, style and Motivation. Different does not mean superior or inferior. We should also not deny biology,in order to shake off the myths that have accumulated regarding female nature. Howard Gardner in his book Frames of Mind (1983) argues that the human intellect is not a single entity. Multiple forms of Intelligence exist, including musical, linguistic, spatial, logical, mathematical, interpersonal and bodily and kinesthetic intelligences. All individuals have an intellectual mix intellectual mix that includes all these types in varying Proportions. The mix may be weighted differently in each sex too.

The genetic engineering has revealed a number of facts regarding the physiological development of male and female. Now the scientists recognise that the creation of a male from the arrival of the chromosome to the testosterone that floods the embryo, is a precarious business, the result at best, is a creature with a single survival advantage over females: greater muscular strength. At every stage of life, men pay dearly to gain this advantage; fall victim to every threat from genetic defects to heart disease. Women are biologically superior to men in every other category but muscles. Boys are more likely to suffer than girls from birth defects and genetic diseases. So called X-linked genetic diseases such as haemophilia and muscular dystrophy strike boys almost exclusively because they are carried on the X-chromosome to protect them. But Y provides no such back up to a boy with a defective X. Infant boys suffer more illness and infection and in the first month of life three of them die for every two-baby girl. At every age, women have lower death rates from heart disease and heart attacks than do men. Even women who have high blood pressure and high blood cholesterol do not die as readily as men do. Women are less likely to die of infectious diseases. The endocrinologist Estelle Ramey says: "So women are an extraordinarily viable sex, right from the moment of conception".

In the modern times medicine has reduced the perils of childbirth and the threat of infectious diseases. Women are simply better prepared mentally and physically, to meet the pace and challenges of life and work in a technologically advanced world.

Women of all ages have more responsive immune systems than men, giving them protection from bacteria and virus. Girls have higher levels of a protective blood protein called immunoglobulin M or IgM than males, and a gene on the X-chromosome seems to be responsible for the immune system. The X-chromosome also carries other genes that influence various parts of the defense system. And after puberty, oestrogens increase the efficiency of the immune responses.

It is becoming increasingly clear as the gap between men's and women's life expectancies grown ever wider that women have better ways of coping with stress, physically, socially. Some of the biggest risks to life today – heart disease, alcoholism, lung cancer, suicide- arise from the way we handle pressure and stress. Although the same stress response takes place in both men and women it is more extreme in men because they need a bigger head of steam to get their larger muscles fueled for action. It has been found that women are about fifteen years behind men in accumulating significant heart damage. Men on average, start to develop heart disease between age of thirty-five and forty, women between the ages of fifty and fifty-five. Men between thirty-five and fifty-five are twice as likely to die of heart disease as are women. Today's women are entering into competitive athletics with the same intensity as men and their performance is improving dramatically. No doubt that there are some biological differences between the sexes that cannot be ignored, although they are not nearly as great as the myths about the women have been propagating.

Information Age

Knowledge is the most precious commodity in the information age. The doors are now wide open for women to push against the frontiers of ignorance and it is very heartening to note that women have begun to take their mental and intellectual capabilities seriously. Keeton and Basrin in their book Women of Tomorrow (1985) write that women are forging new ways to care, applying their concern along with their intellect to much larger human goals. These authors emphasise that women can be system analysts and computer programmers, they can be hardware as well as software engineers; women can enter into the fields of infertility and test-tube baby research, of molecular biology and genetic engineering, women should prefer to study Bionics, (a field that's already produced artificial hearts, artificial pancreases to secrete insulin to diabetics, the first rudimentary artificial ears and eyes connected directly to the human brain, etc.). It's never too late for a woman to start to find a place for herself in any of these frontier fields. The country needs scientists and engineers to improve life on earth and help expand in space.

It can be said with confidence on the basis of the findings of various physiologists and the biologists that the women are not physiologically weak, rather they are by nature superior and their superiority lies in the power to give birth. It is argued that woman and woman alone have the capacity to give birth. Despite all the evolution of socioeconomic conditions and progress of genetic manipulation of medical knowledge, the fact remains that it is the woman and none else that carries the work of reproduction. It is this biological feature gifted by nature to woman, which is at the root of the existence of necessary minimal sexual division of labour.

The modern physiologists reject biological explanation of the inferior status of woman. They argue that the biological view does explain why men have been excluded from the task of reproduction, but it fails to clarify why women have been excluded from some activities, which are not reproductive. This implies that the inferior position of the women is not due to any natural deficiency in them but it has resulted from changing historical circumstances, which have always been tied to the reproductive role. Needless to say in the modern society women have been doing the same work that was once considered exclusively to be of men. For instance, women have gone to space, joined modern guerrilla groups and fought on the battle fronts, headed the country's administration, participated in sports and games and the like. To the chagring of men, women even surpass men in many of the so-called men's activities. Hence It does not stand to reason to attribute women's inferiority in society to biological or physical factors.

In view of the above mentioned facts we may suggest that the education for women must be as liberal and deep as for men. A woman must know the course of history, the rise and fall of different political systems, the co-ordination and contact of different cultures, the fundamental issues that this evolution in history involves. She must also know where she stands, how is she related to society, how can she promote solidarity in social life without injuring the growth of the individual. She must also know how life began. She must have knowledge of Botany and Zoology. She must learn Geography and Literature, which are the fountains of culture and civilisation. In short she must learn all, the areas of liberal education so that she knows her relations to the society and may thus prepare herself for real citizenship.

Hygiene and Economy

The woman must also have training in domestic hygiene and economy. She must learn the art of nursing children and decoration of home. She may also learn fine arts, dancing and music. Her education thus must equip her for twin task of keeping the household and involving in the world of work. We consider that system of education an ideal one which aims at making of each versatile artisan-versatile for changing conditions, a good citizen consciously playing a part in a general scheme and a well-disposed, considerate person in full possessions of all his/her powers.

The education of the women should usher in an era of complete rationalism and equality. Equality between men and-women means equality in their dignity and worth as human beings as well as equality in their rights, opportunities and responsibilities.

Minorities' Plight

In the Indian situation the education of the minority communities have been very much neglected except perhaps in the case of the Christian community. The worst sufferers are the women of the Muslim community. Because of poverty and purdah the Muslims have avoided sending their daughters to the schools. The Muslim clergy is by and large opposed to the liberal education of the girls. According to them the education of the women should be confined to the reading of the religious texts and to those activities which are performed by them for the maintenance of their households.

The Christians on the other hand, have a tradition of educating their daughters. The missionaries have opened a number of good institutions where the Christian girls get quality education. The girls of the Sikh minority except of the Sikhs who fall in the category of Dalits are able to get fairly good education. Hence the Muslim minority is the one which has not been able to educate its daughters to the extent to which they should have been educated. We shall examine in this chapter the socio-psychological factors that have affected the education of the Muslim girls.

The Muslims feel that it is ordained in holy book Quoran that the women are kept under purdah. It is often quoted:

> And say to the believing women
> That they should lower
> Their gaze and guard
> Their modesty; that they
> Should not display their
> Beauty and ornaments except
> What (must ordinarily) appear thereof
>
> Quran (24:31)

According to the above verse among Muslim women veiling or Purdah is projected as the preferred code of conduct. They are supposed to remain veiled whenever they go out or face the males. They are thus restricted to go to those institutions in which they have to discard their veil. The choice of schooling, therefore, remains very limited. Because of pardah Muslim women are also restricted from undertaking jobs in the factories or offices. Their rightful place is considered home and their responsibilities are the domestic work and rearing of the children. It is, therefore, not surprising that very few Muslim women are employed in Government or factories or business services.

Trauma of Partition

It may be mentioned that the Muslim community in India has undergone the trauma of partition. No doubt that to some extent the community in India was partly responsible for the partition of the country in 1947 but once it took place this community suffered a lot. Its elitist, well to do members, shifted to Pakistan and those who were left were separated from many of their near and dear ones who migrated to Pakistan. The trauma of partition that separated the families is very effectively projected in the movie Garam Hawa. The affluent businessman of shoe market at Agra found his relations migrating to Pakistan and ultimately decided to leave the country. It was a difficult and much pain producing decision but there was no escape route. In many other stories and novels including Bhisham Sahani's Tamas, a Television serial, the trauma of partition with which Indians suffered has been dramatised. The effect of it on the Indian Muslims was that they retreated into a world of their own and tried to preserve their culture and religious ideology as interpreted by not very well educated Mullas. The community thereby instead of taking a progressive outlook fell prey to obscuration ideas and values. The worst sufferers of this situation were the Muslim women who were forced to embrace ignorance.

After Independence many laws were made to give equal rights to the Hindu women. The Hindu Code Bill conferred almost equal rights to women in the sphere of property and marriage etc. Unfortunately there has been complete absence of reform in Muslim family laws. The Indian constitution envisaged a single civil code for all the citizens of the country. But because a large section of the Muslims were extremely critical of a common civic code it could not be enacted. Muslims do not want that any changes be made in their personal law. But there are many provisions and interpretations of the Shariat, which go against the interests of the Muslim women. So while the Hindu society is on reformist trending the Muslim clergy favours the status quo. The outcome is that the women are sufferers. It may, however, be noted that there is no feminist movement worth the name sponsored by the Muslim women for the removal of any law that places them in an inferior position than men. The reason for this may be found in the Muslim women psyche. They have been so groomed that to raise any objection to the interpretation of the Shariat by the Ulemas is unthinkable. The restrictions on their education keep them perpetually in the sphere of ignorance.

The enactment of the Muslim Women's (Protection of Rights on Divorce) Bill in 1986 by the Indian Parliament was done because controversy arose over a case that came up for review in the Supreme Court. It is better known as Shah Bano's case. In this case the earlier judgment of the Supreme Court was, that a husband was responsible of maintaining his wife. The orthodox argued against this judgment that is goes against the spirit of Shariat. A wife is entitled for her Mehar only. About this Bill Maitrayee Mukhopadhyay writes: "The Muslim Women's Bill constitutes a major attempt at codifying Muslim personal law, setting up boundaries delineating what Muslim women are entitled to in the event of a divorce. In the process Muslim women's entitlements have been redefined and men's responsibilities to their divorced "fixed" in a way that disempowers Muslim women". It may be asserted that the Muslim women's fight for a fair treatment by their male counterparts faces very tough opposition in the name of keeping the separate identity of Muslims and in the name of not involving any other agency than what Ulemas consider as the right interpretation of religious texts.

Huma Ahmed-Ghosh writes: "The lifestyle, attitudes and cultural identity of Muslim women in India are an outcome of their socio-economic condition, and a tenuous relationship the Muslims share with the Hindus". She in her article entitled "Preserving identity: a case study of Palitpur" examines the various indicators of the socioeconomic status of Muslim women in Palitpur, a village in Meerut district, north India. She found the Muslim community in Palitpur as economically backward. But the economically depressed, Muslim men in Palitpur "Flaunted a moral and cultural superiority over the Hindus." In them there was a feeling that they belonged to the ruling (royal) class, (referring to the four-century rule of India by the Mughals). They felt that due to the creation of Pakistan they have been neglected or harassed by the government and Hindus because they stayed back.

The above finding shows that the Muslims after partition ascribe to their backwardness the neglect by the government and blame the Hindus also. They have a sort of defeatist mentality. They want to keep their Islamic identity not by progressive education but by remaining rooted to the traditional education given in madrassas. In Palitpur there were only two schools, one the government school and the other the madrassa. Muslim children attended the madrassa that only imparted Islamic education. It is through such education that they wanted to keep their Muslim identity. In spite of this there was a sense of helplessness among them. They considered that their future was bleak.

The Muslim women in Palitpur were victims of "their gender as well as their minority status". They were uneducated and conservative. In them the idea of good education was not at all inculcated. They considered the reason for their low socio-economic status lie in their victimisation by the Hindus and the neglect by the government. According to Ghosh: "Education which was the only way out, was still not encouraged. The sense of victimisation was very strong. For the women, conforming to Islamic tenets as rigidly as their socio-economic conditions would allow, was not only perceived, as an improved lifestyle but also the only escape from their 'disadvantaged' situation".

The case study of Palitpur may not be the representative of all the Muslims in India since there exists a diversity of culture and lifestyle among Muslims in different regions and states of India. But certainly it throws some light on the social status, aspirations and motivations of Muslim women of rural India. In Palitpur Muslim community aspires for upward mobility but not through learning or further understanding of the Quran, Hadith or Shariat. They try to achieve it by means of emulating the lifestyle of the Ashrafs, that is those who belong to higher social echelon.

Status and Position

The Indian Muslim women's lower status and position is due to many factors. Some of these we have outlined above. The women are guided by the zeal resulting from their adherence to Islamic tenets as preached by male Muslim leaders. Many of their interpretations of the religious texts go against their interests but because of their ignorance and upbringing they are incapable of raising their voice against them. They also suffer from the feeling of helplessness for improving their lot. They are also fed with the propaganda that their plight is the result of a conspiracy by the Hindu fundamentalists which make them more rigid in the observance of the religious practices and the obedience of religious injections. The Mullahs and Muslim politicians have a stake in keeping them backward and so they feed them with those notions that perpetuate their backwardness. The plight of Muslim women can improve only if they are encouraged to have liberal education and to think independently and assert their individuality.

The Stresses

A modern educated women suffers from various tensions. If she is a housewife she feels stressed because her education has not incurred her any relief from domestic chores. If she is working woman she is stressed because of lack of co-ordination between her home and office life. This chapter identifies stresses typical to the modern educated woman and offers some suggestions for dealing with them.

The ambivalence that women feel as they take on dual roles of housewife and worker is quite tension producing. Undoubtedly, many women are able to combine both roles with smooth adjustments, particularly if the husband and the family members are co-operative and supportive. However, in many families, the conflict between both the roles has created estrangement between either the husband or the wife or the wife and the other members of the family.

Desire for Domination

The psychology of the Indian women in terms of her desire for domination and her will for subordination. The large number of women who have traditional outlook are meeting with their tensions and stresses by overtly subordinating themselves to men and covertly trying to dominate them by their extreme devotion and sense of duty. The modern emancipated women are revolting against this duplicity. They are denying the superiority of the male and seeking an equality between the sexes overtly and covertly both. We have also advocated that through our educational system the women should learn to move towards equality of sexes without involving themselves in any duplicity in their behaviour pattern. But the danger in such a move is the enhancement of tensions and stresses in the individuals, in the families and also in the society.

Ambitious men of lower income group want their wives and daughters to work and earn to help raise the family's standard of living. At the same time these men cannot tolerate the idea of independence such as that they themselves have on the job. They are unable to free themselves from the myths of Sita and Savitri. They become agitated when their women become assertive and begin to express their personal views and opinions and their likes and dislikes. They feel that women are transgressing their freedom, which they have so generously bestowed on them. Their ego is hurt if their wife's income exceeds their own Income. But the women when they go out for work cannot be bound in the chains of orthodoxy. Hence the modern woman's tensions enhance as she has to cope with the demands of her job and the dictates of her male relations.

In a study by Mukta Mittal on "Educated Women Power," it was found that the need for supplementing the family income was the chief motivating factor for encouraging the respondents belonging to "lowly educated" and "moderately educated" groups to become job seekers and get themselves registered at the Employment Exchange Bureaus. But in the case of "highly educated" respondents, the prime motivating factor behind encouraging them in their becoming registrants for job was "desire to be free from dependence on family members and relatives".

Many conflicts arise when both husband and wife are working. The husband desires that the wife should take up job but disapproves the complete involvement of the wife in the job. For him the job of the wife is only a secondary commitment. Her primary duty he feels is towards him and his family. He wants his wife to work and also to take up full time duties of looking after the household. When the wife is unable to cope with this situation the seeds of conflict and estrangement between the husband and wife begin to germinate. After returning from her work the wife is tired but she receives no sympathy or help from her husband or in-laws. When the tensions so created become unbearable the wife has no option but to resign from the job. But this is also not liked by the husband who resents the loss of income and blames the wife for not being able to reconcile between her job outside and her duties to her family.

The tension reduction in such cases is possible when all the family members recognise that the household work is to be shared and is a joint responsibility of all the members of the family. In those families in which the joint responsibility is recognised the tensions are suitably dealt with.

Till nearly three decades earlier the women were giving utmost importance to the role of the housewife. In a study by Cora Vreede

Stuer in 1970 it was reported that quite a substantial number of girls "consider the role of the housewife as the most suitable." But when they were asked that if they had to go outside the home to work, most of them said they would prefer to teach or do social work. One girl in Cora's study remarked: "I would be willing to work in my field, but if my husband opposed it, I would submit to his wishes." Similar views were expressed by 18 of 15 educated women in Rama Mehta's study of the Western Educated Hindu women in 1970. One woman in her study expressed this view: 'Working was not important enough for me to go against my husband's wishes. After marriage, one cannot do as one wants, working is not an important enough issue to create tensions". It may be noted that till seventies or may be later also the working women, generally, perceived their main role as that of wife or mother. By such an attitude they were meeting with their tensions created by their becoming working women. But the situation at the end of the twentieth century is not as simple as that. The aspirations and the motivations of the women have increased manifolds and so also there is increase in their stresses and tensions.

Society now has a more favourable attitude towards the employment of women in the middle income groups. It has become an economic need. Promilla Kapur in her study in seventies took a sample of 300 working women from three major occupations — teachers, office workers and doctors. She observed that because of society's change of attitude, as well as change in attitudes of the educated married women towards their own employment, their number has multiplied to the extent that they now constitute a class by themselves. This class is facing the greatest change and, challenge ever offered anywhere in the world to the feminine population.

Spectre of Unemployment

The number of women seeking jobs has increased manifolds now from that of seventies. The challenges before them have also become quite serious. The educated women have first to face the spectre of unemployment. The job market is very tight. It is difficult for men to get the jobs and when women also compete with them the number of the job seekers becomes quite high. With the limited job opportunities the women also suffer from the various types of restrictions which are put on them by the society. They still search the jobs, which are considered feminine in nature like the teaching, or nursing or office work, etc. They also want a job in the town or place to which they belong. They do not opt for the jobs in the villages or remote areas. It is not only due to the intention of the women that they do not want to work at the distant places from their homes but also due to the living conditions. It is difficult for a single working woman to find a decent living place in most of the towns or big cities. The security environment in the country is also not such as the women may move very freely. The cases of eve teasing are on the increase and the single working woman becomes an easy prey of unscrupulous males.

The women's problems are three-fold with regard to getting employment. First of all, they have to compete in an overcrowded job market. Secondly, their families and society do not allow them to serve in those professions, which are branded as predominantly masculine in nature, even though there may be no restriction from the side of the employing authorities. Thirdly, they have the problem of finding suitable living accommodation if they get a job away from their homes or native place and added to this is the problem of security for a single working woman. All these problems are stress producing in the educated women. But it may be said that the stresses of the women can be reduced if they themselves and the society approach towards the solution of the problems with some dedication. There is no doubt in it that the number of jobs has to be increased. More efforts should be made to educate the women to generate self-employment. They may also be given vocational training. A change is to be brought in their own attitudes and the attitudes of the society and the family that it is a myth that the women are incapable of taking up some jobs which are masculine in nature. The women are capable of taking up all those jobs, which are considered masculine. In previous pages we have forcefully built the case of sexual equality on the basis of the physiology of the male and the female. Lastly, the government and the society must come forward to build "Working Women's Homes." In some towns they have been built. The need is to have a chain of such homes in each town and township.

There is another type of conflict with which the working women suffer. This is in relation to their work environment. The working women rightly demand that they should be accepted and respected as equally capable and efficient workers as males. The conflict occurs when they simultaneously demand special privileges and advantages because they are the women and the weaker sex. For example, they take up jobs that require night duties but after taking the job they may claim that since they are ladies they may be exempted from working in the night. They may press the employer to transfer them to some daytime job and transfer some male to this job. This becomes a conflict-producing situation. Some women also shirk work claiming that they are women and so entitled for light work. To avoid such conflicts the women need to develop professional attitude. There are many examples of successful women.

There is another side of the picture as well. The men resent the working women in their midst. In an office in which men and women both work the men do not feel as free with the women as with their men colleagues. If male becomes too intimate gossips are unleashed. If he ignores them he is branded as the chauvinistic male. There seems to be a need to develop a code of ethics for interpersonal relationships in those situations in which the males and females have to work in close co-ordination.

A very serious situation is developing in some places of work where the boss is male and he tries to sexually exploit his female employees. The women organizations, the government and even the courts are seized with this problem. Some women take the courage to make complaints about this behaviour of their officers or male colleague but there are lots of women who silently suffer at the hands of office sharks. Sometimes men also become victims of women's manipulations. They make false complaints about their exploitation so that the persons concerned are defamed. It is because of this danger that the complaints of women regarding exploitation are being scrutinized cautiously. Such situations can be avoided in case men and women both are made to realise that there shall be no discrimination in the work situations on the basis of sex. Both men and women must view each other as equal partners in work performance and must expect that recognition shall depend on their efficiency and quality of work and not on their sex.

As has already been pointed out that greatest danger resulting from a woman being career oriented is disharmony within her family. In Kapur's study of much marital maladjustment, the husband expected the wife to work as well as serve him and the household. The husbands generally believed in absolute supremacy over their wives and desire complete surrender and devotion from them. Those women who asserted their individuality were severely punished and ruthlessly treated, In cases where women could not tolerate the brutalities, they were separated from their spouses.

If the husband demands that his wife quit work and she refuses, it creates much tension in the family. In those cases in which the husband is transferred and the wife refuses to quit her job and go with him, legal problems arise. The husband may sue his wife for the restoration of conjugal rights. In such cases the attitude of the Indian courts has not been very decisive. Kusum (1976) cited many cases in which the wife was asked to leave her job and join her husband. In one case (Gaya Prasad Vs. Smt. Bhagwati) in Madhya Pradesh, the wife worked as Gram Sevika due to financial circumstances. The husband petitioned for the restitution of conjugal rights. The observations of the court while delivering the judgement were: "Merely on the ground that the husband has a small income, and the wife if allowed to serve at a place away from the marital home, can substantially augment the family, cannot be held to be a sufficient reason to deny the wife's society to the husband".

The above judgement was given in the sixties. From seventies onwards the change in the attitudes of the courts is noticeable, as judgements have become much less traditional. The judges concede that in case of genuine economic necessity, the wife has a right to maintain her job. But the main problem here is not only the economic necessity but also a woman's freedom to take her own decisions. The woman's personal satisfaction, sense of confidence and security and her intellectual needs must be the guiding factors in making a decision about her quitting the job or remaining in service while living away from her husband or family. Whatever may be the decisions of the courts the stressful life between the husband or and wife will continue to be lived till there is the recognition that wife also has aspirations, ambitions and a will of her own. The idea that the women should work only to supplement their husbands income is to give them much inferior position in the family than that of husbands and of considering them as only the instruments for augmenting the family incomes. The women should not be viewed as the objects or instruments, but as entities unto themselves.

Narrow and conservative concepts of in-laws are also tension producing. The in-laws, in many cases want that their daughters-in-law take up jobs but at the same time are extremely critical if she is late in returning from her place of work or is not able to do the household work as efficiently as they expect her to do.

Some studies indicate that women seek work equal to the level of their husband's prestige. In case a wife is not equally educated or trained she may prefer to stay at home rather than accept work below her husband's level. In such a case if she is forced to undertake inferior status work, she remains tense and suffers from inferiority complex. The woman herself can take steps to come out of such situation by undertaking courses or training to improve her qualifications.

Prestige and Emoluments

There is another side of the picture also. If the wife is employed in a job which has higher prestige and emoluments than the husband's job, the husband feels jealous and threatened. In many cases the tension between the husband and wife becomes so intense that living under the same roof becomes a torture leading to divorce or separation or to perpetual quarrels between them. There can develop proper amity and understanding between them if the wife tries to understand the sentiments of the husband and the husband realises that his wife deserves what she is getting. Truly well adjusted couples are those who respect each others individuality. A husband and wife can achieve harmony through mutual support and self-esteem. When both work role differentiation should not exist. The husband should give full emotional support to the wife and the wife should be considerate to the needs of the husband, may they be either psychological, physical, sexual or economical.

The girls including those who are educated find it very difficult to get a husband who does not demand dowry. In fact now the eligible bachelors and their families are demanding that the girls be educated so that they can earn money and also a dowry to meet the initial expenses of setting the home. Dowry demands are increasing day by day with the rising ambitions for equipping the houses with the modern gadgets. The educated girls whose parents search bridegrooms who are well-employed and highly educated face demands of exorbitant amounts as dowries. Such demands many parents are not able to meet with. The sensitive girls feel themselves as the cause of their parent's woes and blame themselves for being born as girls. Sometimes their tensions increase so much that they even commit suicide.

The statistics relating to dowry are very grim. Sometime back it was announced in the Lok Sabha that as many as 878 cases of dowry murders and 1,479 cases of dowry suicides were registered in the country in 1990. The educated girls who resent their husband and in-laws demands of dowry are brutally killed or forced to commit suicide. In order to stop these great human tragedies and combat horrible social evils, it would be necessary to bring about radical transformation, in the old rigid social structure. The parents of the educated girls rear them up in such a rigid environment that they themselves are incapable of finding their own life partners. They have to depend on the traditional system of marriage. The educated girls may be saved from much stress if they are left free to make a choice of their own mates. The rigid social structure can be changed only when a brave new philosophy of life steeped in socio-economic and moral values of equality of all castes and both the sexes is evolved out and adopted. Such a philosohpy will enable the male as well as the female child to spontaneously internalise the principle of equality of man, woman of all castes and creeds.

The Indian women are marching ahead in each and every field of work and activity. They are in the forefront of all the movements for progress and development. But unfortunately the area of social reforms, which touches them directly, is as yet a neglected area. The movement for women emancipation and empowerment are ridiculed and made fun of by the traditionally oriented males. The women have little say in the Parliament or state legislatures because their number is extremely limited in these bodies. The Bill for 30 per cent reservation of seats for women in the Parliament is opposed on one flimsy ground or another. Our Parliament and legislatures are responsible for the governance and the administration of the country. On them are needed such persons who are highly motivated towards efficient management, adequately educated, well-informed and possess a zeal for social service. The country at present has quite a substantial number of such women who can adorn the seats of the Parliament. There are, however, some leaders who want those women in the Parliament who are mere appendages of their husbands or male relatives. The ridiculous thing is that they want to do it in the name of social justice.

The stresses and the tensions of the modern educated Indian women can be minimised if they involve themselves in a strong movement of women emancipation and empowerment. In the Indian context it means the deliverance from the myths which have been woven around them and the false pedestal at which they have been put since long.

Many a Myth

In 1963 Frieden wrote the Feminine Mystique which attempted to explode many myths about women. Her thesis is applicable to both East and West. She writes 'the Victorian culture did not permit women to accept or gratify their basic sexual needs, our culture does not permit women to accept or gratify their basic need to grow and fulfill their potentialities as human beings, a need which is not solely defined by their sexual role". Just as the Indian women have been led to believe that their fulfillment lies in motherhood and wifely duties, so Friedan observes about American women: "In the feminine mystique, there is no other way she can even dream about herself, except as her children's mother, her husband's wife."

Simone de Beauvoir considers that the myth of feminine 'mystery' has several advantages for the male. He can dismiss inexplicable moods, behaviours, and feelings by saying:"Oh Women! Who can understand them any way?" Rohrbaugh Joanna adds: "Since woman cannot be understood, man cannot be expected to build an authentic relationship with her. He is free to relate to her in terms of his own perceptions, fantasies and desires".

Williams referring to the myth of woman as mystery says : "By defining her as mysterious, other, man spares himself the necessity of analysing her behaviours and understanding it as a consequence of her position vis-a-vis him. To do that would require acknowledgement of her oppression, and a possible shift in their power relationship? The price would be very high".

In such a 'mystique' or lifestyle, a woman's intelligence has no meaning and her capability is negated. By following a monotonous daily routine, she loses all interest in the outside world, draws herself into a shell and spends her time in gossips. She is little more than an instrument, which keeps a constant supply of members through her powers of reproduction.

Friedan emphasises that one's individuality when becoming a wife and mother should not be given up, but strengthened. She says: "Maslow found that the individuality is strengthened, that the ego is in one sense merged with another, but yet in another sense remains separate, and strong as always. The two, tendencies, to transcend individuality and to sharpen and strengthen it, must be seen as partners and not as contradictory". Self-actualised educated women should serve their society and contribute their best to humanity, just as men have the opportunity to do so. The world has suffered enough because half of humanity has remained dependent on the other half.

Indian women are often viewed as passive, prudish and fragile. Many of them feel that a mere lustful glance or touch by a non-relative male leads to the loss of their chastity. The women's movements should actively try to alter such a nonsensical perception. It may be remembered that the women in general and the educated women in particular are in danger of becoming not only household slaves but also work place slaves if they do not learn to become individualistic and assertive.

An Indian woman with lustre with a brilliance of her won, with a dynamic attitude towards life and with the charm of a sturdy woman going about her business is always in danger of being branded as aggressive, too outgoing and, perhaps, flirtatious,

This type of woman is incongruent with the image of the ideal that has been imprinted on the minds of the Indians for the centuries. The women's movements should be in the direction of relieving intelligent, modern women from the clutches of orthodoxy. The real women's movement which India need and towards which the Indian feminists seem to be fully conscious is that of removal of orthodoxy, blind faith, poverty, helplessness, dependence and complete subjugation of woman's will. The reformers should try to bring the changes in the attitudes of both male and female regarding marriage and the family. The must attack fanatical religious rites, ill conceived notions of virginity, wrong notions of chastity, custom of giving or taking dowry, wastage in the marriage ceremonies and similar other outdated customs and traditions.

We may agree with Carden when he says that : 'The new feminism is not about the elimination of differences between the sexes, nor even simply the achievement of equal opportunity; it concerns with the individual's right to find out the kind of person he or she is and to strive to become that person".

16

Trends in Twenty First Century

India is a developing country, which depends very much on its vast potential of human resources, if these resources are properly tapped the country is bound to progress efficiently, effectively and rapidly. Women form the most important part of the human resources of the nation and they may contribute very substantially in building a strong, powerful and affluent nation. They can, however, make their best contribution when they are properly educated and are able to explode the myths, which have kept them in a state of backwardness and neglect. In the present chapter we are trying to project the type of education which is needed in future for Indian women in view of their socio-phychological make up.

Today too much theory based on little reality exists. Men talk of morality while all the time degrading their women. The reformists talk of abstinence to reduce population while they themselves might have fathered more, than half a dozen children. The harmony in family life is preached while subjugating the women in the name of old ideal of Pativrata. The quarrels between the husband and wife may involve much cruelty yet the divorce may be very much condemned. There is an urgent need to cry a half to this type of duplicity in talks and action. For example, when there is genuine discord between husband and wife or there is much cruelty involved in their relationship then divorce is the only viable solution. It will injure the ego of the children much less than their upbringing in a daily quarrelsome situation. But this point of no return in the relationship between husband and wife will not come up if both respect each other's individuality and live together with mutual trust, faith, desire and love. In a stable marriage alliance consideration of each other's viewpoint is desirable and Indian men and women have the capability of developing such consideration.

There is enough scientific evidence available, which shows that since birth onwards girl child receives rejection; unequal, indifferent and discriminatory treatment as compared to male children. Access to food and other household assets allocation of domestic duties, participation in community and neighbourhood activities, school education, etc. reflect serious gender based differences and inequalities.

Scientific Techniques

Modern scientific techniques like amniocentesis and ultrasound have been widely misused as "sex determination test" for selective elimination of the female foetuses. Between 1978 and 1983, 78,000 female were aborted in India, following sex determination tests. A Mumbai-based survey in 1984 revealed that out of the 8,000 foetuses aborted following such tests 7,999 were female. Many State Governments have framed or are framing legislation against this practice. But still there is a danger that secretly such tests will continue to be conducted and female foetuses aborted. The tradition of having a male child is so deep-rooted that the women themselves do not hesitate in destroying their pregnancies if the tests reveal that the baby to be born is a female. Proper education is needed to discourage this tendency. It has been noticed that many educated women also indulge in the practice of destroying foetuses hence our emphasis is on proper education by which we mean an education, which frees the woman from gender biases.

Conservative cultural values, coupled with assumption of domestic responsibilities dictate the girl child's withdrawal from formal education in our country the female literacy rates are very low. These are 39.4 per cent according to the 1991 census. The drop out rate for girls in the school is estimated at 55.5 per cent at the primary stage and 77.7 per cent at the middle school stage. There is thus great need for having a crash programme for women education.

It is unfortunate that in spite of Indian women getting all those legal rights which are being demanded by the women of some developed nations they are having quite difficult time in keeping themselves from the old fossilised traditions. The mother cult may be one of the reasons for their remaining tradition oriented. Though that which is motherly is represented as noble, it has its drawbacks as well in those situations in which the women cannot think of any other thing except being mothers. The motherhood syndrome is incompatible with modern woman's development and exists because of cultural conditioning. According to Evelyn Reed: "The subordination of the women is not the result of a predetermined biological handicap i.e. child bearing." She considers that attribution of inferior status of women to her faulty biology is a false preposition.

Self-reliance, self-esteem and a reality-oriented approach to life must be the goal of Indian women. Some people may take exception to this suggestion because of the fear of loss of domestic harmony but unless the women are able to assert their will the family and the social life will remain in a state of disharmony.

Socialist Pattern

After independence India framed planning, strategies and techniques to steer the nation's economic development towards attaining a socialist pattern of society. The first five-year plan was launched in 1950-51 and thereafter nine more five-year plans besides some yearly plans have already been adopted. In each of these plans women's development issues, especially their economic, educational and health issues, have received considerable attention and various welfare measures were taken to ameliorate their conditions. The result of all these measures is that the status and position of the Indian women have much improved. But as we have repeated again and again in this book there is much, which has still to be done.

National Policy

The Draft of the National Policy on Empowerment of Women released by the Ministry of Human Resource Development seeks to eliminate all forms of violence against women as also to abolish discrimination against the girl child. It commits the government to ensure that women are not denied of their human rights and fundamental freedom. This policy also seeks to provide equal opportunities for power sharing and decision-making to women at all levels and processes in public and private sectors. All these are highly desirable goals. But these alone would not be sufficient unless the government policies and its mechanism are supplemented by a social will, a wave and a movement by women themselves for achieving these goals and for promoting rational attitudinal changes.

The National Policy on Education (NPE) 1986 has given very important recommendations for women education. It has paid attention to the basic issues of women's equality. In the section titled 'Education for Women's Equality' the Policy states:

> "Education will be used as an agent of basic change in the status of women. In order to neutralise the accumulated distortions of the past, there will be a well-conceived edge in favour of women. The national education system will pay a positive role in the empowerment of women. It will foster the development of new values through redesigned curricula textbooks, training and orientation of teachers, decision makers and administrators, and the active involvement of educational institutions— women's studies will be promoted as a part of various courses and educational institutions encouraged to take up active programmes to further women's development.

Women's Participation

The removal of women's illiteracy and obstacles inhibiting their access to, and retention in, elementary education will receive overriding priority, through provision of special support services, setting of time targets and effective monitoring. Major emphasis will be laid on women's participation in vocational, technical and professional education at different levels. The policy of nondiscrimination will be pursued vigorously to eliminate sex stereotyping in vocational and professional courses and to promote women's participation in non-traditional occupation, as well as in existing and exerged technologies".

The above recommendations have given very important guidelines for the futuristic education of the women. The government definitely took interest in implementing the policy framework and so there were developed "Programme of Action" in 1986 and 1992. Also a National Perspective Plan for Women's Education 1997-98 to 2000 AD was drawn. The National Perspective Plan formulated some important specific objectives for women education so that women may also participate actively in the social cultural, economic and political areas. These important objectives were to be obtained by 2000 AD. These objectives included elimination of illiteracy and universalisation of elementary education, substantial vocalisation and diversification of courses at secondary level, making education as an effective means for women equality, making necessary intervention in the content and processes of education to inculcate positive and egalitarian attitudes, providing non-formal and part-time courses to women to enable them to acquire knowledge and skills for their social, cultural and economic advancement, and to provide impetus to women to enroll themselves in various professional degree courses so as to increase their number in medicine, teaching, engineering and other fields substantially. To achieve the above mentioned and some other objectives the National Perspective Plan made important recommendations that awareness needs to be generated among the masses regarding the necessity of educating girls so as to prepare them to effectively contribute to the socio-economic development of the country, to strengthen their role in society and to realise their own capacities for improving and minimising drop-outs and wastage of girl students.

The Revised Plan of Action (1992) has laid down suitable strategies for implementing the above mentioned targets.

In spite of all endeavours made so far for promoting women education, we still find that for every 100 boys there are only 62 girls in primary schools, 43 girls in middle schools, 36 girls in secondary schools and 31 girls at different stages of higher education. According to the 1991 census female literacy is 39.4 per cent compared to 63.8 per cent for males, the total number of female illiterates is 197 millions which is more than male counterparts by 70 millions, even though the female population is less than the male population by 32 millions. There are rural urban disparities, and among rural women, literacy is about half of the urban female literacy.

The above figures lead us to conclude that more intensive efforts are needed to educate our women specially those who are living in the rural areas or the slum areas in the towns. Since most of these women who are illiterate and do not go to the school the programmes for educating them may be accompanied with the programmes of improving their financial conditions. The programmes for the poverty alleviation should be intensified. It may be emphasised that the success of any scheme of education depends to a great extent on it being productive both in the material as well as social sense. Actually education should lead to social, economic and moral development. An educated person must be able to earn more than an uneducated one. The national education system will play a positive, interventionist role in the empowerment of women. It will foster the development of new values through redesigned curricula, textbooks, training and orientation of teachers, decision-makers and administrators, and the active involvement of educational institutions. Women's studies will be promoted as a part of various courses and educational institutions encouraged taking up active programmes to further women's development.

The removal of women's illiteracy and obstacles inhibiting their access to, and retention in, elementary education will receive overriding priority, through provision of special support services, setting of time targets and effective monitoring. Major emphasis will be laid on women's participation in vocational, technical and professional education at different levels. The policy of nondiscrimination will be pursued vigorously to eliminate sex stereo-typing in vocational and professional courses and to promote women's contribution effectively towards bringing desirable social change and be honest, sincere and affectionate individual. For our women such education is required which may help them in getting gainful employment and in improving their financial position.

From the above discussion it may be evident that the government is very much aware of the need of providing education to the women of the country. In the recent decades it has made some genuine efforts to bring the women on the national scene by giving them incentives, providing for their education schools and colleges, giving free education to the girls up to a particular stage, developing centres of women studies, opening various avenues of employment to them, providing non-formal centres for their vocational training. It is very much desirable that no discrimination is made on the basis of jobs meant exclusively for males or for females. The interest of the student should be the main consideration. From the lower classes onwards the attention of the students should be directed towards creating social awareness and motivating them for higher achievements in all the areas of concern to them. India needs good housewives as well as efficient women workers. Education for women must be organised around these two powerful needs.

Expansion of Education

It is to be noted that the outlook of the women has changed considerably during the last four decades. Much of it is due to the expansion of education that has taken place in the country. The young women of today are neither afraid of moving out of their homes nor are as dependent on their parents or husbands as were their mothers and grand mothers. The woman wants to be economically independent. She has realised the importance of education and is quite conscious of the need of raising the standard of living of the family through her engagement in the world of work. The educated women are prepared to fight for their rights and to assert their individuality. Hence web may say that the educational efforts made so far have yielded positive results. These efforts are now required to be intensified. Certain changes in the educational system are also needed so that the women learn to be self-reliant, are able to develop self-esteem and become caring, loving and the source of amity and goodwill in the family.

The following are some suggestions regarding the changes to be brought about in the educational system:

1. All out efforts should be made to implement the constitutional directives of compulsory elementary education up to 14 years of age. Education should be free up to this age for both boys and girls.

2. The girls should be taught the same subjects as are being taught to the boys, which means that if home craft is taught to the girls it should also be taught to the boys. The physical education should be given to both boys and girls. At the onset of puberty the girl's menses begin. At this age some training in personal hygiene may be given exclusively to the girls.

3. From the lower classes onwards the attention of the students should be directed towards social evils and in them social awareness should be created. They should also be motivated for higher achievements in all the areas of concern to them. As said earlier India needs good housewives as well as efficient women workers. Education for women must be organised around these two powerful needs.

4. The girls should be encouraged to join technical, managerial, professional institutions of higher learning so that they can compete with boys in the job market.

5. The methods of teaching should be so planned that they inculcate the habits of thinking freely and expressing their views freely.

6. The curricula of all the subjects, which are taught to the school children, should be free from sex bias.

7. The education of the school children must include co-curricular activities in which both boys and girls should participate and learn to take independent decisions.

8. In our educational institutions the courses in the maintenance of inter-personal relationships be introduced. Some of these courses must be compulsory for both boys and girls.

9. Some special courses for girls in mother craft, in the home economics and household affairs should be introduced. Some of such courses may also be open for boys.

10. Non-formal system of education must be strengthened. It should be available to all those girls who are unable to join the formal system of education. Education from the elementary to postgraduate levels must be available through this system.

11. A network of adult literacy centres must be established throughout the country. In these centres the education for social change must be stressed. The women must specially be prepared to fight against social evils and to rise above their mythical existence.

12. A network of counselling centres must be set up. These centres must be equipped with to give educational, vocational and personal counselling. Special emphasis should also be placed to marital and family conselling. Each big school must have adequately

trained counsellors. Counselling is very much needed at the adolescent stage to both the boys and girls. Our educational system must be able to fulfil this need.

13. Precaution should be taken in teaching those topics, which involve the status and position of women. It will all depend on the teachers how they present an episode where the women are depicted as serving their husbands. It may be taught in terms of inferior position of the women or it may be taught as an ideal example of love and affection. The teachers training colleges or colleges of education should pay special attention towards the teaching of such lessons by their teacher trainees so that the myths regarding women perpetuated in our society for centuries are exploded and the modern outlook is inculcated.

14. The educational institutions must also provide placement services so that the boys and girls are not only prepared for jobs but are also able to be placed in jobs.

15. The emphasis on the education of the girls must be specifically on making them strong so that they are able to reverse their image of being delicate and unfit for jobs requiring tough exterior.

The above are some of the suggestions which have emerged out of the discussions made in the different chapters of the present book. Many useful and worthwhile suggestions have been made by various commissions and committees, plans and policies. We have refrained ourselves form repeating them, as they are available in the from of reports in full details. In planning or the futuristic education they may all be taken into consideration.

In conclusion we may say that the Indian women have always been quite strong. They have always been in the forefront of the struggle for the betterment of the mankind. They have been great support to their male counterpart. It is their power of resilience that in spite of the persistent efforts of the male to enmesh them in the web of myth they have never lost their composure and cool and today they are bravely facing the challenges of their subjugation.

ti

17

Future Programme

The Perspective Plan for Women is an effort at a long term overall policy for Indian Women, guided by those constitutional principles and directives relevant to the development process. It is linked to the national targets determined for the end of the century in respect of certain basic indicators especially of health, education and employment. The Plan views women not as the weaker segment of society or as passive beneficiaries of the development process, but as a source of unique strength for reaching national goals.

The Plan aims at:

> Economic development and integration of women into the mainstream of the economy.
>
> Equity and social justice for all women.

These are critical goals for the all round development of women not merely as producers and providers, but also as individuals with a right to human dignity in a society where 'culture', 'caste' and 'class' tend to discriminate against gender.

The overall purpose of this plan is to find the highest common denominator for all national endeavour, running across the spectrum of class and religion; functions, sectors and disciplines; to harness the resource represented by the people-both the women as well as the men. This renewal of efforts, from the fifth decade of political independence, will have meaning only if the full potential of the silent half-comprising the 331 million women and girls of India, (about 150 million of them in material poverty and many more close to it) is harnessed. The direction and design, priorities and pace of national development, must have direct relevance to their lives and future. Every dimension of development-political, economic and cultural, not just social-has to assist and hasten their generation.

If the results and lessons of the past are any guide, a larger allocation of resources for women within the prevailing patterns and structures of development, does not promise a reversal of trends. A parallel sub-stream of women's development even if possible, will only perpetuate discrimination and subordination. An alternative strategy of national development which will provide not just some additional space for women, but create a democratic, egalitarian, secular, cooperative social structure has to be defined and tried. In such a scheme, it will be necessary to accelerate the women's component of composite programmes, to ensure the integrity of the enterprise as well as a measure of compensatory justice. The goals of holistic human development must not be at the expense of one another and the ascent to equality must be collective.

Current Situation

For outlining a development perspective, a review of the existing situation of the Indian woman is an essential prerequisite. Both, positive indicators as well as negative indices that are a growing cause of concern to policy makers, planners, administrators and activists are projected to present her overall status. A brief review of the Five-Year Plans and the programmes for women launched in the last few decades, is also included.

Among the positive developments affecting women are:

The expectation of life at birth has improved from 44.7 years in 1961-71 to 52.9 years in 1971-81.

The sex ratio has registered a slight rise-from 930 women per thousand men in 1971 to 933 per thousand men in 1981. The average age at marriage for girls has reached 18.3 years in 1981 as against 17.2 years in 1971, achieving for the first time an average higher than the minimum prescribed age for marriage.

The focus in the programmes for women has shifted from welfare to development. This shift can be perceived in the creation of a separate department for the development of women.

The Programme of Action of the National Policy on Education (1986) lays stress on women's equality and has identified for the first time three areas for special attention, viz. (i) review of school textbooks to remove sexist bias and developing approaches to promotion of the value of equality through school curricula; (ii) reorientation of teachers to promote gender equality through their teaching and (iii) increasing the coverage of women and women's issues in the research and teaching activities of higher education.

Women's Studies and Development Centres have been set up in constituent colleges of several universities with the objective of using students and teachers as resource groups for creating social awareness and bringing about attitudinal changes in society.

There is an effort to sensitize administration to the women's perspective in development programmes, through the introduction of a women's component in training programmes for senior administrators conducted by the Department of Personnel in the Government of India.

There is a special effort launched to involve women at all levels in the planning and implementation process of programmes for women.

There is an increasing emphasis on professionalizing women's programmes by providing technical expertise for their implementation.

For the first time since Independence the elected representation of women in Parliament has gone up to almost 10 per cent of its total membership.

The Prime Minister's office has now identified 27 beneficiary oriented schemes exclusively for women. These schemes though falling under various Ministers are monitored by the Department of Women and Child Development, Ministry of Human Resource Development.

A National Advisory Committee on Women has been set up with the Prime Minister as Chairman.

Several legislative enactments/amendments have come into force to protect the interests of women.

Overshadowing the positive indicators, there are certain distressing negative indices as follows:

Though a marginal improvement has been registered in the sex ratio, the projected ratio for 2000 AD is depressing with 500 million males to 480 million females.

Amniocentesis tests are being misused to determine the sex of the child in the womb, resulting in the female foetus being aborted.

Age specific death rates indicate higher rates for female children and women up to 35 years of age.

As per the 1981 Census, 75 per cent of women are illiterate. This is compounded by the high drop out rate for girls which is estimated at 55.5 per cent at the primary stage and 77.7 per cent at the middle school stage. Enrolment of girls in higher education has been almost static from 1975 to 1985. There are also substantial disparities in the enrolment of girls and boys at the university stage, and in technical and professional colleges.

The work participation rate for females declined in the census decades up to 1981. In 1981, it recorded a marginal improvement.

The fertility rates in 1981 showed only a very marginal decline-average number of children born to a woman during her lifetime being 4.6. There are in addition many incomplete pregnancies. Over 50 per cent of women suffer from anaemia in pregnancy, which accounts directly for 15-20 per cent of all maternal deaths.

Approximately 90 per cent of the women workers are engaged in the unorganized sector. Of these over 80 per cent are in agriculture and allied occupations. In the organized sector women constitute only 13.3 per cent of all employees. In the public sector, they account for 11 per cent of total employment and in the private sector for 17.8 per cent.

The number of female job seekers through employment exchanges increased from 11.2 lakh in 1975 to 51 lakh in

1986. After showing an increase between 1975 and 1982, the percentage of placements declined in the subsequent years, i.e., 1983-86.

Studies show that modernization and mechanization are tending to marginalize women in many sectors. They are either pushed down or out of the workforce. There are also indications that agricultural modernization/ industrial growth policies have tended to widen gender disparities.

Estimates of the average hours of unpaid work done by women outside their homes vary from 6.1 and 7.5 hours per day, with some women working up to 10 hours and more. Apart from their domestic duties, women are engaged in agricultural operations for an average of 12 hours a day. Despite this, their access to ownership of land, credit and other productive resources remains negligible.

Recent surveys indicate that, 30-35 per cent of rural households are headed by women due to male migration, neglect, abandonment.

Only 994 women hold senior management/administrative posts as against 15,993 men in similar jobs in the All India Services, constituting only 5.8 per cent. There are only 21 women officers in the Indian Police Service as against 2418 men (0.9 per cent). In the Indian Administrative Services, there are 339 women against 4209 men (7.5 per cent).

Women comprise only 7.5 per cent of the membership of registered trade unions and approximately one per cent of the office bearers and executive committee members.

Proportional representation of women in elected offices either remained stagnant or declined in the last decade.

This is not withstanding their increased voting turnout in the general elections.

Crimes against women continue unabated, there were 6668 reported victims of rape in 1987 and 1517 dowry deaths including by burning (provisional figures).

The *First Five-Year Plan* (1951-56) envisaged welfare measures for women. To spearhead welfare measures, the Central Social Welfare Board (CSWB) was established in 1953 which symbolized the welfare approach to women's problems. The CSWB was also reflective of the community development approach, which envisaged for the first time, the need for organizing women into Mahila Mandals or Women's Clubs. A number of studies have shown that the community development (CD) worker, perceived more as a harmonizer of interests rather than a stimulator of awareness, worked closely with the rural elite. Moreover, although rural women came within the purview of the CD programmes, they were not specifically catered to as a target population based on economic or other specific class related criteria. A large majority of poor rural women thus remained untouched.

The *Second Five-Year Plan* (1956-61) was closely linked with the overall approach of intensive agricultural development. The welfare approach to women's issues persisted. The plan recognized the need for the organization of women as workers. It also perceived the social prejudices/disabilities they suffered. The Plan stated that women should be protected against injurious work, should receive maternity benefits and creches for children. It also suggested speedy implementation of the principle of equal pay for equal work and provision for training to enable women to compete for higher jobs.

The *Third Five-Year Plan* (1961-66) pinpointed female education as a major welfare strategy. In social welfare, the largest share was provided for expanding rural welfare services and condensed courses of education. The health programme concentrated mainly on the provision of services for maternal and child welfare, health education, nutrition and family planning.

The *Fourth Five-Year Plan* (1969-74) continued the emphasis on women education. The basic policy was to promote women's welfare within the family as the base of operation. The outlay on Family Planning was stepped up to reduce the birth rate from 40 to 25 per thousand through mass education. High priority was accorded to immunization of pre-school children and supplementary feeding for children, expectant and nursing mothers.

The *Fifth Five-Year Plan* (1974-79) emphasized the need to train women in need of income and protection. It also recommended a programme of functional literacy to equip women with skills and knowledge to perform the functions of a housewife (including child care, nutrition, health care, home economics, etc.)

This Plan coincided with the International Women's Decade and the submission of the Report of the Committee on the Status of Women in India (CSWI). The overall task of the CSWI was to undertake a comprehensive examination of all the questions relating to the rights and status of women in the context of changing social and economic conditions in the country and problems relating to the advancement of women. The report stressed that the dynamics of social change and development had adversely affected a large section of women and had created new imbalances and disparities such as:

- The declining sex ratio;
- Lower expectancy of life;
- Higher infant and maternal mortality;
- Declining work participation;
- Illiteracy; and
- Rising migration.

The CSWI Report led to a debate in Parliament and the emergence of a new consciousness of women as critical inputs for national development rather than as targets for welfare policies. A second significant outcome was the recognition of women as a group adversely affected by the processes of economic transformation. It was realized that constitutional guarantees of equality would be meaningless and unrealistic unless women's right to economic independence is acknowledged and their training in skills as contributors to the family and the national economy is improved. A major outcome of the CSWI report was the National Plan of Action (1976) that provided the guidelines based on the UN's World Plan of Action for Women. The National Plan of Action (1976) identified areas of health, family planning, nutrition, education, employment, legislation and social welfare for formulating and implementing action programmes for women as called for planned interventions to improve the conditions of women in India.

An immediate outcome of the National Plan of Action was the setting up of the Women's Welfare and Development Bureau in 1976 under the Ministry of Social Welfare, to act as a nodal point within the Government of India to coordinate policies and programmes and initiate measures for women's development. The Women's Welfare and Development Bureau was charged with the nodal responsibility of:

(a) Co-ordinating and collaborating with multifarious programmes in other Central Government Ministries;

(b) Initiating necessary policies, programmes and measures;

(c) Collecting data to serve as a clearing house;

(d) Monitoring programmes for women's welfare,

(e) Servicing the National Committee on Women;

(f) Following up on the recommendations of the CSWI by formulating proposals and providing guidelines;

(g) Working out financial and physical targets;

(h) Liaising with multinational / UN agencies in the field of women's welfare;

(i) Legal issues and problems concerning women; and

(j) Implementing programmes and schemes.

In 1977-78 as an exercise for the Sixth Plan, the Government appointed the Working Group on Employment of women. Two other critical reports on village level organizations and participation of women in agriculture and rural development were prepared as part of the exercise. This plan was undoubtedly influenced by the CSWI Report of 1975. It devoted a whole chapter to Women and Development. For the first time a shift was perceived from welfare to development approaches for women. Influenced by the era that heralded concepts of social justice, the Sixth Plan recognized women's lack of access to resources as a critical factor impeding their development and, among others, the programme providing joint *pattas* (titles) to men and women was initiated. However, though the plan defined the magnitude of women's problems and suggested development strategies, the 'Family' rather than the 'women' remained the basic unit of development programming.

The *Seventh Five-Year Plan* operationalized the concern for equity and empowerment articulated by the International Decade for Women. For the first time, the emphasis was qualitative, focusing on inculcating confidence among women; generating awareness about their rights and privileges; and training them for economic activity and employment. In keeping with the spirit of the decade which aimed at integrating women into mainstream national development, the Plan emphasized the need to open new avenues of work for women and perceive them as a crucial resource for the development of the country.

The access of women to critical inputs and productive resources such as land (joint title on *patta* scheme initiated in the Sixth Plan period) were expanded in the Seventh Plan period to include support through credit (or small scale capital), marketing, training in skills/management and technology. At the same time, it was emphasized that technology that causes unemployment or displacement of women must be resisted. Another salient and crucial recognition was the need for organization of women workers and unionization that could:

(a) Make demands for improving legal services to safeguard rights; and

(b) Reduce occupational and health hazards.

The Plan acknowledged the long hours spent by women in activities within the household especially in the collection of fuel, fodder, water, etc., as well as their labour on the family farm or in family business. While the Seventh Plan did not call for the computation of women's work in these two areas as part of women's contribution to the GNP, the identification of these hitherto invisible areas was a significant beginning. Complementing the productive endeavour were the supportive services offered to women, especially maternal and child care facilities as part of the total package of services for women.

Schemes in Operation

Currently, the Government of India has over twenty-seven schemes for women, some women specific and others both for the male and female population. These schemes are located in different departments and ministries of the Government of India such as Rural Development, Labour, Education, Health Science &

Technology, Welfare, Women and Child Development, etc. The total outlay on the women-specific schemes in the Seventh Plan is 2.4 per cent of the total while a gender break-up of beneficiaries or targets is unavailable for general schemes (RLEGP, NREP, etc.)

In 1985 the Government of India constituted a separate Department in the Ministry of Human Resource Development, for the development of women and children. This Department funds the Central Social Welfare Board that has developmental and welfare programmes for women. The Department also plans and executes programmes for women besides monitoring programmes for women in other Ministries /Departments. A number of these programmes were envisaged in the Sixth/Seventh Plan period-viz., Women's Development Corporations, Support to Training and Employment Programme (STEP), Training-cum-Production Centres for Women, Generation Awareness Camps for Rural and Poor Women, Women's Training Centres or Institutes for Rehabilitation of Women in Distress, Short Stay Homes for Women and Girls, Voluntary Action Bureau and Family Counselling Centres, Free Legal Aid & Para Legal Training, Working Women's Hostels, etc.

Women specific programmes implemented by the Department of Women and Child Development include:

(i) Strengthening and improvement of women's work and employment in agriculture, small animal husbandry, dairying, fisheries, handlooms, handicrafts, khadi and village industries, and sericulture;

(ii) Economic rehabilitation of women from weaker sections of society in the form of training and employment on a sustained basis;

(iii) Better employment avenues for women to bring them into mainstream national development;

(iv) Providing Short Stay Homes for women and girls in moral danger together with counselling, medical care, psychiatric guidance and treatment and services, and development of skills; and

(v) Preventive and rehabilitative services to women and children who are victims of atrocities and exploitation.

The thrust of these various programmes is to provide five principal categories of services:

(a) Employment & Income Generation Services;

(b) Education & Training Services;

(c) Support Services;

(d) General Awareness Services; and

(e) Legal Support Services

The Prospects

Poverty is a consequence as well as a cause of several factors that limit life. The obstinacy of this self-perpetuating cycle needs to be broken before its grip can be loosened and overcome in the measurable future. The poverty-induced cycle affects all the people but impinges hardest on girls and women. Material poverty starts a chain of consequences, namely, infections, nutritional deficiencies, ill-health, growth retardation, slow learning, small body size, low productivity, repeated child bearing, excess of unpaid and unrecognized work, low earning capacity, unemployment and perpetuation of poverty. The strategic response need not tax the nation's resources and can yield decisive social benefits if it spans the spectrum of needs through the life cycle-the girl's education, food, security, safer environment in the home and neighbourhood, vocational training, support services to save time and energy, income and employment opportunity, safe motherhood, breast feeding and proper weaning, immunity against childhood diseases, management of common illnesses like diarrhoea and respiratory infection, growth promotion and early childhood stimulation as educational foundation leading to full and equal participation in socio-economic life. The process of inter generational (and now intragender,) improvement, which is what development planning is about, has to ascend these steps in an unbroken sequence.

These may not necessarily cover women in specially difficult circumstances such as refugees and migrants, prostitutes and victims of atrocities, the mentally and physically handicapped, etc., as these would require separate and detailed studies as has been done in the case of women in custody. However, for the majority of women, especially the rural poor, an integrated and decentralized approach to planning is envisaged. While the plan perceives main-streaming as long-term goal, it also realizes that some sector-specific measures will have to be undertaken to elicit higher participation of women in the development process during the interim period.

Recognizing the need for a holistic approach, the Perspective Plan offers sectoral reviews of the situation of women in rural development, employment, supportive services, education, health, legislation, political participation, media and communication and voluntary action, while suggesting inter-linked and converging strategies towards a holistic development of women in the new Millennium.

18

Conclusion

Woman has been the subject of love-hate, appreciation-ridicule, acceptance-rejection and good-evil ambivalence since ancient times. Whatever media, man had at every stage of history, used to describe and express his feelings towards women, songs were sung, dramas were staged, poems were composed, paintings were drawn, sculptures were carved, and models were constructed to concretely reveal these dichotomous emotions. Literature is full of the chaste, noblest and most revered saint-like women as well as most vile and evil witch like women. Man found woman a natural object for the satisfaction of his passion. Like food, she satisfied his natural urge and became an essential part of his existence. However, because she was a dynamic being capable of expressing her own wants and needs, man could not control her as easily as he wished. This created a frustration within him since he could neither rule her nor ignore her. Thus all of the finer and basal qualities of humanity became associated with woman. She was viewed as goddess, the representative of all that's good in human nature, and as a witch, the harbinger of all the evils in society.

In many verses of the ancient Hindu scripture, Rig Veda, women are praised as mothers and wives. In other verses, they are blamed for their evil nature. Verse 5-616 reads: "Yea, many a woman is more firm and better than the man who turns away from God and offers not". A different view is expressed in verse 17-8-33: The mind of woman brooks not discipline. Her intellect hath little weight." A most derogatory reference to woman is found in verse 10-95-15: "With women there can be no lasting friendship: hearts of hyenas are the hearts of women. "

Indra cites Shatapatha Brahman as stating that women who are mothers are considered the best and foremost preceptors of children. Indra further elaborates by stating that "a woman is a hundred times superior to a man in instructing and elevating a child." Indra cites Manu's view that women are to be goddesses in their homes. Wives and mothers who secure many blessings, who are worthy of worship and irradiate their dwellings are equated to goddesses of fortune who reside in the houses of men." Indra summaries Manu's views by stating that the prosperity of the family lies with the happiness of the females in the household where the female relations live in grief, the family soon wholly perishes; the family where they are not unhappy ever prospers. The epic Mahabharata enjoins all to honour women because the virtues of men depend on women and because all pleasure and enjoyment also entirely depend on them.

The ambivalence with which Manu views Indian women is apparent in his description of them as morally low creatures: "It is the nature of the woman to seduce men in this world, for that reason the wise are never unguarded in the company of females. For women are able to lead astray in this world even a learned man and make him a slave of desires and anger." Women are described as lustful and impure in their desires and are debarred from receiving sacramental rites with sacred texts: "For women no sacramental rites is performed with sacred texts, thus the law is settled. Women are destitute of strength and destitute of the knowledge of Vedic texts and are as impure as falsehood itself." The Mahabharata depicts women as deceitful and unfathomable": The faces of women are like flowers, their words are like the drops of honey and their hearts like sharp razors, the interior of them no one can know. Shukra, a writer of the post-epic age holds women as inherently weak and given to eight vices: "falsehood, inconstancy, deceitfulness, stupidity, greediness, impurity, cruelty and insolence." Carstairs presents this duality in terms of the spiritualistic perception of the goddess Kali, protective mother to her worshippers. She stands on top of her male adversary, cuts off his head and drinks his blood. A woman whose demands cannot be met may be viewed as one who assumes demonic powers and extracts her due. It is clear that in Indian thought the concept of protective power in women along with demonic reprisal when offended are consistently interwoven.

The Mahabharata attributes this fear of woman to her great sexual powers: "Fire is never satiated with fuel. Ocean can never be filled with waters that the rivers bring to it. The destroyer is never satiated with killing even all-living creatures. Likewise women are never satisfied with men." Women are described as powerful, demanding, seductive and ultimately destructive. Sexual love is believed to be destructive to a man's spiritual and physical natures.

The dread of a woman's vagina is very much present in Indian culture just as it has been found in many other cultures. Horney says, "Men have never tired of fashioning expressions for the violent force by which man feels himself drawn to the woman and side by side with his longing, the dread that through her he might die and be undone." To the male Indians, the vagina was an ever opening, engulfing, unsatiable organ. They found it difficult to save themselves from the attractions of the female vagina while being afraid that upon entering it, all would be lost. They conceived it as a snatcher of their powers.

According to the famous story of the birth of Shakuntla, the great sage Vishwamitra lost his power to dislodge the heavenly king Indra as he was lured by Menka who was a celestial being of Indra's court. To lose the powers achieved after great penance is symbolically worse than physical death. Most of the Indian sages in the post Vedic period extolled the spiritual and moral virtues of celibacy and continence. They considered that excessive physical strength could be obtained through Brahmacharya, the control of the sexual urge. Hanuman, the monkey god of the epic Ramayana, was endowed with colossal strength and became recognised as the ideal of the celibates. His strength and power were attributed to his Nitya Brahmacharya, which meant that he was able to repeal successfully the attraction of the vagina.

It was considered a crime if a woman who was in her ritu period was not sexually satisfied. According to the Indians, "the ritu was twelve days after the stoppage of the flow of the menstrual fluid. This would be a woman's fertile time of ovulation. In the Epic period of India ritu was considered the most important part of a woman's life: With the ritu, love begins; with it, it ends, in it, it has always its central point". The urge for coitus was supposed to be great during this time and for a woman passing through this period, satisfaction was her holy right as well as command.

Many myths illustrate the woman arguing with a reluctant male for intercourse as if she were in her ritu. It was considered a sin for him not to satisfy her and give her motherhood. One such example is that of Carmishta Devyani was the energetic daughter of a Brahmin and was married to king Yayati. Another king's daughter, Carmishta, who had insulted Devyani was given as a slave girl in marriage. Her father asked Yayati not to touch his daughter. Carmishta got her ritu while the king was visiting her quarters. She convinced him to make love to her on the basis of the holy law. When she complained to her father about the incident, King Yayati explained that he did not want to be known as an embryo slayer and out of that fear he went to Carmishta when she requested it of him."

The leanings towards celibacy did not minimize the attraction of the vagina among the people of India. It was assigned mythical powers in many tales where men could not be saved from its attraction. Because the entire human race sprang from this mysterious opening; it became the symbol of creation. The philosophical mind extended this symbolism to the extent that the female vagina became the goddess who created the mankind.

Sculptures are available which depict the sexual triangle, the Yoni as prominently visible. Desai describes two types of these goddesses as the opulent goddess and the personified yoni type of goddess. The opulent goddess has broad hips and exposed sexual triangle and is seen in a frontal pose on a pre-Asokan gold plaque of Lauriya in Champaran district. The personified Yoni figures existed in early centuries of the, Christian era at Bhita, Jhusi and Kausambi in Uttar Pradesh, Ter and Nevasa in Maharashtra and Nagar jupakonda in Andhra Pradesh. The goddess is usually headless with a lotus replacing her head. She is nude and sits with her legs apart like a frog, Uttanapad, with her yoni fully visible. According to Desai, even today, women worship such figures of the goddess and apply butter and kumkuma on the yoni for begetting children. Thus the fertility aspect of this goddess can be established beyond a doubt.

These creative powers are also associated with destructive powers, which are attributed to women. The Hindus describe earth as Mother Earth and death as a return to Mother Earth since the dead are put on the earth. Thus death is philosophically and symbolically considered a return to the womb. Horney says: "We have learned to understand the longing for death as a longing for reunion with the mother. This psycho-analytical observation is very much in keeping with the emphasis of the Hindu symbolisation of death. According to Desai, the image of the Opulent Goddess could have been worn as either a fertility ornament or was associated with the burial grounds. In either case, its magico-religious function is significant. The vagina as a magic symbol of destruction is also implied in the curbing of sexual energy and the magical powers of chastity." In the Apastamba DharaMasutra, this view is stated: They who keep the vow of chastity, accomplish their wishes merely by conceiving them, for instance the desire to produce rain, to bestow children. This power is considered lost if the vagina is entered into.

Another factor involved in the dread of vagina is the severe restrictions placed on the menstruating women. The Hindus believe that the presence of such a woman is offensive and the gods will not take sacrifice that she has looked upon. The food she prepares or looks upon must not be eaten, and she should not be spoken to. These taboos illustrate the fear with which ancient Indians viewed the menstrual flow as well as the fluids during and after childbirth. Some of these notions are still prevalent among a large number of illiterate and orthodox people of this country. Only the educated few have been able to transcend these myths.

It may be due to the inescapable attraction of woman that she is conversely labelled as evil in many cultures. Men can find no retreat for woman and are, therefore, led to brand her as destructive. According to the text of the Islamic Shia sect, women are of value only as vehicles for entry into the world of spirits condemned temporarily to take on flesh in punishment for their sins; they themselves being, however, without soul.

Lederer quotes from the very revered fathers Henry Kramer and James Sprenger in Part 1, question VI, of their Malleus, 1486 AD., now nearly all the kingdoms of the world have been overthrown by women... Therefore it is no wonder if the world suffers through the malice of women. It is said he who trusts a woman, he also trusts a deceiver. Talmund describes how God chose which part of Adam's body to make Eve from. God decided that the rib would be the chastest part, but even with all this precaution, woman has all the faults God tried to avoid. Adam, upon seeing Eve, said, This is my never silent Hell.

Christian sages regarded woman as evil. Tertulliarn wrote the following for the edification of his contemporaries:

> "You must know that you are Eve. You are the devil's gateway... How easily you destroyed man, the image of God. Because of the death which you brought upon us, even the Son of God had to die."

Women are viewed differently in Hindu religion in that the Hindus branded women as goddesses possessing energy. The Shakti or power is embodied in the female and not in the male.

Man alone is not the beginning and end. Man without woman is nothing. Maya Shakti is personified as the world protecting feminine, maternal side of the Ultimate Being, and as such, stands for the spontaneous, loving acceptance of life's tangible reality. Thomas Aquinas on the other hand says, In a secondary sense the image of God is found in man, and not in woman for man is the beginning and the end of every creature. The Hindus personify the energy of a God and speak of it as his wife (Shakti). Not separate from Himself, for a better understanding of the active aspect of the deity, she is brought within the compass of human perceptive capacity and endowed with an entity of her own, states P. Thomas.

In spite of this recognition of the female as active principle, the Indian male failed to continue to revere and respect woman. Instead he became obsessed with controlling and subduing her. Except in the Vedic times and the Epic times, women were always ill-treated. With the passage of time, a wide gulf was created between the spiritual aspect of woman's existence and her physical being. Traditional observance to the goddess replica of woman was continued while, in reality, her status and power within society and the family was continually undermined. Eventually, women were considered mere possessions and burned alive with their deceased husbands. The Indian woman lost her image as a goddess and her witch nature became the standard of belief.

The process of subjugating the virile, strong Aryan women was difficult task. The assertive male had to search out many means by which to accomplish this domination. She had to be pulled down from her goddess pedestal. This was accomplished by completely domesticating her. She was taught that she must keep harmony in the family and submit completely to her husband's wishes. If she worshipped her husband as lord and master, then she might regain her status and be put again on her throne. The myths, stories and preaching of the sages put forth an intense psychological impression upon the mind of the woman and brain washed her into a life of secondary existence. Horney highlights this phenomenon in her essay.

The Dread of Woman, in which she discusses the fears that men have of women which might have contributed to the male originated concept of penis envy which may have been defensively constructed to booster a threatened ego. Kelman agrees with this in the introduction of this book:

> "Throughout history man has seen, woman as a sinister and mysterious being, particularly dangerous when she is menstruating. Man attempts to deal with his dread by denial and defiance ... Men deny their dread by love and adoration and defend themselves from it by conquering, debasing and diminishing the self-respect of women."

In the Indian context, men express their dread of women by first giving them supernatural powers as goddesses. Then they defend themselves by weaving an intricate web of mythology around chastity and sub-servience. Thus, women were put under constant surveillance by either their parents, or husbands and even by their sons. The ancient law giver Manu was of the opinion that Her father protects her in childhood, her husband protects her in youth and her son protects her in old age: a woman is never fit for independence.

Juanita Williams summarizes a number of myths that have been used to categorize women. She says: There is woman as earth mother, a fertile creature who is somehow more in tune with nature than iş her male counterpart. Then there is woman as seductress, another magical creature whose charms lure the man away from the narrow path of rectitude and responsibility.

Due to ambivalence regarding the women's status and position in the Indian culture, society and philosophy, her education was not given proper attention in various periods of the history of India except perhaps in the Vedic period. The Rig-Vedic society was founded on the base of home and family with the proper place assigned to women under an advanced system of material laws. There was no seclusion of women and consequently no Purdah. Aryan taught their women music and dancing, the religious lore and warfare, literature, fine arts and languages.

During the Upanishad period women enjoyed an equal eminence with men. The two sexes were considered as the two wheels of the same chariot. The women received domestic education. She also learnt the art or some handicrafts. She was taught the elements of hygiene, physiology, and nutrition along with literature, language, fine arts, etc.

The women of Ramayana and Mahabharata were given proper opportunities for education. Women like men were entitled to Upanayana or initiation into Brahamcharya or Vedic studentship. Women were versed not only in the highest philosophy but also in the other branches of knowledge.

During Buddhism there was acceptance of female education, including religious and spiritual education. It opened a new gate for the salvation of women. But Lord Buddha never thought women to be fit for ruling a nation as they were thought to be easy victims of the senses, passion, anger, hate, greed, etc.

Jainism believed that there were very few women who had strength of mind and body adequate to study the faith and to endure the hard life of an ascetic. Men were considered more physically fit than women for undertaking a course of self-mortification and self-effacement.

The invasion on India by the Muslims brought about deterioration in the position of the women. Restrictions on her freedom and rights were imposed. Muslim women were practically denied access to learning. Excluded from worshipping with the men, they were excluded from the mosques where most education occurred and also from the Kuttabs and Madarasah system. Essentially, woman's education and training, the Muslims maintain should be confined to their domestic and nurturing functions so as to make them more useful to their families and homes.

At the time when the Indians came in vital contact with the British in the later half of the eighteenth-century, the position of the Indian women had reached the maximum degree of degeneration. But the European usherance brought breath of fresh air. The close contacts with Western cultural traditions, literature and education had deep impact on the minds of Indian leaders. The result was that a number of social reform movements started in the nineteenth century. These resulted in a strong movement for the emancipation of women. Thus the pre-independence period marked the beginning of the awareness of the oppressive social customs which had reduced the status of a woman to that of a slave. The advent of Mahatma Gandhi stimulated women to fight for their honourable existence. This period in India may be described as a period of renaissance for the Indian womanhood. During this period there was a revolt against the Purdah system and fight against the old and established but decadent conventions.

India won her independence in 1947. Soon after this, Indian Constitution was framed and adopted in 1950. The women were granted equal status and position under Article 14 of the Constitution. But still the women were not able to achieve their rightful place in the social setup. Customs, traditions and the myths ingrained through centuries of prejudice continued to operate to prevent women from exercising their rights and from benefiting from whatever opportunities were offered to them. One of the basic reasons for this was the mass illiteracy among Indian women. It is well-recognized that in the struggle for empowerment of women education plays the most significant role. In India women education was, by and large, neglected till very recently. Why has this happened? It is the main theme of the present book. The book concentrates on the socio-psychological dimensions of women's education, mainly, in a historical perspective.

The socio-psychological dimensions refer to the socio-psychological make-up of the women and the cultural factors responsible for their status and position in the society. The socio-psychological make-up involves the attitudes, aspirations, motivations, interests etc.

Bibliography

Adnan, K.N., *Status of Women*, Paras Pub., Lucknow: 2003.

Altekar, A.S.: *The Position of Women in Hindu Civilization*, Motilal Banarsidas, Varanasi: 1962.

Arora, K.K.: *Women and Career*, Tata Institute of Social Sciences, Bombay: 1963.

Asthana, P.: *Women's Movement in India*, Vikas Publishing House, Delhi: 1974.

Badel, Auguste: *Women: Past, Present and Future*, Bone and Liveright, New York: 1918.

Baig Tara Ali: *India's Woman Position*, S. Chand and Company Pvt. Ltd., Delhi: 1976.

Bebel, August: *Women in the Past, Present and Future*, ed. By Mukerjee, Subrata and Rama Swami, Sushila, Deep and Deep Publication, New Delhi: 1996.

Bhasin, K. (ed.), *The Position of Women in India*, Leslie Sawny, Bombay: 1971.

Bhushan, Jamila Brij: *Muslim Women*, Vikas Publishing House, New Delhi: 1980.

Billington, Mary Frances: *Women in India*, Amarka Book Agency, Delhi: 1973.

Bose, Moni Mohan: *Female Education in India*, B.B. Gupta Publication, Kanpur: 1921.

Carden, Maren Lockwood: *The New Feminist Movement*, Russall Sage Foundation, New York: 1974.

Carstairs, G. Morris: *The Twice Born*, Indiana University Press, Bloomington: 1958.

Chakrapant, C. Kumar: *Changing Status and Role of Women in Indian Society*, M.D. Pub., New Delhi: 1994.

Chattapadhya, Kamladevi: *The Awakening of Indian Women*, Everyman's Press, Madras: 1939.

Chaturvedi, Geeta: *Women Administration in India: A study of the Socio-economic Background*, RBSA Publication, Jaipur: 1985.

Cormack, Margaret: *The Hindu Women*, Asia Pub. House, Bombay: 1961.

Deckard, B.S, *The Women's Movement*, Harper and Row, New York: 1979.

Desai Devangana; *Erotic Sculpture of India*, Tata McGraw Pub., New Delhi: 1975.

Desai, Neera: *Indian Women*, Popular Prakashan, Bombay: 1975-85.

De'Souza Alfred: *Women in Contemporary India and South Asia*, Manohar Pub., Delhi: 1980.

Devasia, L.: *Empowering Women for Sustainable Development*, Ashish Pub. House, New Delhi: 1994.

Engineer, Asghar Ali: *Islam and Liberation Theology*, Sterling Pub., New Delhi: 1990.

Everett, J.M.: *Women and Social Change in India*, Heritage Pub., New Delhi: 1979.

Gandhi, M.K.: *The Role of Women*, Bhartiya Vidhya Bhavan, Bombay: 1964.

Ghadially, Rehana: *Women in Indian Society*, Sage Pub., New Delhi: 1988.

Goldstein, Rhoda L.: *Indian Women in Transition*, The Scarecrow Press Inc., New Jersey: 1972.

Gorwaney, N., *Self Image and Social Change*, Sterling Publishers, Delhi: 1977.

Gullahorn, J.E.: *Psychology and Women in Transition*, John Wiley, New York: 1979.

Gupta, A.K.: *Women and Society*, Criterion Pub., New Delhi: 1986.

Gupta, A.R.: *Women in Hindu Society*, Jyotsna Prakashan, Delhi: 1985.

Hasan, Zoya: *Forging Identities, Gender, Communities and the State*, Kali for Women, New Delhi: 1994.

Hate, C.A., *Changing Status of Women in Post-Independence India*, Allied Publications, Bombay: 1969.

Horney, Karen: *Feminine Psychology*, W.W. Norton & Co., New York: 1967.

Jain, D: *Indian Women*, Publication Division, Government of India, Delhi: 1975.

Jain, P.C., Jain Sudha: *Scheduled Caste Women*, Rawat Pub., Jaipur: 1997.

Jain, Pratibha and Mahan, Rajan: *Women Images*, Rawat Pub., Jaipur: 1996.

Jayashree: *India and Indian Women*, Granthayan, Aligarh: 1980.

Jogdand, P.G.: *Dalit Women, Issues and Perspectives*, Gyan Publishing House, New Delhi: 1995.

Kalarani: *Role Conflict in Working Women*, Chitra Pub., New Delhi: 1976.

Kapur, Promilla: *The Changing Status of the Working Woman in India*, Vikas Pub., Delhi: 1974.

Keeton Kathy: *Woman of Tomorrow*, Harvard Univ. Press, New York: 1985.

Khanna, G: *Indian Women Today*, Gyan Publishing House, New Delhi: 1978.

Kidwai, Shaikh M.H.: *Women under Different Social and Religious Law*, Seema Pub., New Delhi: 1976.

Kumar Ashok, *Women in Contemporary Indian Society*, Anmol Pub., New Delhi: 1993.

Kuppuswamy, B., *Social Change in India*, Vikas Publishing House, Delhi: 1972.

Lara, Bimla Churn: *Women in Buddhist Literature*, N.E. Bastian, Colombo: 1927.

Lateef, Shahida: *Muslim Women in India:* Kali for Women, New Delhi: 1990.

Lederer, Wolfgang: *The Fear of Women*, Arun and Strattan, New York: 1968.

Mehta, Hansa: *Indian Woman*, Butala & Co., New Delhi: 1981.

Mehta, Rama: *Socio-legal Status of Women in India*, Metropolitan Book Co., Delhi: 1982.

Mehta, Sushila: *Revolution and Status of Women in India*, Metropolitan Book Co., Delhi: 1982.

Menon, M. Indu: *Status of Muslim Women in India*, Uppal Pub. House, Delhi: 1981.

Minault, Gail: *Secluded Scholars, Women's Education and Muslim Social Reform*, Oxford Univ. Press, Delhi: 1998.

Misra, Rekha: *Women in Mughal India*, Munshiram Manoharlal, Delhi: 1992.

Misra, R.S.: *Women Education and the Upanishadic System of Education*, Chugh Pub., Allahabad: 1993.

Mittal Mukta: *Women in India: Today and Tomorrow*, Anmol Pub., New Delhi: 1995.

Moddie, A.D.: *The Brahamanical Culture and Modernity*, Asia Pub. House, London: 1968.

Mohanty, Jagannath: *Education for All*, Deep and Deep Pub., New Delhi: 1994.

Montagu, Ashley: *The Natural Superiority of Women*, The Macmillan Co., New York: 1968.

Myrdal, A. and Klien, V.: *Woman's Two Roles*, Routledge & K. Paul, London: 1968.

Nanda, B.R.: *Indian Women*, Vikas Pub. House, Delhi: 1976.

Pal, B.K.: *Problems and Concerns of Indian Women*, ABC Pub. House, New Delhi: 1989.

Pandey, Rekha: *Women from Subjection to Liberation*, Mittal Pub., New Delhi: 1989.

Pandit, S.K.: *Women in Society*, Rajat Pub., Delhi: 1998.

Phandis, Urmila: *Women of the World*, Vikas Pub. House, Delhi: 1978.

Pinkham, Mildreth Worth: *Women in the Sacred Scripts of Hinduism*: AMS Press Inc., New York: 1941.

Pujari, Premlata: *Women Power in India*, Kanishka Pub., Delhi: 1994.

Rajgopal, T.S.: *Indian Ideal of Womanhood*, Ramakrishna Mission, Calcutta: 1969.

Ramabal: *The High Caste Hindu Woman*, Jas. B. Podgers Printing Co., Philadelphia: 1888.

Ranganathan, Sarala: *Women and Social Order*, Kanishka Publishers, New Delhi: 1998.

Rege, Y.M.: *Whither Women*, The Popular Book Depot, Bombay: 1938.

Rehman, M.M.: *Education, Work and Women*, Commonwealth Publishers, New Delhi: 1993.

Roby, Pamela, *Women in the Work Place*, M.A. Schenkrnan, Cambridge, 1981.

Rohibaugh, Joanna Bunker: *Women: Psychology's Puzzle*, Basic Books Inc., New York: 1979.

Sachidananda: *Women's Right: Myth and Reality*, Printwell Pub., Jaipur: 1984.

Sengupta, Padmint: *The Story of Women of India*, Indian Book Co., New Delhi: 1974.

Sharma, Anuradha: *Women and Work, Human Resource Management Perspective*, Gyan Pub., New Delhi: 1999.

Sharma, S. Ram: *Women's Education in Ancient and Muslim Period*, Discovery Pub. House, New Delhi: 1996.

Sharma, Usha: *Committees and Commissions on Women Education*, Commonwealth Pub., New Delhi: 1995.

Sikkri, Rehana: *Women in Islamic Culture and Society*, Kanishka Pub., New Delhi: 1999.

Singh, Indu Prakash: *Women, Law and Social Change in India*, Radiant Pub., New Delhi: 1989.

Singh, Uttam Kumar and Nayak, AR: *Women Education*, Commonwealth Pub., New Delhi: 1996.

Srinivasan, M.N.: *The Changing Position of Indian Women*, Oxford Univ. Press, Delhi: 1970.

Subbamma, Malladi: *Women, Tradition and Culture*, Sterling Pub., Delhi: 1985.

Suguna, B: *Working Women and Religion*, Discovery Publishing House, New Delhi: 1994.

Tandon, R.K.: *Women, Nature, Education, Teaching and Rights,* Commonwealth Pub., New Delhi: 1996.

Thomas, P.: *Epics, Myths and Legends of India,* D.B. Teraporevala, Mumbai: 1961.

Thomas, P.: *Indian Women through the Ages,* Asia Pub. House, New York: 1964.

Tikoo, Prithvi Nath: *Indian Women,* B.R. Publishing Corporation, Delhi: 1985.

Usha, Rao N.J.: *Women in Developing Society,* Ashish Pub. House, Delhi: 1983.

Vashishta, B.K.: *Encyclopaedia of Women in India,* Parveen Encyclopaedia, New Delhi: 1976.

Vyas, Anju: *Women's Studies in India,* Sage Pub., New Delhi: 1993.

Yaqin, Anwarul and Anwar Badr: *Protection of Woman under Law,* Deep and Deep Publications, New Delhi: 1982.

Index

J